Nutshell Series

of

WEST PUBLISHING COMPANY

P.O. Box 3526

St. Paul, Minnesota 55165

April, 1981

NUTSHELL SERIES

Constitutional Analysis, 1979, 388 pages, by Jerre S. Williams, former Professor of Law, University of Texas.

Constitutional Power—Federal and State, 1974, 411 pages, by David E. Engdahl, Adjunct Professor of Law, University of Denver.

Consumer Law, 2nd Ed., 1981, 418 pages, by David G. Epstein, Dean and Professor of Law, University of Arkansas and Steve H. Nickles, Professor of Law, University of Arkansas.

Contracts, 1975, 307 pages, by Gordon D. Schaber, Dean and Professor of Law, McGeorge School of Law and Claude D. Rohwer, Professor of Law, McGeorge School of Law.

Corporations—Law of, 1980, 379 pages, by Robert W. Hamilton, Professor of Law, University of Texas.

Corrections and Prisoners' Rights—Law of, 1976, 353 pages, by Sheldon Krantz, Professor of Law, Boston University.

Criminal Law, 1975, 302 pages, by Arnold H. Loewy, Professor of Law, University of North Carolina.

Criminal Procedure—Constitutional Limitations, 3rd Ed., 1980, 438 pages, by Jerold H. Israel, Professor of Law, University of Michigan and Wayne R. LaFave, Professor of Law, University of Illinois.

Debtor-Creditor Law, 2nd Ed., 1980, 324 pages, by David G. Epstein, Dean and Professor of Law, University of Arkansas.

Employment Discrimination—Federal Law of, 2nd Ed., 1981, 402 pages, by Mack A. Player, Professor of Law, University of Georgia.

Estate Planning—Introduction to, 2nd Ed., 1978, 378 pages, by Robert J. Lynn, Professor of Law, Ohio State University.

Evidence, 2nd Ed., (May, 1981), approx. 450 pages, by Paul F. Rothstein, Professor of Law, Georgetown University.

Family Law, 1977, 400 pages, by Harry D. Krause, Professor of Law, University of Illinois.

Federal Estate and Gift Taxation, 2nd Ed., 1979, 488 pages, by John K. McNulty, Professor of Law, University of California, Berkeley.

Federal Income Taxation of Individuals, 2nd Ed., 1978, 422 pages, by John K. McNulty, Professor of Law, University of California, Berkeley.

Federal Income Taxation of Corporations and Stockholders, 2nd Ed., 1981, 362 pages, by Jonathan Sobeloff, Late Professor of Law, Georgetown University and Peter P. Weidenbruch, Jr., Professor of Law, Georgetown University.

Federal Jurisdiction, 2nd Ed., 1981, approx. 258 pages, by David P. Currie, Professor of Law, University of Chicago.

Federal Rules of Evidence, 1981, 428 pages, by Michael H. Graham, Professor of Law, University of Illinois.

Future Interests, 1981, 361 pages, by Lawrence W. Waggoner, Professor of Law, University of Michigan.

Government Contracts, 1979, 423 pages, by W. Noel Keyes, Professor of Law, Pepperdine University.

Historical Introduction to Anglo-American Law, 2nd Ed., 1973, 280 pages, by Frederick G. Kempin, Jr., Professor of Business Law, Wharton School of Finance and Commerce, University of Pennsylvania.

NUTSHELL SERIES

Injunctions, 1974, 264 pages, by John F. Dobbyn, Professor of Law, Villanova University.

International Business Transactions, 1981, 393 pages, by Donald T. Wilson, Professor of Law, Loyola University, Los Angeles.

Judicial Process, 1980, 292 pages, by William L. Reynolds, Professor of Law, University of Maryland.

Jurisdiction, 4th Ed., 1980, 232 pages, by Albert A. Ehrenzweig, Late Professor of Law, University of California, Berkeley, David W. Louisell, Late Professor of Law, University of California, Berkeley and Geoffrey C. Hazard, Jr., Professor of Law, Yale Law School.

Juvenile Courts, 2nd Ed., 1977, 275 pages, by Sanford J. Fox, Professor of Law, Boston College.

Labor Arbitration Law and Practice, 1979, 358 pages, by Dennis R. Nolan, Professor of Law, University of South Carolina.

Labor Law, 1979, 403 pages, by Douglas L. Leslie, Professor of Law, University of Virginia.

Land Use, 1978, 316 pages, by Robert R. Wright, Professor of Law, University of Arkansas, Little Rock and Susan Webber, Professor of Law, University of Arkansas, Little Rock.

Landlord and Tenant Law, 1979, 319 pages, by David S. Hill, Professor of Law, University of Colorado.

Law Study and Law Examinations—Introduction to, 1971, 389 pages, by Stanley V. Kinyon, Late Professor of Law, University of Minnesota.

Legal Interviewing and Counseling, 1976, 353 pages, by Thomas L. Shaffer, Professor of Law, Washington and Lee University.

NUTSHELL SERIES

Legal Research, 3rd Ed., 1978, 415 pages, by Morris L. Cohen, Professor of Law and Law Librarian, Harvard University.

Legislative Law and Process, 1975, 279 pages, by Jack Davies, Professor of Law, William Mitchell College of Law.

Local Government Law, 1975, 386 pages, by David J. McCarthy, Jr., Dean and Professor of Law, Georgetown University.

Mass Communications Law, 1977, 431 pages, by Harvey L. Zuckman, Professor of Law, Catholic University and Martin J. Gaynes, Lecturer in Law, Temple University.

Medical Malpractice—The Law of, 1977, 340 pages, by Joseph H. King, Professor of Law, University of Tennessee.

Military Law, 1980, 378 pages, by Charles A. Shanor, Professor of Law, Emory University and Timothy P. Terrell, Professor of Law, Emory University.

Post-Conviction Remedies, 1978, 360 pages, by Robert Popper, Professor of Law, University of Missouri, Kansas City.

Presidential Power, 1977, 328 pages, by Arthur Selwyn Miller, Professor of Law Emeritus, George Washington University.

Procedure Before Trial, 1972, 258 pages, by Delmar Karlen, Professor of Law, College of William and Mary.

Products Liability, 2nd Ed., 1981, 341 pages, by Dix W. Noel, Late Professor of Law, University of Tennessee and Jerry J. Phillips, Professor of Law, University of Tennessee.

Professional Responsibility, 1980, 399 pages, by Robert H. Aronson, Professor of Law, University of Washington, and Donald T. Weckstein, Dean and Professor of Law, University of San Diego.

Real Estate Finance, 1979, 292 pages, by Jon W. Bruce, Professor of Law, Stetson University.

Real Property, 1975, 425 pages, by Roger H. Bernhardt, Professor of Law, Golden Gate University.

Remedies, 1977, 364 pages, by John F. O'Connell, Professor of Law, Western State University College of Law, Fullerton.

Res Judicata, 1976, 310 pages, by Robert C. Casad, Professor of Law, University of Kansas.

Sales, 2nd Ed., 1981, 370 pages, by John M. Stockton, Professor of Business Law, Wharton School of Finance and Commerce, University of Pennsylvania.

Secured Transactions, 2nd Ed., (July, 1981), approx. 380 pages, by Henry J. Bailey, Professor of Law, Willamette University.

Securities Regulation, 1978, 300 pages, by David L. Ratner, Professor of Law, Cornell University.

Titles—The Calculus of Interests, 1968, 277 pages, by Oval A. Phipps, Late Professor of Law, St. Louis University.

Torts—Injuries to Persons and Property, 1977, 434 pages by Edward J. Kionka, Professor of Law, Southern Illinois University.

Torts—Injuries to Family, Social and Trade Relations, 1979, 358 pages, by Wex S. Malone, Professor of Law Emeritus, Louisiana State University.

NUTSHELL SERIES

Hornbook Series

and

Basic Legal Texts

of

WEST PUBLISHING COMPANY

P.O. Box 3526

St. Paul, Minnesota 55165

April, 1981

―――――

Common Law Pleading, Koffler and Reppy's Hornbook on, 1969, 663 pages, by Joseph H. Koffler, Professor of Law, New York Law School and Alison Reppy, Late Dean and Professor of Law, New York Law School.

Common Law Pleading, Shipman's Hornbook on, 3rd Ed., 1923, 644 pages, by Henry W. Ballantine, Late Professor of Law, University of California, Berkeley.

Constitutional Law, Nowak, Rotunda and Young's Hornbook on, 1978 with 1979 Pocket Part, 974 pages, by John E. Nowak, Professor of Law, University of Illinois, Ronald D. Rotunda, Professor of Law, University of Illinois, and J. Nelson Young, Professor of Law, University of Illinois.

Contracts, Calamari and Perillo's Hornbook on, 2nd Ed., 1977, 878 pages, by John D. Calamari, Professor of Law, Fordham University and Joseph M. Perillo, Professor of Law, Fordham University.

Contracts, Corbin's One Volume Student Ed., 1952, 1224 pages, by Arthur L. Corbin, Late Professor of Law, Yale University.

Contracts, Simpson's Hornbook on, 2nd Ed., 1965, 510 pages, by Laurence P. Simpson, Professor of Law Emeritus, New York University.

Corporate Taxation, Kahn's Hornbook on Basic, 3rd Ed., 1981, 614 pages, by Douglas A. Kahn, Professor of Law, University of Michigan.

Corporations, Henn's Hornbook on, 2nd Ed., 1970, 956 pages, by Harry G. Henn, Professor of Law, Cornell University.

Criminal Law, LaFave and Scott's Hornbook on, 1972, 763 pages, by Wayne R. LaFave, Professor of Law, University of Illinois, and Austin Scott, Jr., Late Professor of Law, University of Colorado.

Damages, McCormick's Hornbook on, 1935, 811 pages, by Charles T. McCormick, Late Dean and Professor of Law, University of Texas.

Domestic Relations, Clark's Hornbook on, 1968, 754 pages, by Homer H. Clark, Jr., Professor of Law, University of Colorado.

Environmental Law, Rodgers' Hornbook on, 1977, 956 pages, by William H. Rodgers, Jr., Professor of Law, University of Washington.

Equity, McClintock's Hornbook on, 2nd Ed., 1948, 643 pages, by Henry L. McClintock, Late Professor of Law, University of Minnesota.

Estate and Gift Taxes, Lowndes, Kramer and McCord's Hornbook on, 3rd Ed., 1974, 1099 pages, by Charles L. B. Lowndes, Late Professor of Law, Duke University, Robert Kramer, Professor of Law Emeritus, George Washington University, and John H. McCord, Professor of Law, University of Illinois.

Evidence, Lilly's Introduction to, 1978, 486 pages, by Graham C. Lilly, Professor of Law, University of Virginia.

Evidence, McCormick's Hornbook on, 2nd Ed., 1972 with 1978 Pocket Part, 938 pages, General Editor, Edward W. Cleary, Professor of Law Emeritus, Arizona State University.

Federal Courts, Wright's Hornbook on, 3rd Ed., 1976, 818 pages, including Federal Rules Appendix, by Charles Alan Wright, Professor of Law, University of Texas.

Future Interest, Simes' Hornbook on, 2nd Ed., 1966, 355 pages, by Lewis M. Simes, Late Professor of Law, University of Michigan.

Income Taxation, Chommie's Hornbook on, 2nd Ed., 1973, 1051 pages, by John C. Chommie, Late Professor of Law, University of Miami.

Insurance, Keeton's Basic Text on, 1971, 712 pages, by Robert E. Keeton, former Professor of Law, Harvard University.

Insurance, Keeton's Case Supplement to Basic Text, 1978, 334 pages, by Robert E. Keeton, former Professor of Law, Harvard University.

Labor Law, Gorman's Basic Text on, 1976, 914 pages, by Robert A. Gorman, Professor of Law, University of Pennsylvania.

Law of the Poor, LaFrance, Schroeder, Bennett and Boyd's Hornbook on, 1973, 558 pages, by Arthur B. LaFrance, Professor of Law, University of Maine, Milton R. Schroeder, Professor of Law, Arizona State University, Robert W. Bennett, Professor of Law, Northwestern University and William E. Boyd, Professor of Law, University of Arizona.

Law Problems, Ballentine's, 5th Ed., 1975, 767 pages, General Editor, William E. Burby, Professor of Law Emeritus, University of Southern California.

Legal Writing Style, Weihofen's, 2nd Ed., 1980, 332 pages, by Henry Weihofen, Professor of Law Emeritus, University of New Mexico.

New York Practice, Siegel's Hornbook on, 1978, with 1979–80 Pocket Part, 1011 pages, by David D. Siegel, Professor of Law, Albany Law School of Union University.

Oil and Gas, Hemingway's Hornbook on, 1971 with 1979 Pocket Part, 486 pages, by Richard W. Hemingway, Professor of Law, Texas Tech University.

Partnership, Crane and Bromberg's Hornbook on, 1968, 695 pages, by Alan R. Bromberg, Professor of Law, Southern Methodist University.

Property, Boyer's Survey of, 3rd Ed., 1981, 766 pages, by Ralph E. Boyer, Professor of Law, University of Miami.

Real Estate Finance Law, Osborne, Nelson and Whitman's Hornbook on, (successor to Hornbook on Mortgages), 1979, 885 pages, by George E. Osborne, Late Professor of Law, Stanford University, Grant S. Nelson, Professor of Law, University of Missouri, Columbia and Dale A. Whitman, Professor of Law, University of Washington.

Real Property, Burby's Hornbook on, 3rd Ed., 1965, 490 pages, by William E. Burby, Professor of Law Emeritus, University of Southern California.

Real Property, Moynihan's Introduction to, 1962, 254 pages, by Cornelius J. Moynihan, Professor of Law, Suffolk University.

Remedies, Dobbs' Hornbook on, 1973, 1067 pages, by Dan B. Dobbs, Professor of Law, University of Arizona.

Sales, Nordstrom's Hornbook on, 1970, 600 pages, by Robert J. Nordstrom, former Professor of Law, Ohio State University.

Secured Transactions under the U.C.C., Henson's Hornbook on, 2nd Ed., 1979, with 1979 Pocket Part, 504 pages, by Ray D. Henson, Professor of Law, University of California, Hastings College of the Law.

Torts, Prosser's Hornbook on, 4th Ed., 1971, 1208 pages, by William L. Prosser, Late Dean and Professor of Law, University of California, Berkeley.

Trusts, Bogert's Hornbook on, 5th Ed., 1973, 726 pages, by George G. Bogert, Late Professor of Law, University of Chicago and George T. Bogert, Attorney, Chicago, Illinois.

Urban Planning and Land Development Control, Hagman's Hornbook on, 1971, 706 pages, by Donald G. Hagman, Professor of Law, University of California, Los Angeles.

Uniform Commercial Code, White and Summers' Hornbook on, 2nd Ed., 1980, 1250 pages, by James J. White, Professor of Law, University of Michigan and Robert S. Summers, Professor of Law, Cornell University.

Wills, Atkinson's Hornbook on, 2nd Ed., 1953, 975 pages, by Thomas E. Atkinson, Late Professor of Law, New York University.

Advisory Board

THE LAW OF
CORPORATIONS
IN A NUTSHELL

By

ROBERT W. HAMILTON

Vinson & Elkins Professor of Law
The University of Texas at Austin

ST. PAUL, MINN.
WEST PUBLISHING CO.
1980

Library of Congress Cataloging in Publication Data

Hamilton, Robert W   1931–
  The law of corporations in a nutshell.

  (Nutshell series)
  Includes index.
  1. Corporation law—United States. I. Title.
KF1414.3.H35   346.73'066   80–21532

ISBN 0-8299-2108-7

Hamilton Law of Corp.
1st Reprint—1981

OUTLINE

CHAPTER THREE. FORMATION OF CORPORATIONS

CHAPTER FOUR. THE LIMITED ROLE OF ULTRA VIRES

CHAPTER FIVE. PREINCORPORATION TRANSACTIONS

CHAPTER SIX. "PIERCING THE CORPORATE VEIL" AND RELATED PROBLEMS

CHAPTER SEVEN. FINANCING THE CORPORATION

CHAPTER EIGHT. THE DISTRIBUTION OF POWERS WITHIN A CORPORATION: THE SPECIAL PROBLEMS OF THE CLOSELY HELD CORPORATION

CHAPTER NINE. SHARES AND SHAREHOLDERS

CHAPTER TEN. DIRECTORS

CHAPTER ELEVEN. OFFICERS

CHAPTER TWELVE. THE CLOSELY HELD CORPORATION

CHAPTER THIRTEEN. THE PUBLICLY HELD CORPORATION

CHAPTER FOURTEEN. FIDUCIARY DUTIES OF DIRECTORS AND OFFICERS

CHAPTER FIFTEEN. INSPECTION OF BOOKS AND RECORDS

CHAPTER SIXTEEN. CORPORATE DISTRIBUTIONS AND REDEMPTIONS

CHAPTER SEVENTEEN. SHAREHOLDER'S SUITS

CHAPTER EIGHTEEN. ORGANIC CHANGES: AMENDMENTS, MERGERS AND DISSOLUTION

TABLE OF CASES

References are to Pages

TABLE OF CASES

TABLE OF CASES

*

THE LAW OF CORPORATIONS IN A NUTSHELL

CHAPTER ONE

THE CORPORATION IN PERSPECTIVE

§ 1.1　What is a Corporation?　The Concept of an Artificial Entity

In most states today a corporation may be formed simply by filing an appropriate document with a State official, usually the Secretary of State, and paying the appropriate fee. (Some states, however, require additional steps; see § 3.3.) Assuming that the necessary steps have been followed, what has been created?

The simplest and usually the most useful way of viewing a corporation is to consider it a *fictitious being* or *artificial entity* independent of the owners or investors. This artificial entity may conduct a business or businesses in its own name much in the same way that a "real" person could. Business is done, assets acquired, contracts entered into, and liabilities incurred, all in the name of the corporation rather than in the name of any individual. Also, the artificial entity may sue or be sued as though it were a person, it pays taxes, it may apply for business licenses in its own name, it may have its own bank account, it may have its own seal, and so forth.

Conducting a business in this way often has several advantages over conducting business in the name of one or more individuals. For example:

(a) The corporation is unlimitedly liable for the debts and obligations of the business but the shareholders are not, since in theory all debts are the artificial entity's obligations, not the shareholders. In effect, the shareholders risk what they have invested but no more; in legal language the shareholders enjoy "limited liability."

(b) The existence of the corporation is not dependent on who the owners or investors are at any one time. If shareholders die, or decide to sell out, or what have you, the corporation continues to exist as a separate entity. If it is necessary to raise additional capital, new shareholders or investors may be brought in without changing or disturbing the corporate form.

There are other advantages of the corporate form (and some disadvantages as well) which are discussed below when the corporation is contrasted with a partnership (§ 2.1). The basic point is that the concept of a corporation greatly simplifies things by permitting a business to have a separate legal identity independent of the flesh-and-blood persons who own and operate it.

The artificial entity approach has come under some criticism from legal writers and thinkers who view themselves as "legal realists". The starting point for this criticism is a fundamental truth about corporations: flesh-and-blood people underlie every corporation, and are essential to everything a corporation does. Some individual must decide what the corporation is to do; some individual must actually do the required act on behalf of the corporation, because manifestly an artificial entity has no arms, legs, mouth, or eyes. Some individual will ultimately reap the profits earned by the corporation, and some person must ultimately bear any loss. Realistically, a corporation is simply a device by which individuals conduct a business and other individuals share in the profit or loss. Professor Hohfeld represented one modern view of the corporation when he said, "strangely enough, it has not always been perceived with perfect clearness that transacting business under the forms, methods and procedure pertaining to so-called corporations is simply another mode by which individuals or natural persons can enjoy their property and engage in business. Just as several individuals may transact business collectively as partners, so they may as members of a corporation—the corporation being nothing more than an association of such individuals . . .." He added, when "we speak of the corporation . . . contracting in the corporate name, . . . we are merely employing a short and convenient mode of describing the complex and peculiar process by which the benefits and burdens of the corporate members are worked out . . .", Hohfeld, Fundamental Legal Conceptions 197 (1923). Hohfeld's analysis illustrates the fallacy of accepting too literally the "artificial entity" theory. A corporation is treated as an entity for most purposes but it need not be treated as an entity for all purposes. At some point the reality which Hohfeld describes may control over the fiction being relied on. For this reason, arguments grounded solely on the artificial entity thesis and not supported by considerations of fairness, justice, or policy have sometimes not prevailed.

Most provisions of modern corporation statutes are consistent with the hypothesis that a corporation is a separate legal entity. As a "short and convenient mode" of describing most of the powers of a corporation and the legal relationships surrounding it, therefore, the artificial entity concept is extremely useful. It should be emphasized, however, that a corporation possesses these attributes not so much because it is an artificial entity as because the statute so provides. To repeat, it does not necessarily follow that because a corporation possesses many entity attributes under the statutes, it necessarily possesses certain other entity attributes as well.

§ 1.2 What is a Corporation? Other Theories

The artificial entity theory is the most useful one in the context of most modern problems. However, there have been other attempts to describe the theoretical concept of a corporation. These other formulations usually arise in situations involving the power of states to regulate corporations or the rights or duties of participants in a corporation among themselves. They include:

(a) The corporation may be viewed as a "privilege," "concession" or "grant" from the state which allows the owners and investors to conduct business as a corporation. Conceptually, when documents are filed with the Secretary of State, he issues a piece of paper called a "charter" or "certificate of incorporation" which can be viewed as evidencing the State's grant of the privilege to conduct business in corporate form. This conception had greater importance in an earlier day when significant limitations or conditions were often imposed on the privilege of incorporating. Indeed, in an earlier age, individual charters were granted by the State legislature; when a charter was obtained through the legislative process, the concept of privilege or grant had considerable meaning. Today, incorporation involves only routine or ministerial acts. However, the concession theory is still sometimes referred to usually in connection with the social policy debate about the appropriate role of corporations in modern society (see § 1.3).

(b) The corporate charter may also be viewed as a "compact" or "contract." Depending on the circumstances, the parties to this contract may be:

(i) The shareholders themselves; or

(ii) The shareholders and the corporation; or

(iii) The corporation and the state.

For example, the contract theory often appears in situations where disputes have arisen between classes or members. In such disputes the rights of each class are resolved by a careful reading of the various provisions of the charter. In a dispute between preferred and common shareholders, for example, it is not uncommon to refer to the provisions of the charter that describes the rights of preferred shareholders as "the preferred shareholders' contract" which constitutes the full and exclusive description of the rights of that class of shareholders.

In the famous decision in Dartmouth College v. Woodward, 4 Wheat. (17 U.S.) 518 (1819), the Court considered the charter of Dartmouth College to be a contract between the corporation and the state which was protected against unilateral impairment by the state under the contracts clause of the United States Constitution. This case is of only historic interest today since all states have adopted constitutional provisions or incorporation statutes that specifically require every charter granted by that state to be subject to later amendments by the state.

The theories of corporateness discussed in these first two sections—the "artificial entity" theory, the "realistic" theory, the "concession" theory, and the "contract" theory—all help to explain the modern concept of a corporation. None is totally correct, none is totally wrong, and each has its place in defining the concept of corporateness.

§ 1.3 The Development of Corporation Law in the United States

While the concept of a corporation was clearly developed by the time of Blackstone and can be traced much earlier, the modern law of corporations is largely a product of developments in the latter part of the nineteenth and, particularly, the twentieth centuries. Prior to that time, business in the United States tended to be local in nature and of primary concern to individual states (though there were some exceptions such as the national bank). Corporations during this period were often created for public or near public purposes—e. g. to build bridges or toll roads—and often enjoyed some monopoly privileges. However, after roughly 1825 intensive industrial development began. The corporation proved to be an ideal instrument for this development since it could raise large amount of capital from numerous investors and yet provide centralized direction of large industrial concerns. Even though many corporations rapidly became national in scope during this period, they were and remained the descendants of local state-related enterprises, and received their charters from states rather than from the Federal Government.

At a relatively early stage, several states enacted general incorporation statutes permitting all lawful businesses to incorporate without specific legislative approval, though restrictions were often imposed in terms of size, capital invested, or powers of the corporation. Beginning roughly in the early twentieth century, a number of states systematically eliminated restrictions in their statutes to attract the incorporation business that otherwise might gravitate to other states. This rather unseemly competition among states is vividly described in Mr. Justice Brandeis's dissent in Liggett Co. v. Lee, 288 U.S. 517, 548 (1933). The incorporation business provided tax revenues for the state, fees for members of the local bar, revenues for local newspapers, and the like. Other states, in an effort to preserve whatever incorporation business they already had, found themselves forced to follow suit. The result was a race "not of diligence but of laxity," to use Mr. Justice Brandeis's phrase, or a "race for the bottom," to quote a modern commentator.

The uncrowned winner of this race unquestionably has been the small state of Delaware. More than one-half of the twenty-five largest corporations listed on the New York Stock Exchange are incorporated in that single state. The popularity and primacy of the state of Delaware is explained partially on the basis of history and partially on the continued efforts by the Bar of that state to provide an effective, flexible, and modern body of corporate law. Indeed, the major question about the Delaware law today is whether it is too flexible or too liberal. The Delaware approach has been the subject of scathing attacks and staunch defenses. Whether or not it is too flexible depends to a large extent on the social views of the observer.

In addition to Delaware, a second major influence on modern corporation law has been the Model Business Corporation Act, developed and maintained by a committee of the American Bar Association. The MBCA, as it is usually referred to, has been influential in the development of state incorporation statutes in some thirty states. Originally based on the Illinois statute, the MBCA is subject to a continuing process of revision and review.

Not all states have followed the trend toward increasingly permissive statutes. California is the principal example of a state that has recently attempted to reimpose greater substantive regulation on corporations subject to its jurisdiction. Other states may be tempted to follow the same approach in the future.

Finally, mention should be made of developments at the federal level. In the early 1930s, Congress enacted two statutes relating to corporate matters. The Securities Act of 1933 and the Securities Exchange Act of 1934 have formed the spring board for considerable federal regulation of the internal affairs of publicly held corporations; at one stage a trend appeared to be developing toward an inclusive "federal law of corporations" based on these two statutes. While this trend has apparently been stopped in its tracks by a series of narrow and restrictive holdings by the United States Supreme Court, federal regulation is still of great importance in many areas of corporate governance.

§ 1.4   The Debate Over Social Responsibility and the Publicly Held Corporation

The discussion in the last section leads naturally to a brief exploration of the debate over the social responsibility of large publicly held corporations in modern society. It is clear that such corporations wield immense economic power when they make decisions. A decision where to locate a plant, what environmental equipment to install, what products to manufacture, what to charge for them, what safety devices to build into them, and so forth, are all decisions which may fairly be described as "social" as well as "economic." These decisions, furthermore, are usually made by corporate management without public input or the approval of voters, investors, shareholders, or anyone else. The concentration of power in such corporations has been decried by some commentators and defended by others. The debate goes back to before the New Deal era and shows no sign of abating today.

The social responsibility debate has several different levels. At the most basic level the issue can be phrased in terms of whether corporate management should take social policies expressly into account when they make important decisions or whether they should make the decision on the "bottom line" of what produces the best profit for investors. While these two positions may at first seem polar, in fact there is a considerable degree of overlap since profit-maximizing decisions are not made in the abstract but in the broader societal context, possible governmental intervention, and the like. Further, since the aim is to maximize *long run* rather than short run profits, these social factors must expressly enter into the overall calculation. A decision to raise prices to monopoly levels (assuming that that is feasible), for example, may maximize short run profits but have devastating long run consequences in terms of adverse publicity and governmental intervention.

A second branch of the social responsibility debate considers whether the interests represented in the governance of large publicly held corporations should be broadened. Suggestions range from direct representation of government, labor, consumers, etc. on the board of directors to more modest proposals of improved democratic processes within the traditional corporate structure.

In the middle nineteen-seventies the debate over social responsibility took a new turn and received new impetus from the disclosure by hundreds of publicly held corporations that they had paid domestic or foreign bribes, made illegal payments overseas to obtain business, or had made illegal campaign contributions in the United States. These disclosures led not only to new calls for greater social responsibility of corporations but also focused on the role of the board of directors and the need for better control mechanisms to insure that corporate management conform with legal and moral principles of conduct. In a few instances, specific control mechanisms were imposed on corporations, but the most tangible impact of these developments to date has been on the board of directors. In recent years many public corporations have responded to these developments by increasing the number of independent, non-management directors, often to more than a majority of the board. Boards have also given such directors increased responsibilities through new committees, by providing more adequate compensation, and by increased emphasis on the oversight responsibilities of directors.

One proposal that dates back to the early years of this century has been reconsidered in recent years: the proposal to have a federal incorporation act for very large publicly held corporations. "Federal chartering," it has been argued, will improve the social accountability of corporations and guarantee better democratic procedures. An ingenious, intermediate proposal made by Professor Cary of Columbia was to enact a "Federal Minimum Standards Act" that would require every state statute to guarantee certain minimum procedural rights in large corporations.

§ 1.5 The Corporate Population: Closely Held and Publicly Held Corporations

Throughout the cases and literature dealing with the law of corporations appear references to "publicly held" corporations and "closely held" corporations. There are many similar references scattered throughout this book. This section explores what is meant by these terms.

A "publicly held" corporation is one that has outstanding shares held by a large number of people. While there is no minimum number that defines when a corporation is "publicly held", corporations with shares traded on the securities exchanges, or shares for which there are published price quotations, are clearly "publicly held" corporations. Corporations with more than $1,000,000 of assets and an outstanding class of securities held by more than 500 shareholders of record are subject to special regulation under the Federal Securities and Exchange Act of 1934, including requirements that the corporation register with the SEC and submit periodic financial information. Corporations registered with the SEC (often called, not surprisingly, "registered corporations"), of course, are all publicly held corporations. However, there may be corporations that are considered publicly held that are not large enough or whose securities are not widely enough held to require registration with the SEC.

Publicly held corporations may also be defined in terms of whether they have ever made a public distribution of securities. The Federal Securities Act of 1933 and state statutes colloquially called "blue sky laws" require corporations to register issues of securities with the SEC or state security commissions before they are sold publicly. Registration of a public *issue* under the Securities Act of 1933 is entirely independent of the registration of the *issuer* under the size and holding requirements of the Federal Securities and Exchange Act of 1934 described in the previous paragraph. (If you think it peculiar that the federal government requires two different registration procedures often for the same corporation, do not be surprised; you are not the first). In any event, a "publicly held corporation" may also be defined as a corporation that has registered a public distribution of securities in the past.

The "closely held" corporation is one with relatively few shareholders. Again there is no definite maximum number, but everyone agrees that a corporation with less than fifteen shareholders is a closely held corporation, and one may argue that a corporation is still closely held if the number of shareholders is as large as, say thirty-five. Typically a "closely held" corporation is one in which all or most of the shareholders participate in management, where there is no outside market for shares if a person wants to sell, and in which the free transferability of shares may be restricted. Indeed the presence of restrictions on transfer and the absence of a ready market for shares are usually considered typical characteristics of a closely held corporation, more important than the number of shareholders. Almost by definition a closely held corporation is one that never had a registered public distribution of securities and certainly is not registered with the SEC under the 1934 Act. Obviously, most closely held corporations are small and most publicly held corporations are large, but that is not universally true since there are some very large closely held corporations.

The corporate model that appears in state incorporation statutes is an idealized model that is tailored neither for the close corporation nor for the publicly held corporation. It is a model that is sufficiently broad and generalized that portions of it are appropriate for the very large and the very small.

In one sense the distinction between publicly held and closely held corporations is unsatisfactory because there are many corporations that do not precisely fit either definition. A study by Professor Melvin Eisenberg using a variety of different sources approximates the actual population of corporations as follows:

No. of Shareholders	Approximate No. of Corporations
1–10	1,630,000
11–99	70,000
100–499	26,500
500–1499	5,000
1500–2999	1,700
3000–10,000	1,200
Over 10,000	600

Source: M. Eisenberg, The Structure of the Corporation (1976) at 42.

The table reveals that the closely held corporation is by far the most numerous, that publicly held corporations probably number under 10,000, and that "in-between corporations" are probably ten times as numerous as publicly held corporations. Because the asset holdings of publicly held corporations are immense, however, they have tremendous economic importance. The 200 largest industrial publicly held corporations owned 60 per cent of all manufacturing company assets in 1970.

[For unfamiliar terms see the Glossary]

CHAPTER TWO

SELECTION OF THE MOST APPROPRIATE
BUSINESS FORM FOR A VENTURE

§ 2.1 The Corporation Compared to a Partnership and Limited Partnership

A venture must select the form in which it is to operate. In most instances, the basic choices are (a) a partnership (or proprietorship if there is only one owner), (b) a limited partnership, or (c) a corporation. Where a business cannot be incorporated because of professional or ethical considerations, *e. g.,* a law firm, the choice is between a traditional partnership and a professional corporation. If a conscious selection is not made but a new venture is simply launched the partnership or proprietorship form has been chosen, for better or for worse.

A *partnership* is the simplest form of organization involving more than one person. It is formed merely by agreement of the partners, who share the right to manage and the right to participate in the profits. Each also shares the unlimited obligation to answer personally for all the liabilities of the business. A *proprietorship* is a business owned by a single person who has the sole right to manage, is solely entitled to the profits, and is unlimitedly liable for the debts of the business. A proprietorship is essentially a one person partnership.

A *limited partnership* is a partnership of two or more persons in which there are one or more general partners unlimitedly liable for the debts of the business with general powers of management and one or more limited partners who have no personal liability for the debts of the business (except to the extent of their capital contributions) and very limited powers of management. In order to create a limited partnership a certificate must be filed with an appropriate state or county official and a fee paid. The limited partnership certificate bears little resemblance to corporate articles of incorporation and the state official authorized to accept limited partnership certificates may or may not be the official who is authorized to accept articles of incorporation. Partnership agreements state that certain people are "limited partners" or that specified persons "are not personally liable for the debts of the business" without a certificate being filed are not effective of themselves to limit the personal liability of partners. To ensure limited liability, a certificate of limited partnership must be filed.

The fundamental differences between partnerships, limited partnerships and corporations may be summarized as follows:

(1) *Limited Liability.* A corporation possesses the attribute of limited liability: usually the shareholders are not personally liable for the business debts of the corporation. A shareholder risks what he has agreed to invest in the corporation and nothing more. As described above, a partnership involves unlimited liability, while a limited partnership has two classes of partners: general partners who are jointly and severally liable for business obligations, and limited partners who, like shareholders, risk only what they have agreed to invest in the venture.

(2) *Federal Income Taxation.* A corporation is a separate tax paying entity. Corporations have their own tax rates, and distributions by a corporation to its shareholders are usually taxable to the shareholders even though previously taxed to the corporation. A partnership on the other hand is treated as an extension of the partners themselves. A separate partnership return is required to reflect the receipts and expenditures of the business. However, no tax is paid with this return; rather, the net income or loss is allocated among the partners and then carried directly over to each partner's individual return. Since the income is taxable to each partner whether or not actually

distributed, distributions from the partnership to a partner are normally not themselves taxable. A limited partnership is usually treated as a partnership for tax purposes.

(3) *Centralized Management.* A corporation has the attribute of centralized management: the management of corporate affairs is vested in the directors and officers who may consist of all or some of the shareholders or of persons having no financial interest in the corporation. A partnership on the other hand is managed by the partners. Each partner possesses authority to bind the partnership and a right to participate in management. In a limited partnership the general partners are vested with the power to manage the partnership affairs. As between the general partners, power to manage is diffused as in a general partnership. Limited partners do not participate in management; if they do, they lose the shield of limited liability and assume the obligations of a general partner. A major uncertainty about limited partnerships is to what extent limited partners may participate in management decisions without losing their shield of limited liability.

(4) *Continuity of Life.* Corporations are usually formed with perpetual existence. This simply means that the corporation continues indefinitely, that the death or withdrawal of a shareholder does not terminate the corporate existence, and that a shareholder does not have the power to compel or force a dissolution. A partnership's existence is more flimsy. Numerous events automatically cause the dissolution of a partnership, and each partner has the inherent power to dissolve the partnership at any time, though in some circumstances such a dissolution may constitute a breach of contract. In a limited partnership, the general partners have the dissolution powers of a partner in a general partnership, while the limited partners usually have power only to obtain dissolution by decree of court.

(5) *Free Transferability of Interest.* In the absence of contractual restriction, shares of stock of a corporation may be freely

sold, assigned, or otherwise disposed of by the owner. A purchaser of a share of stock becomes a shareholder in the corporation with whatever rights pertain to that status. In contrast, the holder of a partnership interest has only limited rights to dispose of his interest. An assignee of a partnership interest receives only the most limited rights unless the other partners agree to accept him as a partner. General partners in a limited partnership have no more power to dispose of their interest than do partners in a general partnership, while a limited partner's interest usually is made assignable by appropriate provision in the limited partnership agreement.

(6) *Simplicity of Operation.* A corporation involves a considerable degree of formality and paperwork. In even the smallest one-man corporation, the business corporation act assumes that there will be a board of directors, a corporate president, a vice-president, a secretary, and a treasurer (though some of these offices may be held simultaneously by a single person). Minutes should be kept; annual reports and separate franchise tax returns filed. A registered office and registered agent must be maintained. If the corporation desires to do business in another state, it may have to qualify to transact business in that state. In contrast, partnerships and limited partnerships are permitted relatively great freedom in their form of operation and are subject to relatively few formal legal requirements.

(7) *Costs of Creation and Operation.* Both corporations and limited partnerships involve filing fees; a general partnership does not. A corporation may also be required to pay franchise taxes, share transfer taxes, and other miscellaneous taxes to the incorporating state. Partnerships and limited partnerships generally are not subject to such taxes.

So far as the costs of creation are concerned, legal fees are apt to be the single most important item. The cost of preparing formation documents is likely to be more dependent on the complexity of the venture than on the form it takes, and, of course, creation costs are only paid once.

§ 2.2 Principal Factors in the Selection of the Business Form

In the real world lawyers often must give advice as to which form of business enterprise is most suitable for a specific venture. The choice usually comes down to weighing three basic variables: (1) the advantages of limited liability for shareholders in corporations and limited partners in limited partnerships, (2) the differences in federal income tax treatment of corporations and partnerships, and (3) the various costs and complexities of creating and operating corporations and limited partnerships. In some instances, the restrictions on the power of a limited partner to participate in the control of the business may rule out that form of business organization. It is not generally possible to evaluate all these variables in the abstract; as described below each must be weighed in the context of the particular business under discussion.

§ 2.3 Federal Income Taxation

For many students, the role of federal income taxation in the selection of the business form is the most difficult to understand. Often, they are not familiar with the broad structure of the federal income tax which, of course, is the subject of a separate law school course. Indeed, in many corporations courses, the role of federal income taxes is not covered for just this reason. However, it is covered briefly in many courses and this section is included for the benefit of students in those courses.

(a) *In General.* The fundamental difference in the tax treatment of partnerships and corporations is that the corporation is taxed as a separate entity with its own tax rate whereas the partnership is taxed as an extension of the individual. For the same amount of taxable income, corporate tax rates are lower than individual tax rates. However, there is an element of double taxation in the corporate form if the corporation pays dividends. The corporate earnings are taxed to the corporation, and when the diminished earnings are distributed as dividends, they are treated as income in the hands of the shareholders, and taxed again. In contrast, in a partnership, the total income is taxed only once, directly to the partners. If it is assumed that all the corporate earnings not eaten up by income taxes are distributed to the shareholders as dividends, the aggregate tax bill will usually be reduced by conducting business in partnership form and having the earnings taxed only once. This simple comparison, however, is misleading for two reasons:

First, it is usually possible to reduce substantially the tax at the corporate level through the payment of salaries, rent or interest to the shareholders. If reasonable in amount, such payments are deductible by the corporation as ordinary and necessary business expenses. Of course, the payments received by the shareholders are taxable as ordinary income, but if the same money were distributed as dividends, it would also be taxable as ordinary income. Ideally, if all the corporate income can be paid out in the form of salaries (and the reasonableness of the salaries is accepted by the Internal Revenue Service), the venture in effect eliminates the double tax. However, it often may not be feasible to distribute earnings in these fashions in the same proportion as shares are held.

Second, the assumption that all earnings will be paid out in the form of dividends is usually untrue. If earnings are accumulated in the corporation, the value of the shares of stock will increase. If the shares are held over one year and subsequently sold, the gain is usually taxed at favorable capital gains rates. Whether accumulation of earnings in the corporation is cheaper tax-wise than accumulation in the partnership depends on a comparison of the corporate tax rate and the applicable rate to the individuals involved. Since the corporation rate is generally lower and only mildly progressive, accumulating earnings in a corporation generally increases in attractiveness as the outside income of the shareholders increase. Because the double taxation problem may be avoided relatively easily in many situations, profitable ventures are often made subject to corporate tax rates rather than being taxed on an individual basis.

A caveat should be added: there are special taxes which, if applicable, eliminate the advantage of accumulating earnings in the corporation. These two taxes are the personal holding company tax and the tax on unreasonable accumulations of income. However, the danger of running afoul of these taxes is often overstated.

Where it is expected that tax losses will be generated for a few years, partnership treatment is usually desirable, since the losses may be used to "shelter" other income from tax. It is true that a corporation generating tax losses may carry them over to other years to offset taxable income. However, this alternative is usually not as attractive as taking an immediate deduction of the losses from the participants' personal income. Of course, the losses referred to are losses for tax purposes; because of depreciation or similar deductions, an enterprise may simultaneously have a positive cash flow and a loss for tax purposes.

An additional factor often favoring corporate tax treatment is the availability of tax-free employee fringe benefits for shareholders who are also employees of the corporation. Such benefits include pension plans, group life insurance, free medical insurance, and so forth. In the aggregate, these benefits may be very substantial in amount. A partnership cannot provide these benefits for partners because for tax purposes a partner is generally considered to be an owner, not an employee, of the partnership. The desire of persons such as lawyers or doctors, who are prohibited by law from incorporating, to obtain these tax benefits led to the development of the professional corporation as a new type of business form.

(b) *Subchapter S.* A "subchapter S corporation" is a regular business corporation which qualifies for, and has elected to take advantage of, the special federal income tax treatment provided by subchapter S of the Internal Revenue Code of 1954. This special tax treatment is sometimes loosely referred to as a corporation being "taxed as a partnership" or "electing partnership taxation." However, there are often significant differences in detail between the tax treatment of a partnership and tax treatment under a subchapter S election. In broad outline they are similar: under subchapter S, only a single tax on corporate income is imposed at the shareholder level. The income is taxable to the shareholder whether or not the income is actually distributed to him. Ordinary losses pass through within certain limits that are not applicable to partners.

To be eligible for subchapter S, a corporation must meet the following conditions on the date of election:

(a) It must be a domestic corporation;

(b) It must not be part of an affiliated group of corporations;

(c) It must have no more than 15 shareholders;

(d) Each shareholder must be an individual, a decedent's estate, or certain types of trusts; but no shareholder may be a nonresident alien;

(e) It may have only one class of stock outstanding; and

(f) No more than 20 per cent of its income may come from passive sources such as rents or interest.

A subchapter S corporation is a true corporation with all attributes of a corporation other than the peculiar tax treatment. Thus, a subchapter S corporation has the corporate characteristics of limited liability and centralization of management.

§ 2.4   Uses of Multiple Business Forms for Tax and Other Benefits

Imaginative uses of multiple business forms are often possible. Assume that X and Y desire to obtain partnership taxation, take part in the operation of the business, and yet have limited liability. Subchapter S is a possibility (even though taxation under this election is not identical to partnership taxation). If subchapter S in unavailable for some reason, however, X and Y might conduct their business as follows: A limited partnership is formed with X and Y as limited partners; the general partner is a newly formed corporation (owned by X and Y) with more than nominal assets. There is a good possibility that X and Y may function as corporate officers, operate the business, and receive the various attributes that are desired, including limited liability.

Of course, such a combination of forms contains some elements of risk. It is possible that X and Y might be held to have participated in the business (since they are corporate officers) and thus be liable as general partners. Also, it is possible that they might be held personally liable on the theory that the corporate veil of the general partner should be pierced. (See § 6.4). However, there is a good chance that neither of these arguments would be accepted, and there is no other way of obtaining all the desired characteristics in the absence of subchapter S.

Other imaginative uses of multiple business forms may doubtless be found.

§ 2.5   The Importance of Limited Liability

The protection against unlimited liability for business obligations provided by the corporate form is often stressed as a significant reason for incorporating a business. If all other things are equal (which they often are not), this advantage of the corporate form should perhaps tip the scales toward incorporating. In practice, however, limited liability is not as important as often thought.

Both corporations and partnerships buy liability insurance against claims based on tort. Both buy fire, theft, and extended coverage insurance to protect its property. Employees with access to large amounts of money are bonded whether the business is a partnership or a corporation. Thus the existence of such risks does not materially affect the question whether or not to incorporate, since the great bulk of such risks are in fact borne by others.

So far as contract obligations are concerned, banks and extenders of substantial credit are aware of the limited liability of a corporation, and if in their view the assets of the corporation are insufficient to provide reasonable security, they routinely insist that the persons behind the corporation give their personal guarantees. Such guarantees are often also required on leases and other long term corporate commitments.

Of course, some creditors may not require personal guarantees, and it is here that limited liability is advantageous. Small creditors—sellers of office supplies, minor parts, and the like—usually rely on corporate credit exclusively; when added together such obligations may be substantial. Employee wage and tax claims are also typically unguaranteed and substantial in amount. Finally, some creditors may be careless, or may make a mistake, and not require a guarantee.

On balance, it is fair to say that limited liability is a distinct plus for the corporate form of business from the investors' standpoint but is usually not the determinative factor in deciding whether to incorporate a small business.

Where limited liability and partnership taxation are simultaneously desired, the following alternatives may be considered: a limited partnership, a corporation electing to be taxed under subchapter S, and a combination of a limited partnership with a corporation being the general partner.

§ 2.6   The Importance of Continuity of Life

A partnership lacks the attribute of continuity of life in the sense that the death or resignation of a partner dissolves the partnership; the existence of a corporation, however, is unaffected by such an event. This legal difference, however, is seldom of practical importance.

At the outset, a distinction should be made between economic continuity and legal continuity. In many businesses, the death or retirement of the key man may render the continuation of the business impractical as an economic matter. In such situations the business will (or should) in fact end upon the death or retirement of the key man whether the business is conducted in partnership or corporate form. It is only where the death or retirement will not have such a devastating economic impact that the legal differences in continuity of life between a corporation and partnership may become significant. However, by appropriate provisions in a partnership agreement, virtually as much continuity of life may be built into a partnership as exists in a corporation so that with appropriate planning this factor is not crucial.

§ 2.7   The Importance of Centralized Management

Sometimes it is desired to vest the power to manage the affairs of the enterprise in the hands of less than all the participants, or in the hands of a person who is not himself a participant. In such circumstances, a corporation rather than a general partnership is generally the preferred form of organization. In a corporation, management is vested in the directors and officers who may but need not be the shareholders. In a general partnership, on the other hand, the power to exclude specific partners from participating in management is limited. With respect to third parties, each partner has power to participate in management. Even if the agreement excludes certain partners from management, the excluded partner may negotiate on behalf of the partnership with third persons who are unaware of the restriction on his authority.

As an enterprise increases in size and in the number of investors, the partnership form of business rapidly becomes increasingly unwieldly. For this reason most large enterprises are conducted in corporate form though some ventures with a large number of investors have been successfully conducted as limited partnerships.

§ 2.8   The Importance of Transferability of Interest and Access to Capital

Shares of corporate stock are usually freely transferable while the assignability of partnership interests is sharply restricted. However, free transferability of interests can largely be provided by agreement in the case of partnerships or avoided by appropriate provision in the bylaws or articles of incorporation of a corporation. Hence this attribute should not ordinarily bulk large in the decision whether or not to incorporate.

In a small business, the participants often desire to retain a veto power over who is admitted to the enterprise. This veto power is usually automatically present in the partnership, and can be provided in the corporation by appropriate share transfer restrictions. However, in the latter case, it may be necessary for the corporation or other shareholders to raise capital to purchase the shares of the person desiring to withdraw. Absolute prohibitions on transfer are against public policy.

In a small business, there is often need to raise capital by borrowing. There is little difference in borrowing ability between a partnership and a corporation; the unlimited liability of partners is relatively unimportant since shareholder guarantees of payment provide the same protection to creditors of a corporation. If it is contemplated that additional capital will be raised by selling equity interests in the venture, the corporate form is generally preferred. Partnership interests carry with them unlimited liability, and may be unattractive to investors. On the other hand, shares in a closely held corporation have no market, and may be sold only to other participants in the corporation, who may not be disposed to pay very much for the shares.

§ 2.9 The Importance of Informality, Privacy, Cost, and Ease of Interstate Operation

There remain a variety of factors that clearly favor the less formal partnership form of business. In a small business particularly, costs of organization and operation should obviously be kept to a minimum, as should formal requirements without substantive impact. The usually sound advice, "when in doubt, don't incorporate," is based primarily on the fact that partnerships have advantages over other forms of organizations in informality, privacy, cost, and ease of interstate operation. Other things being equal, the simpler and cheaper form should be preferred over the more expensive and more complex.

[For unfamiliar terms see the Glossary]

CHAPTER THREE

FORMATION OF CORPORATIONS

§ 3.1 In General

The process of corporate formation is essentially a very simple one, and much (though not all) of it may be performed by a competent legal secretary. Indeed, one of the great modern innovations in corporate formation is the magnetic tape or computer controlled typewriter which permits the mass production of corporate documents with only special name and other minor changes. There are two significant pitfalls in such a process. The first is the danger of overlooking some obvious matter. The second is the use of "boiler-plate" forms which may contain some provision that was suitable for the last corporation but is egregiously inappropriate for the next one. Overall, however, the process is simple and routine and not in any way mysterious.

§ 3.2 Selection of the State of Incorporation

Theoretically, a small corporation has the same freedom as a large, publicly held corporation to select its state of incorporation among any of the fifty states. However, practical considerations usually dictate that the small corporation be formed in the jurisdiction in which it is solely or principally doing business. The alternative usually is Delaware, with its liberal statute. The advantages of Delaware as a state of incorporation, however, have lessened as other states have modernized their corporation statutes. And there are real costs if any foreign state is selected: the corporation will have to qualify as a foreign corporation in its "home state;" it will be subject to two taxing authorities; and it may be subject to suit in a distant state. For these various practical reasons, most local businesses are incorporated in the state in which they primarily conduct business.

§ 3.3 Mechanics of Creating a Corporation

The mechanics of creating a corporation vary from state to state, and the specific statute must be consulted for details.

Every state requires the filing of a document with a state official, usually the Secretary of State, together with the payment of a filing fee. Depending on the state, the document may be called the "articles of incorporation," the "certificate of incorporation," the "charter" or some other name. In every state, the filing is reviewed by the state officer or his staff. If the document is approved, the corporate existence is usually deemed to begin as of the date and time the document is filed. The filing authority reflects its approval of the document by some step, such as the issuance of a formal "certificate of incorporation," attaching it to a duplicate original or copy of the document, or increasingly, by the mere issuance of a receipt for the filing fee. The original document is retained by the Secretary of State in most states, and the same information may also be kept in computer-readable form. Some states have additional filing requirements. Delaware, for example, requires local filing in the county in which the corporation's registered office is located (as well as filing in a state office) [Del.Code Ann.Tit. 8, § 103(c)(5)]. Arizona requires that the articles be published in a newspaper of general circulation in the county in which the corporation's known place of business is located three consecutive times within 60 days after the articles are filed (Ariz.Rev.Stat.Ann. § 10–055). A handful of states still require recording in every county in which the corporation transacts business. It is generally believed that these additional requirements serve little or no practical benefit; they are retained usually because of the political power of county clerks or newspaper publishers who have come to rely on the fees or charges generated by those requirements.

These additional filing requirements may also create legal problems as to when the corporate existence begins if some, but not all of them, are complied with. A few states have statutes that deal with this question. Delaware, for example, provides that corporate existence begins with the acceptance of the filing by the Secretary of State, and the failure to file locally within the specified period increases the filing fee but does not affect the existence of the corporation [Del.Code Ann.Tit. 8, § 103(d)]. Some states, however, condition the existence of the corporation on the completion of all filing and advertising requirements.

§ 3.4 Incorporators

The person or persons who execute the articles of incorporation are called "incorporators." The number required varies from state to state, with three being the traditional number but with a large number of states requiring only a single incorporator. A few states may still have residency or age requirements, or limit incorporators to natural persons, but most states now permit an incorporator to be anyone over the age of 18 without regard to residency and many states also permit artificial entities such as corporations to serve as incorporators. Pennsylvania requires that each incorporator subscribe for at least one share of stock [Pa.Stat.Ann. Tit. 15, § 1204(a)(8)], but most states do not have a similar requirement.

The relaxation of the requirements relating to incorporators reflects the minor role they play in the formation of a modern corporation. Depending on the state, incorporators may serve one or more of the following roles:

(1) They execute and deliver the articles or certificate of incorporation to the Secretary of State;

(2) They, or their representatives, receive the charter or certificate of incorporation back from the Secretary of State;

(3) They meet to complete the organization of the corporation;

(4) They call the first meeting of the initial board of directors (named in the articles of incorporation), at which meeting the organization of the corporation is completed;

(5) They may voluntarily dissolve the corporation if the corporation has not commenced business and has not issued any shares; and

(6) They may amend the articles of incorporation by unanimous consent if the corporation has not commenced business and has not issued any shares.

In most states today the initial directors named in the articles complete the organization of the corporation. In these states, the role of incorporators is basically limited to the ceremonial function of signing the articles of incorporation. As a result, acting as incorporator does not appear to give rise to any risk of liability. Indeed, many attorneys or their secretaries or other law office employees routinely serve as incorporators.

An "incorporator" must be sharply distinguished from a "subscriber." The latter agrees to buy shares in the corporation; in other words, he is an investor and participant in the venture. An "incorporator" on the other hand serves the largely ceremonial or ministerial functions described in this section. At one time many states required that an incorporator also be a subscriber of shares; however, as indicated above, such requirements have disappeared in all but a few states.

§ 3.5 Articles of Incorporation: In General

The document filed with the Secretary of State must contain certain mandatory information. While the requirements vary from state to state, the following modest list (drawn from § 54 of the Model Business Corporation Act) is typical:

(a) The name of the corporation;

(b) The period of duration which may be perpetual;

(c) The purpose or purposes of the corporation, which may be generally described as "for any lawful business purpose;"

(d) The number of shares authorized to be issued, including information about the rights and preferences of such shares;

(e) The address of its registered office and the name of its registered agent at that office;

(f) The number of directors and the names and addresses of the members of the initial board of directors; and

(g) The names and addresses of each incorporator.

In addition, state statutes provide that a corporation may elect to be governed by certain statutory provisions, the election of which must be reflected by an appropriate provision in the articles of incorporation. For example, many statutes provide that a majority shall constitute a quorum of shareholders except that the quorum may be reduced to as low as one-third by specific provision in the articles of incorporation (MBCA § 32). Of more practical importance, many statutes provide that shareholders shall have a preemptive right to acquire new shares (see § 7.16) or to vote shares cumulatively (see § 9.4) unless these rights are specifically negated by appropriate provisions in the articles of incorporation. Some states instead provide "opt in" provisions for these rights—*e. g.,* a corporation's shareholders will not have preemptive rights unless the articles of incorporation specifically provide for them. The statute of each specific state must be consulted to determine the pattern adopted by that state.

Finally, corporations may elect to place optional provisions relating to internal governance in the articles of incorporation in order to make them more permanent, more difficult to amend, and, hopefully, binding on persons who may not have actual knowledge of them. Such provisions may also be placed in the corporation's bylaws. However, many lawyers and judges expect important provisions, or unusual provisions denying customary rights to shareholders or others, to appear in the articles of incorporation rather than the bylaws.

§ 3.6 Articles of Incorporation: The Corporate Name

Most statutes set up minimum requirements with respect to the corporate name. Typical provisions include:

(1) The name must contain a word indicating corporateness, such as "corporation," "company" or "incorporated," or an abbreviation of one or more such words.

(2) The name may not contain any word or phrase which indicates that it is organized for a purpose that it is not permitted to engage in. As a practical matter, with the development of very general purposes clauses, the principal impact of this restriction is to preclude the use of names which suggest a purpose for which corporations may not be organized under the state business corporation act. Thus, in many states, "bank," "bank and trust," "certificate of deposit," "title guaranty," and "cemetery" may not appear in corporate names since there are special regulatory requirements in statutes relating to formation of corporations for such purposes.

(3) The name may not be the "same or deceptively similar" to any other corporate name. The purposes of this requirement are apparently in part to make sure that each corporation has a unique name, and in part to prevent unfair competition.

(4) If the name is "similar" (as contrasted with the "same or deceptively similar") to any other corporate name, it may be used only if a "letter of consent" is obtained from the owner of the similar name which expressly permits the name to be used. The purpose of this requirement appears to be solely to prevent unfair competition.

Secretaries of States usually maintain lists of corporate names that are not currently available, and check proposed new names against that list. However, the issue as to whether a name is available or whether it is "deceptively similar" often involves questions of judgment; some Secretaries of State have developed "rules of thumb" or "house rules" to guide their discretion on judgments as to name availability. As a practical matter, the issue whether or not a specific name is available is seldom litigated. Even if an attorney strongly disagrees with the Secretary of State as to the availability of a name, it is much simpler and cheaper to select another name than to litigate over name availability. However, when two corporations or businesses have used similar names in the past, the right to the continued use of such name may be so valuable as to lead to bitter litigation over whether the use of the name constitutes unfair competition. Secretaries of State are usually directed by statute to accept the results of such litigation in establishing name availability.

Because corporate names are handled on a first-come first-serve basis, many state statutes permit the *reservation* of a proposed corporate name for a limited time for a nominal fee while corporate papers are prepared. This *reservation* of a corporate name should be contrasted with the *registration* of a name by a foreign corporation permitted in some states. A *registration* of a corporate name allows a foreign corporation with long-term plans to expand into the state to reserve the exclusive use of its name and prevent a local corporation from using the same name. A *reservation* of a name is for a brief period, usually three months, and is usually not renewable; a *registration* is for a year or more and may be renewed indefinitely.

§ 3.7 Articles of Incorporation: Period of Duration

All business corporation acts now permit a corporation to have perpetual existence. In the past some statutes limited corporations to a fifty year or some other specified life span. These provisions are now obsolete though rarely articles may be filed providing for a term less than perpetual as part of internal corporate planning: Such provisions are apt to create more problems than benefits in the long run since expiration of the term may result in the corporation having uncertain status.

§ 3.8   Articles of Incorporation: The Purposes Clause

Many state statutes provide that a corporation may be organized for any lawful purpose or purposes, which purposes shall be "fully stated" in the articles of incorporation. This language has often been interpreted to mean that extremely broad phrases such as "for general business purposes" or "to engage in any lawful business" are unacceptable.

The requirement that the purposes of a corporation be "fully stated," however, has one major drawback. There is no limitation on the number of purposes for which a single corporation may be formed. It is theoretically possible for a corporation's purposes clause to list every conceivable business in which a corporation may engage, including mining diamonds on the moon. Purposes clauses therefore had a tendency to become increasingly prolix, increasingly unreadable, and often completely uninformative as to what business the corporation planned to engage in. As a result the modern trend is clearly away from the "fully stated" approach of purposes clauses, and toward the direction of requiring either no specific statement of purposes at all or a very general one, e. g., "this corporation may engage in any lawful business." Where a state permits such a clause to be used, the requirement of a purposes clause has been reduced to a formality, and there seems to be little reason to require such a clause. Even in such states, articles may sometimes be filed with a narrow purposes clause as part of internal corporate planning. Like the limited duration clause, such a provision is apt to create more problems than benefits since, as discussed in the Chapter on ultra vires (§ 4.2), it does not effectively limit the scope of the corporation's activities.

Corporate "purposes" should be distinguished from corporate "powers." Every state business corporation act contains a list of corporate powers that every corporation organized under that act automatically possesses. In most states this list is broad and not exclusive and it is generally undesirable in such states to include powers clauses in articles of incorporation since the inclusion of certain powers may be construed as negating the existence of non-enumerated ones. Because of peculiar problems in some states, however, it may be desirable to refer to certain specific powers in the articles. It should be clear that a clause that permits a corporation, for example, "to enter into partnerships or joint ventures" states a "power" and not a "purpose." The corporation is utilizing the "power" of entering into a partnership to achieve a "purpose," *e. g.*, a purpose of buying, selling and trading in real estate. The partnership power clause in the above example, incidentally, changes the common law rule that a corporation could not be a general partner in a partnership, and therefore may be appropriate in states which do not refer specifically to this power in their business corporation acts.

§ 3.9   Articles of Incorporation: Capitalization

Articles of incorporation must include information about the types or kinds of securities the corporation is authorized to issue. A separate chapter of this Nutshell is devoted to corporate securities, and the disclosure requirements applicable to articles of incorporation are discussed there. (See Chapter Seven, particularly § 7.2)

The required information about types or kinds of securities in articles of incorporation relates to securities the corporation *is authorized to issue*. In addition, the statutes of several states require disclosure of what securities *will actually be issued*, or more commonly, prohibit the corporation from commencing business before it has received a specified minimum amount of capital. The most popular amount is $1,000, but some statutes require $500 or some other amount, and some require some specified percentage of authorized capital. Minimum capital requirements in state statutes were practically universal twenty years ago, but a large number of states, including all of the important commercial ones, have eliminated such requirements on the theory that any minimum amount of capitalization is arbitrary and does not provide meaningful protection to creditors.

The major problem with minimum capital provisions is that they take no account of the specific capital needs of the particular business. Also, the requirement of $1,000, while perhaps meaningful in the 1950's and 1960's, has become the victim of inflation and is much less significant today. The Model Business Corporation Act eliminated its minimum capitalization requirement in 1969. In states that have eliminated the minimum capitalization requirement it is theoretically possible to form a corporation with a capitalization of one cent.

In most states with a minimum capital requirement, the principal enforcement mechanism is to make directors who assent to the corporation commencing business before it has received the required capital liable jointly and severally for such part of the capital as has not been received. Usually this liability terminates when the required consideration is received. A few states have *in terrorem* statutes that make the directors personally liable for *all* corporate obligations incurred before the minimum capital was paid in, even if the shortfall of capital was small and the liabilities incurred are large.

§ 3.10 Articles of Incorporation: Registered Office and Registered Agent

Every corporation must maintain a registered office and a registered agent at that office. The registered office may but need not be also the corporation's business office. The primary purpose of a registered office and registered agent is to provide an agent for service of process. The underlying idea is that it should be possible at all times to find a corporation and to have a person upon whom, and a place at which, any notice or process required or permitted by law may be served. A second purpose is to have an office to which tax notices and other official communications from the state may be sent. The original registered office and registered agent must usually be specified in the articles of incorporation; if either is changed thereafter a statement describing the change must be filed with the Secretary of State.

Often a corporation designates its principal business office to be its registered office. In such a case, the registered agent usually is a corporate officer or employee. The principal disadvantage of this is the possibility that summons, legal documents, or other communications may be mixed in with routine business mail and not receive the attention they deserve. For this reason, many attorneys suggest that they be designated as the registered agent and their office be designated as the registered office.

§ 3.11   Articles of Incorporation: Initial Board of Directors

In states where the incorporators meet to complete the formation of the corporation, there is usually no requirement that the initial board of directors be named in the articles of incorporation since they will be selected by the incorporators at the initial meeting or by the shareholders at a meeting immediately thereafter. However, in most states the role of incorporators is nominal and the organization of the corporation is completed by the initial directors who are named in the articles.

Where the initial board of directors is named in the articles, it serves as the board until the first annual meeting of shareholders or until the directors' successors are elected and qualify. The first annual meeting of shareholders may be set immediately after the organizational meeting of the initial board of directors so that elected directors take office almost immediately. It is therefore possible to refer to nominal directors (that is, directors who have no continuing interest in the business and cease to serve as directors immediately after the organizational meeting) in the articles. In this way disclosure of the identity of the permanent board of directors may be avoided. Whether or not this is desirable depends on the wishes of the clients.

Unlike incorporators or registered agents, directors may sometimes incur liabilities by virtue of their office. Hence, it may be unwise for an attorney or his employees to serve as directors, nominal or otherwise, though the risk may be slight as a practical matter if the directorship is for a short period.

§ 3.12   Completion of the Organization of the Corporation: In General

In addition to preparing and filing the articles of incorporation, attorneys often handle a number of other routine details in connection with the formation of a corporation. They may:

(1) Prepare the corporate bylaws;

(2) Prepare the call of meeting of the initial board of directors or the incorporators, minutes of this meeting, and waivers of notice if necessary;

(3) Obtain a corporate seal and minute book for the corporation;

(4) Obtain blank certificates for the shares of stock, arrange for their printing or typing, and ensure that they are properly issued;

(5) Arrange for the opening of the corporate bank account;

(6) Prepare the call of meeting of the shareholders, minutes of this meeting and waivers of notice, if necessary; and

(7) Prepare employment contracts, voting trusts, pooling agreements, share transfer restrictions, and other special ar-

rangements which are to be entered into with respect to the corporation and its shares.

§ 3.13   Nature and Purpose of Bylaws

The bylaws of a corporation are a set of rules for governing the internal affairs of the corporation. They are adopted by the corporation and technically are binding only on intra-corporate matters. They are often viewed as a contract between the corporation and its members, and between the members themselves.

Bylaws are generally not filed with the Secretary of State, and are not a matter of public record. They usually may be amended with considerable more facility than the articles of incorporation. In case of conflict between the articles and the bylaws, the former, of course, control.

As indicated earlier, it is often optional whether a specific provision is included in the articles or in the bylaws. If the provision is unusual or important, maximum legal efficacy is obtained by placing the provision on public record in the articles. On the other hand, corporate officers are much more likely to be conversant with the provisions of the bylaws. For this reason, procedural matters and mandatory provisions that appear in the statute are often repeated in the bylaws. In short, the bylaws should set out what amounts to an operating manual of basic rules for ordinary transactions, sufficiently complete to be relied upon by the officers of the corporation as a checklist in administering the affairs of the corporation.

See § 8.8 for a discussion of the power to amend bylaws.

§ 3.14   The Corporate Seal

In most states a formal corporate seal is no longer necessary. A handwritten facsimile seal has the same legal effect as a metal die, and some states have attempted to dispense entirely with the requirement of a seal. Nevertheless, a seal is probably desirable since it helps to delineate corporate transactions from individual transactions. Also, title and abstract companies and attorneys in real estate work are accustomed to corporate conveyances being under seal, and it may be easier to satisfy them if a formal seal is available. No one need fight city hall unnecessarily.

The corporate seal is usually affixed to share certificates, bonds, debentures, evidences of indebtedness, corporate conveyances of land, and important contracts.

§ 3.15 Organizational Meetings

Most of the miscellaneous matters relating to the launching of a new corporation are accomplished at a meeting of the initial directors, or in some states, the incorporators. Typical actions will include the acceptance of share subscriptions or contracts; the issuance of shares and the establishment of the consideration for them (see chapter seven); the selection and election of officers; the approval of contracts, loans, leases and other business-related matters; approval of the bylaws and the seal; the approval of the payment of the expenses of incorporation (see § 5.7); the adoption of a resolution opening a bank account and the designation of the officers authorized to sign checks; and numerous other possible business-related matters. As a practical matter, the attorney will normally draft the minutes of this meeting before the meeting takes place. Also, in some circumstances it may be necessary to have a meeting of the shareholders to elect permanent directors; the attorney normally also drafts the minutes of this meeting before the meeting takes place. If meetings are held pursuant to waivers of notice, the attorney also prepares the waiver to be executed before or at the meeting.

The question often arises as to whether it is necessary to actually hold meetings to reflect what the minutes describe. If the corporation is closely held and there is no disagreement about what is to be done, it seems to be a waste of time and silly play-acting to actually hold a meeting. In many states a written consent signed by all the directors or shareholders is effective. If the consent procedure is not available or cannot be utilized (as may be the case, for example, where one director is absent) it is generally desirable to actually hold an informal meeting, using the minutes as a form of script. Such meetings do have a play-acting atmosphere but the validity of actions taken without a meeting may be questioned otherwise.

[For unfamiliar terms see the Glossary]

CHAPTER FOUR

THE LIMITED ROLE OF ULTRA VIRES

§ 4.1 The Common Law Doctrine of Ultra Vires

The doctrine of *ultra vires* (literally beyond the scope of the powers of a corporation) is now largely obsolete in modern corporation law. In an earlier day, however, the doctrine had considerable practical importance and was given major attention. Before turning to the vestigal remnants of the doctrine in modern law, a brief description of the scope of the doctrine at common law should be given.

An ultra vires act was one beyond the purposes or powers of a corporation. The earliest view of the matter was that such acts were totally void. A corporation was formed only for limited purposes, the argument ran, and it could do nothing more than it was authorized to do. This early view, however, was unworkable and unrealistic. Carried to its logical conclusion it would permit a corporation to accept the benefits of a contract and then refuse to perform its obligations on the ground that the contract was ultra vires. (Indeed such may have been the view taken early by the English courts.) It would also impair the security of title to property in fully executed transactions in which a corporation participated. As a result, even though dicta supporting the view that ultra vires acts were totally void appeared in many cases, most courts actually adopted the view that such acts were voidable rather than void. The doctrine continued to be firmly grounded on the notion that a corporation possessed only limited power, but a rather elaborate body of principles developed defining when the defense of ultra vires might be asserted. Basic principles included the following:

(a) An ultra vires transaction might be ratified by all the shareholders. Ratification could be express or implied, *e. g.,* by the receipt of benefits without objection. Ratification, however, had to be by unanimous consent.

(b) The doctrine of estoppel usually precluded reliance on the defense of ultra vires where the transaction was fully performed by one party. In some cases, however, the corporation was held not to be estopped even where the other party had performed fully because the corporation had not received a "direct" benefit from the transaction. When benefits were classed as "direct" or "indirect" appeared to be erratic.

(c) A fortiori, a transaction which was fully performed by both parties could not be attacked. This principle was generally applied to assure security of land titles in transactions that had been closed.

(d) If the contract was fully executory, the defense of ultra vires might be raised by either party.

(e) If the contract was partially performed, and the performance was held to be insufficient to bring the doctrine of estoppel into play, a suit in quasi-contract for recovery of benefits conferred was available.

(f) If an agent of the corporation committed a tort within the scope of his employment, the corporation could not defend on the ground the act was ultra vires. This conclusion was reached because of the overriding necessity of protecting innocent third parties from corporate abuses over which they had no means of control.

These principles somewhat tamed the doctrine of ultra vires. That doctrine, however, continued to defeat legitimate expectations where the contract was still executory and possessed an unfortunate capacity to be applied in an erratic fashion in other situations as well. As a result, the modern trend has been to eliminate this doctrine from the law of corporations, or at least to sharply restrict its availability.

§ 4.2　The Modern Role of Ultra Vires

Several modern developments relating to corporate formation have limited the probability that ultra vires acts will occur. Thus, the widespread use of multiple purposes clauses and general clauses permitting corporations to "engage in any lawful business" indirectly limits the role of the doctrine. Further, it is now very simple to amend purposes clauses to broaden them to cover new activities. However, despite these factors, cases involving narrowly drawn purposes clauses still occasionally arise. In order to eliminate the complicated and arbitrary ultra vires rules in these cases, states have adopted statutes patterned on the following Model Act provision:

> "No act of a corporation and no conveyance or transfer of real or personal property to or by a corporation shall be invalid by reason of the fact that the corporation was without capacity or power to do such act or to make or receive such conveyance or transfer." (MBCA § 7.)

However, the statute permits the lack of capacity or power to be asserted in the following types of proceedings:

(1) In a proceeding by the corporation (or by a shareholder in a representative capacity) against the incumbent or former officers or directors of the corporation for exceeding their authority;

(2) In a proceeding by the Attorney General to dissolve the corporation, or to enjoin it from the transaction of unauthorized business; or

(3) In a proceeding by the shareholder against the corporation to enjoin the commission of an ultra vires act or the ultra vires transfer of real or personal property if all parties are before the court and circumstances make such an action equitable.

A limited purposes clause may be included because one or more of the participants desire to restrict the freedom of a corporation to go into new or different ventures (see § 3.8). The possibility of enjoining a corporation from violating such a limited clause is recognized in clause (3) if such an action is equitable. However, rights of third persons who may be unaware of the restrictions must be taken into account in assessing equity; in view of the routine and pro forma nature of the modern incorporation process it is unlikely that a third person would be held subject to a limited purposes clause unless he was actually aware of it. The notion that a filing in a public office creates "constructive notice," whatever its merits in other contexts, probably should not extend to unusual provisions in articles of incorporation or to limited purposes clauses.

§ 4.3 Ultra Vires Problems in Connection with Corporate Powers

The concept of ultra vires may arise in one other modern context. As described earlier, modern corporation statutes contain a list of powers that every corporation formed under the statute automatically possesses. The language of these powers clauses vary and in some states corporations may not be specifically authorized to engage in certain actions even though they appear to be in furtherance of the stated purposes of the corporation. This problem is also declining in importance as the language of statutes are modernized, but the following kinds of activities may create ultra vires problems in some states.

(1) *Charitable or Policital Contributions.* Under early decisions corporations did not have implied power to make donations to charitable, religious, or civic organizations. Most states now generally authorize such contributions though doubt may exist whether power exists to make gifts that are large in comparison to the income or assets of the corporation. A leading Delaware case, Theodora Holding Corp. v. Henderson, 257 A.2d 398 (Del.Ch.1969) upholds such gifts so long as they are reasonable in amount given the corporate assets and do not exceed the maximum deduction allowed under the federal income tax law. Also a distinction may be drawn between gifts to established charities such as universities, hospitals, or the Red Cross and gifts

to organizations or foundations chartered by a controlling shareholder or director.

Political contributions by corporations are unlawful and subject to severe civil and criminal sanctions.

(2) *Pensions, bonuses, stock option plans, job severance payments, and other fringe benefits.* Such arrangements obviously serve legitimate business purposes, and it is clear that a corporation in an appropriate case may award such benefits.

Most doubts about the propriety of such arrangements arise in either of two contexts: where the compensation appears to be excessive or based on self-dealing (discussed in § 14.6), or where arguably there is an absence of consideration. For example, consideration may be lacking where, as a humanitarian gesture, a corporation supplements the modest pension of a retired employee. Or a bonus may be paid to an employee at the end of the year without a prior agreement that a bonus would be paid. Or a voluntary payment may be made to the widow of a deceased employee. Technically, the argument about lack of consideration is not based on lack of corporate power but on substantive contract law. In most cases consideration may be found if the court is willing to look for it. For example, a bonus in one year may lead to an inference that a bonus will be paid the following year; a promise to remain in the corporation's employment may be implied; or the payment of an apparently gratuitous pension may yield contemplated benefits to the corporation in the form of superior employee morale and a happier labor force. In the absence of excessive compensation or blatant self-dealing, courts generally strive to uphold rather than strike down compensation arrangements.

(3) *The power to enter into a partnership.* The statement that it is ultra vires for corporations to enter into partnerships appears in numerous cases. The contemplated concern is that the fiduciary duties owed to other partners may conflict with the directors' duties to the shareholders. Because of the prom-

inence of these statements the Model Act specifically authorizes every corporation "to be a promoter, partner, member, associate, or manager of any partnership, joint venture, trust or other enterprise." (MBCA § 4(p).) Under such a statute there seems to be no doubt that a corporation has the power to become a partner. However, not all states have adopted such a broad provision.

(4) *The power to acquire shares of other corporations.* The power of corporations at common law to acquire shares of other corporations was sharply restricted on the theory that a general power to invest in shares of another constituted an indirect way for corporations to avoid limitations in its own purposes clauses. These restrictions are obsolete; corporations today generally have power to "purchase, take, receive, subscribe for, or otherwise acquire . . . shares or other interests in, or obligations of, other domestic or foreign corporations . . . ." (MBCA § 4(g).)

(5) *Guaranty of indebtedness of another.* At common law, it was ultra vires for a general business corporation to guarantee the indebtedness of another person, *e. g.,* a potential customer (an exception was made for corporations who were formed for the specific purpose of writing surety bonds for a fee). This principle, which has little to commend it as an abstract matter, gave rise to a considerable amount of injustice since third persons might readily rely on a corporate guarantee. Fortunately, it has been reversed by statutory provision or judicial decision; the Model Act, for example, authorizes corporations "to make contracts and guarantees and incur liabilities . . ." (MBCA § 4(h)).

(6) *Loans to officers or directors.* A provision in the present Model Business Corporation Act provides that a corporation "shall not lend money to or use its credit to assist its directors without authorization in the particular case by its shareholders." (MBCA § 47.) The 1960 version of this section was un-

qualified; it stated that "no loans shall be made by a corporation to its officers or directors." In one form or the other, this restriction has found its way in the statutes of a number of states where it has been construed as a "limitation on a specific power granted, not a positive prohibition." In other words, such a loan is ultra vires but not illegal. The 1960 version of the Model Act also provides that directors who vote for or assent to the making of a loan to an officer or director are jointly and severally liable for the amount of the loan until it is repaid. It may be argued that this specific provision constitutes the sole remedy for a violation of this restriction on the general powers of a corporation; the latest version of the Model Act does not contain a similar provision.

The prohibition against loans to officers or directors sometimes also includes a general prohibition (which was in the 1960 version of the Model Act) against loans "secured by shares of stock of a corporation." Apparently this provision was included to emphasize that from the standpoint of the corporation such a loan is completely unsecured. (See § 7.16, discussing the role of treasury shares.) However, the desirability of including such a limitation on powers seems questionable and the clause has been eliminated from the Model Act and either eliminated from or not included in the statutes of a number of states.

[For unfamiliar terms see the Glossary]

CHAPTER FIVE

PREINCORPORATION TRANSACTIONS

§ 5.1 Introduction

The formation of a new corporation is often not a clean birth. Transactions on behalf of the corporation, or in the corporate name, may occur before the articles of incorporation are filed and the corporate existence begins. Such transactions may be entered into with full knowledge that the corporation is not yet formed (such as subscription agreements or contracts by promoters to ensure that the necessary business assets are available), or inadvertently resulting from unexpected delays in the formation of the corporation. Preliminary transactions are usually classified under several different headings: promoters transactions, de facto corporations, and so forth. They are, however, all closely related and often factual situations may be classified under more than one of these headings.

§ 5.2 Subscriptions for Shares

A "subscription" is simply an offer to purchase and pay for a specified number of theretofore unissued shares of a corporation. Subscriptions may be divided into "preincorporation subscriptions," that is, subscriptions for shares of a corporation that has not yet been formed, and "postincorporation subscriptions," that is, subscriptions for unissued shares of an already existing corporation. Older texts devote a great deal of attention to preincorporation subscriptions as a device by which a new venture may be assured of adequate capitalization before it is launched. At common law, uncertainty existed whether a subscriber might withdraw from such subscriptions before the corporation came into existence and accepted them. The reason for this uncertainty was that subscriptions which were obtained individually were usually viewed as individual offers running from each subscriber to the corporation rather than as a contract among subscribers with the promise of each subscriber supporting the promises of other subscribers.

This problem has largely faded away. Corporation statutes make preincorporation subscriptions enforceable by the corporation for a limited period (six months in the Model Act) after the formation of the corporation is completed without regard to technical questions of consideration; until that period has expired, the statute makes the preincorporation subscription irrevocable by the subscriber.

A subscription may be conditioned on the occurrence of certain events, such as obtaining a specified amount of capital, or a specified loan, or a specified lease. The fulfillment of such conditions is a condition precedent to the obligation of the subscribers. The common law developed a rather confusing distinction between such conditions and "subscriptions on special terms" which constituted a type of condition subsequent. There was little practical difference, however, because failure of the corporation to comply with a "special term" also permitted the subscriber to rescind his subscription. A subscription induced by fraud may be rescinded as any other contract. The fraud may be committed by an agent of the corporation or a promoter of the corporation.

Modern distribution techniques for securities permit the meeting of all capital needs of publicly held corporations without resort to subscriptions. Indeed, the use of subscriptions by such a corporation is precluded as a practical matter by the Federal Securities Act of 1933 and state "blue sky laws," because the subscriptions themselves constitute securities and must be registered as provided by those acts. Since the underlying securities themselves also must be registered, the use of subscriptions results in two expensive registrations.

In closely held corporations where there are only a few shareholders, a contractual agreement among the shareholders to form a corporation and purchase specified shares is, of course, a binding agreement whether or not it is described as a "subscription agreement." Such agreements have largely supplanted the common law subscription, though the wording in such agreements is usually that each investor "agrees to purchase *and subscribe* for . . ." the securities he agreed to purchase. Such agreements, of course, are enforceable as simple bilateral contracts without reference to the special statutory provision relating to preincorporation subscriptions described above.

A person who subscribes or agrees to purchase shares does not become a shareholder until the subscription price has been fully paid, though some states permit shares to be issued for promissory notes for the unpaid portion of the purchase price.

§ 5.3 Promoters in General

A promoter is a person who takes the initiative in developing and organizing a new business venture. He may act either alone or with co-promoters. The term "promoter" is not one of opprobrium; indeed, the promoter is often an aggressive, imaginative entrepreneur who fulfills the essential economic function of taking an idea and creating a profitable business to capitalize on the idea.

The activities of promoters fall into three principal areas. (1) The promoter must arrange for the necessary capital for the corporation. He may invest only his personal funds, or use his personal funds plus loans from banks to obtain the necessary capital. He may seek outside capital from a small number of investors, who may be friends or neighbors. If so, he must negotiate with the outside investors to determine their share in the forthcoming enterprise, and arrange either by contract or subscription to ensure that the capital will be forthcoming when needed. If a public offering is to be made (which is rare for a newly-commenced business) he must secure compliance with the Federal Securities Act of 1933 and state "blue sky" laws as well as arranging for the distribution and sale of the securities, often through an underwriter. (2) The promoter must obtain the necessary assets and personnel so that the corporation may function. He may obtain a lease or an option to purchase needed land, or may enter into a contract to purchase with a view of assigning the contract to the corporation. He may negotiate construction contracts to build or remodel the necessary buildings. He must secure the necessary employees which often will include himself. He must secure the necessary machinery, equipment or fixtures. He may contact customers or arrange for advertising. Obviously, in this area, the kinds of activities promoters engage in are numerous and varied, depending on the nature of the business being promoted. (3) The promoter must arrange for the formation of the corporation itself. He must arrange for the filing of the articles of incorporation, the preparation of the necessary papers, the issuance of shares, and the like. If the promoter first forms the corporation, subsequent contractual problems are usually minimized since he may thereafter conduct all the necessary steps in the name of the corporation, and there is little chance of confusion between the promoter's individual liability and the corporate liability on the arrangements he negotiates. Thus, actions may be taken in the corporate name, and only if a third person desires the personal liability of the promoter as well as the corporation, as may be the case with banks, will the promoter execute an obligation individually or separately guaranteeing its performance.

Often, however, the formation of the corporation turns out to be one of the last steps in the promotional process. The promoter may begin investigation of the profitability of the proposed business, determine that the prospects of success are good, and proceed at once with business negotiations in the areas of capital formation and obtaining business assets and contracts without actually forming the corporation. In this situation there is great likelihood of confusion and uncertainty, and most of the contractual litigation involving promoters arises in this way.

§ 5.4 Promoters Contracts

Let us assume that a promoter enters into a contract to purchase machinery for the new business he is promoting, and consider whether the promoter is personally liable on that contract. No single, simple answer is possible. In some circumstances he is, in other circumstances he is not. If the corporation has been duly formed and the contract is entered into and executed by the promoter in the corporate name, he would normally not be personally liable since he has executed the contract merely as an agent and not as a principal. On the other hand, if the corporation has not been formed, and the promoter enters into the contract in his own name without referring to the corporation with the thought of subsequently assigning the contract to the corporation, he is clearly personally liable. These are the easy cases. The more difficult cases fall into two major categories:

(1) *Contracts Entered In the Name of the (Not Yet Formed) Corporation.* In this class of case the promoter executes a contract in the corporate name in a way that makes it appear that the corporation has been formed when it actually has not been. Many cases say that such a promoter is personally liable on the theory that a person acting as agent represents that his principal exists, and the promoter is liable because of a misrepresentation. Other cases merely state that a person who purports to act as agent for a nonexistent principal thereby automatically becomes a principal. The latter theory is based on contract and the former on tort, though in most cases they should lead to the same result.

These cases holding the promoter personally liable when the corporation has not been formed often give the third person a windfall because that person is usually not relying on the promoter's credit when entering into the contract; rather he is relying on the corporation's credit or, more likely, on the possibility that the corporation will do well and be able to pay off the obligations. (If he was relying on the promoter's credit he would require the promoter to guarantee the "corporation's" obligation.) However, virtually all courts in this situation hold the promoter personally liable despite the potential windfall.

If the corporation is thereafter formed and adopts the contract, the promoter may then seek to avoid liability on the basis of several possible arguments. He may contend that the subsequent formation of the corporation corrected any misrepresentation or deception that may have occurred. He may also argue that the manner of execution of the agreement indicates that the third person was content to accept the liability of the corporation, and that therefore the adoption of the contract should release him—in other words, that the transaction should be construed as a novation. Also, depending to some extent on the wording of the agreement, the promoter may be able to argue that he should not be held liable on the basis of the parol evidence rule (since only the corporation was referred to in the contract). Finally, the promoter may also seek to defend on the ground that the corporation was sufficiently formed so that it was a "corporation de facto," or a "corporation by estoppel" and therefore it was "in existence" when the contract was entered into. Even though these arguments are superficially plausible, the chances of success are problematic.

To summarize: if the promoter enters into a contract with a third person in the name of the corporation without disclosing that it is not in existence, he is personally liable on the contract. If the corporation is thereafter created and takes over the contract, the promoter has a better chance of being relieved of liability but he still probably will be found liable.

(2) *Contracts Referring to the Fact the Corporation is Not Yet Formed.* In this class of case the contract is executed by the promoter and the third party when both are aware that the corporation has not been formed. The contract itself usually reveals this fact, as for example when it is executed in a name such as "ABC Corporation, a corporation to be formed." Or the promoter may advise the third person that the corporation has not yet been formed when he executes the contract in the corporate name. It will be noted that this situation differs from situation (1) in that both parties are aware that the corporation is not yet in existence and there is no possible misrepresentation as to that fact.

This pattern may be analyzed in several different ways with widely divergent consequences. For example, it may be analyzed as an offer to the corporation which is revocable by either party and will result in a contract only if the corporation is thereafter formed and accepts the offer before it is withdrawn. Or it may be analyzed as an irrevocable option running to the corporation, with the consideration being a promise, express or implied, by the promoter to form the corporation and use his best efforts to cause the corporation to adopt the contract. Or, it may be analyzed as a present contract between the third person and the promoter by which the promoter is bound, with the understanding that if the contract is adopted by the corporation the promoter will nevertheless remain secondarily liable in the contract.

Which of these various alternatives is the proper one in any specific situation depends on the elusive "intention of the parties." If an attorney is called upon to draft a preincorporation agreement it is relatively simple for him to ascertain the parties' intention and describe it in a written agreement in terms so precise that there can be no cause for misunderstanding.

If the promoter is to be bound until the corporation adopts the contract, and then is to be released from liability, the contract that specifically so provides should avoid later disputes.

Litigation in this area generally involves agreements in which the intention is not clearly spelled out. The contract may have been negotiated by the parties without legal assistance, or the language chosen may not illuminate the specific problem one way or the other. Or the parties may have been unable to agree on their respective rights in the event of some remote contingency. Rather than forego a lucrative transaction, the parties use language such as "ABC Corporation, a corporation to be formed," hoping that the question of the liability of the promoter will not arise. In such situations, the search for intent is truly hopeless, though the courts must resolve the dispute one way or another.

Generalizations about tests which courts use to find "intention" are hazardous. Probably most courts feel that it is likely that the third person intended for *someone* to be liable. Hence, there is a distinct tendency to hold the promoter at least initially liable, especially where the corporation is never formed. Indeed, some cases flatly state that the promoter is personally liable in this situation unless there is specific agreement to the contrary. This view is strengthened where the third person is to receive payments or partial performance before the corporation is formed; presumably the promoter intends to make those payments or render the performance himself until the corporation is formed.

Professor Williston has suggested that most persons assume that even if the promoter is initially liable, he is nevertheless to be released if the corporation is later formed and adopts the contract. In other words, there is to be a novation. The testimony of the plaintiff in Bradshaw v. Jones, 152 S.W. 695, 697 (Tex.Civ.App.1912; writ refused) is representative of this understanding: "I understood that I was working for [Mr.

Jones] personally until the railroad was organized; and after the railroad was organized, I was working for the railroad, of course." Not surprisingly, the court concluded that a novation was intended. There are, however, some holdings and a considerable amount of dicta to the contrary. One problem with the Williston approach is that it may encourage promoters to create "straw" corporations to take over contracts even after it is clear that the venture should be abandoned.

If the promoters are held liable, they are considered to be partners, and liable for all promotional contracts on a joint and several basis.

Where both parties are aware that the corporation has not yet been formed, several recent cases have held the promoter not personally liable on the contract. In Quaker Hill, Inc. v. Parr, 364 P.2d 1056 (Colo.1961), for example, the court concluded that on the facts the third party never intended to rely on the promoters' performance of the contract and therefore should not be able to hold the promoters personally liable. These recent cases may signal the beginning of a more realistic judicial attitude towards ascertaining the "intention of the parties," since it is probable in many cases that the third person intended to look only to the corporation for performance of the contract.

§ 5.5 Liability of Corporations for Promoters Contracts

A corporation, after it is formed, is not automatically liable on obligations incurred by its promoters in its behalf. The reason usually given is that the promoter cannot be the corporation's agent since the corporation is not in existence. This conceptualistic argument can be partially justified on the practical ground that the rule permits investors in a corporation an opportunity to consider and reject undesirable arrangements agreed to by the promoter. Of particular importance, it permits review by subsequent investors of contracts entered into between the promoter himself and the corporation (see § 5.6). This practical justification is not particularly persuasive since it does not provide a systematic review of all promoters' contracts by subsequent investors.

The theory on which corporations voluntarily become liable on contracts negotiated by their promoters has been the subject of a great deal of confusing discussion. Much depends on how the relationship between the third person and the promoter is originally categorized. If the arrangement constitutes an "offer" by the third person to the corporation or an "option" running to the corporation (without personal liability on the promoter) the corporation becomes liable by "accepting" the offer. If the arrangement constitutes a contract between the promoter and third person where it is understood that a corporation will be formed, the corporation "adopts" the contract. Technically, "ratification" is not the proper word to describe this situation because "ratification" assumes that the corporation was in existence at the time the contract was entered into. Courts nevertheless sometimes use the words "ratification" and "adoption" interchangeably. If the promoter is then relieved from liability, the "adoption" or "ratification" becomes a "novation." If the arrangement between the promoter and third person is contractual and the third person was unaware that formation of the corporation was contemplated, the corporation may be an "assignee" of the promoter, and becomes liable by "agreeing to assume" the obligation.

In the last analysis, the legal words used are not particularly important. What is necessary is some form of assent by the corporation to the contract after it has been formed. If this assent is manifested, it may serve as an "acceptance," an "adoption," or an "assumption," as the case may be.

The necessary assent may be express, or it may be implied from the circumstances. If a corporation takes the benefits of a contract made by its promoter, it will usually be concluded that it has assented to the burdens of the contract. For example, if a promoter negotiates a contract by which a third person agrees to become an employee of the corporation for a specified period, the corporation "accepts" (or "adopts" or "assumes") the contract if it permits the employee to render services for the corporation, and thereafter cannot fire the employee without cause during the contract period.

Since the corporation becomes liable on the contract only when it assents, it has been held that the contract term begins when the assent occurs. This may be of importance for purposes of the statute of limitations or the one year statute of frauds provision.

§ 5.6   Promoter's Fiduciary Duties

Co-promoters of a single venture owe fiduciary duties to each other. In effect they are treated as partners in a venture to organize the business.

Much more difficult questions are raised where a promoter enters into transactions with the corporation before outside creditors, investors, or shareholders are brought into the venture. The transaction may involve the receipt of shares of the corporation by the promoter, or the creation of corporate indebtedness in favor of the promoter for services or property. The transaction may be entered into when the promoter is the sole shareholder, or with the approval of the then-shareholders. Later or subsequent creditors, investors or shareholders may object to the transaction on the ground that the services or property were overvalued or the amount awarded to the promoter was excessive. In many cases of this kind the courts have used language of fiduciary duty in reviewing and often setting aside such transactions to the extent they are believed to be unfair. The leading case finding a fiduciary duty is Old Dominion Copper Mining & Smelting Co. v. Bigelow, 89 N.E. 193 (Mass.1909), announcing the so-called "Massachusetts rule."

Not all courts have agreed, however; see particularly Old Dominion Copper Mining & Smelting Co. v. Lewisohn, 210 U.S. 206 (1908), involving the same transaction and announcing the "federal rule" that subsequent shareholders or investors may not set aside previously approved promoters' transactions.

As a practical matter, the issue in these cases is not so much whether or not a fiduciary duty exists as whether or not there has been full disclosure of the transaction. If there has been full disclosure subsequent creditors, investors, or shareholders may readily protect themselves by refusing to deal with the corporation or by reducing the price at which they acquire shares to reflect the reduction in value caused by the promoter's transaction. Indeed, the fiduciary duty described above is basically a duty of full disclosure rather than a duty of fair dealing. Cases continue to arise, however, in which subsequent investors attack promoter's transactions, and some courts have set them aside on the basis of vague discussion of "fiduciary" duties.

Since failure to disclose may constitute a violation of federal or state securities acts, many cases that fifty years ago would have been analyzed as "promoter's fraud" cases are now analyzed as securities act cases.

§ 5.7   Organizational Expenses Incurred by Promoters

Logically, expenses incurred in connection with the organization of a corporation should be treated no differently than other contracts entered into by promoters. For example, if an attorney is employed by promoters to draw up the articles of incorporation, the promoter should be liable for the attorney's fee unless the attorney agrees to look only to the corporation. If the corporation is formed and adopts the contract, it becomes liable for the fee, and whether or not the promoter is released from his obligation depends on whether the transaction is deemed a novation.

There are complications, however. Organizational expenses such as attorneys' fees are peculiar in that the mere corporate existence is in effect a use of the benefits of the contract by the corporation. Arguably, therefore, by its mere existence the corporation has agreed to pay whatever fee was negotiated by the promoter. Some courts have so held, but the majority view is that the corporation is not automatically bound. Rather the corporation—since it cannot refuse the services—can only be compelled to pay a reasonable fee under the circumstances.

Many states have statutes that permit the payment of reasonable charges and expenses of organization of a corporation out of the capital received by it in payment for its shares without impairing capital or rendering such shares not fully paid and non-assessable.

Often the promoter or the attorney will wish to take shares in the corporation for organizational expenses and services. There is nothing inherently wrong with this practice: indeed, it somewhat resembles a contingent fee based on the success of the business rather than on litigation. The value of shares received by an attorney or promoter for services is, of course, taxable income to them and may be deducted by the corporation as an expense over a 60 month period.

Promoters naturally expect to be compensated for their efforts, and in view of the nature of their innovative efforts, they often may legitimately expect compensation which would be considered generous by a salaried person. Typically, a promoter will form a corporation with nominal capital, and then seek outside financial support to make his promotion a success. The subsequent investors will usually purchase shares in the corporation at a higher price than the shares previously issued to the promoter. The investors' interest is thereby diluted and the promoters' interest increased in value. In a sense this increase in value represents partial compensation to the promoter; it is often a subject of negotiation between promoters and investors. However, both hope that the major portion of the promoter's compensation will occur because the business does well and the value of everyone's shares is enhanced.

§ 5.8   Premature Commencement of Business and the De Facto Doctrine

The procedure to form a corporation under most corporation statutes is basically a very simple one. As a matter of fact, it is so simple and routine that attorneys may become careless and fail to comply with all the requirements that do exist. Mistakes may range from the trivial, such as using an incorrect address, to the more serious, where the attorney becomes so careless that he prepares but fails to file the articles of incorporation at all (this has actually happened). Delays in filing are not uncommon. Perhaps the Secretary of State declines to accept the first filing because of some minor defect which the attorney subsequently corrects. In the meantime, the "corporation" has commenced business. What is the liability of shareholders for the interim debts in such situations?

At common law, these problems were usually handled under the "de facto corporation" doctrine, though occasionally they appeared as promoters contracts; today many courts still apply this common law concept though it has been largely superseded by a statutory analysis. A "de facto corporation" according to the common law was not a fully formed corporation (a "de jure corporation"), but was nearly as good since it was sufficiently formed to be immune from attack by everyone but the State. The usual test for de facto existence was threefold: there must be a statute under which incorporation was permitted, there must have been a "good faith" or "colorable" attempt to comply with the statute, and there must have been actual user of the corporate privilege. However, the cases arising under this doctrine were confusing, particularly with regard to the second requirement and legal commentators convincingly proved that the traditional tests provide little guidance for the decisions of concrete cases. After examining more than 200 de facto corporation cases arising prior to 1950, for example, Professor Frey concludes that the de facto doctrine is "legal conceptualism at its worst."

At common law a "de jure corporation" might exist even though there were some minor defects in its formation. The common law drew a distinction between "mandatory" and "directory" requirements; failure to comply with the latter did not prevent the creation of a de jure corporation. An example of a "directory" requirement was the listing of addresses of directors or incorporators.

These problems today are usually resolved by reference to the specific language of the state's incorporation statute. Every state has a statute that provides in substance that "upon the issuance of the certificate of incorporation, the corporate existence shall begin." The Model Business Corporation Act, § 56, and the statutes of a number of states, adds "and such certificate of incorporation shall be conclusive evidence that all conditions precedent required to be performed by the incorporators have been complied with and that the corporation has been incorporated under this Act" except in suits brought by the State. Thus, if the Secretary of State accepts a filing and issues his certificate a de jure corporation is in existence despite mistakes or omissions in the articles. Some courts have relied on this language to make the negative inference that the corporate existence has *not* begun before the certificate is issued, so that personal liability exists for all preacceptance transactions. A few states have adopted an additional statute that provides in substance that "all persons who assume to act as a corporation without authority so to do shall be jointly and severally liable" for all debts and liabilities (MBCA § 146). However, despite even this statute some courts have refused to hold participants personally liable for a preincorporation transaction. One court has construed the phrase "all persons who assume to act" as referring only to active participants in the venture, thereby immunizing inactive participants from liability. Timberline Equipment Co., Inc. v. Davenport, 514 P.2d 1109 (Or.1973). All in all, the predictability of result under the modern statutes has not been much greater than under the de facto-de jure tests of common law.

The basic problem is that a simple rule conditioning the existence or nonexistence of a corporation on the issuance of a certificate of incorporation has a substantial capacity for unfairness. Under such a rule, if the Secretary of State has not issued the certificate of incorporation, the shareholders and promoters are all presumably liable as partners for the preincorporation debts of the business. The result is that negligence in filing on the part of A may cause crushing liabilities to be imposed on B who may have bought "shares" in the honest belief that the corporation's articles had been properly filed. Of course, B might first check with the Secretary of State's office, but most investors would not normally think to do so. The issue whether B should be in fact liable is discussed further in the following Section.

§ 5.9 Corporations by Estoppel

Inherently the phrase "corporation by estoppel" is not meaningful. It is necessary to ask who is "estopped," under what circumstances, and for what reason. The classic requirements for equitable estoppel (or "estoppel in pais") are that there be a false representation or concealment of a fact to a person ignorant of the truth with the intention by the person making the representation of causing reliance, and actual reliance on the basis of the misrepresentation. "Corporations by estoppel" do not involve these principles. For example, consider the situation where a third person deals with a "corporation" as such relying only on its credit, and then, finding that a certificate of incorporation was never obtained, seeks to hold the promoters and shareholders liable as partners. The defendants in turn may well argue successfully that the plaintiff is "estopped" by his prior dealings from holding the promoters or shareholders personally liable. This is certainly not equitable estoppel in the classic sense, since the third person who is being "estopped" never made any representation of any kind which was relied on by any other party. In effect, courts are applying the label "corporation by estoppel" to reach a desirable result: used in this way "estoppel" is a conclusion-oriented term not an explanation. Nevertheless, there may be strong equitable grounds for limiting the third person's claim to the business assets. The third person receives a windfall if, after dealing and relying solely on the "corporation," he is permitted to hold the promoters or shareholders personally liable. Further, it may be harsh to hold investors personally liable because of the negligence or neglect of some other person, particularly where the investors honestly and reasonably believed that the articles of incorporation had been filed. For these various reasons, a number of courts have held that the third person is "estopped" from suing the promoters or shareholders, or that there is a "corporation by estoppel."

It should be noted that this reasoning apparently results in the recognition of limited liability despite the fact that the promoters may have failed to comply with every statutory requirement for obtaining this privilege. Indeed, if this principle were universally recognized one could save the filing fee by ignoring the statute and simply conducting business in the corporate name. As a result, courts have split on the question whether "estoppel" should be applied in this type of situation though the variations in decisions possibly may be explained by factual variations and variations in statutory wording. There is much to be said for the proposition that a "corporation by estoppel" should be recognized where (a) the plaintiff dealt with the corporation as such, and (b) the defendant believed that the certificate of incorporation had been obtained and was not himself negligent in failing to obtain the certificate. This position does justice to all parties and does not seriously undermine the statutory policy requiring filing of articles of incorporation, since persons knowing that the articles have not been filed would not receive the benefits of limited liability under any circumstances. It is believed that the results of the case law are basically consistent with this view.

5.10 Agreements to Form Corporation

A so-called preincorporation agreement is a contract between proposed shareholders to develop a business to be conducted in the form of a corporation. It may be a summary memorandum outlining the main points of an oral agreement, or a complete formal document describing all the details of the understanding. In a formal document, all aspects of the agreement between shareholders may be stated, as may understandings as to employment, capitalization, or any other matter which is the subject of preliminary agreement. Copies of proposed articles of incorporation, bylaws, and even minutes of meetings may be attached as exhibits.

The major problem with a preincorporation contract is whether it will be fully executed by the formation of a corporation as provided in the agreement or whether specific provisions will survive the creation of the corporation. If it is desired to have certain provisions of the agreement survive and continue to bind the parties, the agreement should specifically so state, since otherwise a court may easily infer that only the provisions of the articles of incorporation, bylaws, and minutes were intended to survive. If the agreement is to survive it should usually be specifically assumed by the corporation after its incorporation.

An agreement to form a corporation usually places the parties to the agreement in the relationship of joint venturers, the object of the venture being the formation of the corporation and the establishment of its business. There is still a conceptual difficulty since after the corporation is formed the parties are simultaneously being treated as having the rights of shareholders in the corporation and the rights of joint venturers in an underlying arrangement to form the corporation. To avoid possible conflicts, some courts have taken the position that when the parties adopt the corporate form, with the corporate shield to protect them, they necessarily "cease to be partners and have only the rights, duties and obligations of stockholders." Other courts however, have taken the more sensible position that the joint venture may continue after the formation of the corporation, at least where the parties' intention to this effect is clear. The question appears to be one of "intention" since there is no reason why both relationships cannot exist simultaneously if that is what the parties desire.

[For unfamiliar terms see the Glossary]

CHAPTER SIX

"PIERCING THE CORPORATE VEIL" AND RELATED PROBLEMS

§ 6.1 "Piercing the Corporate Veil" In Context

Assume for a moment that a corporation has been properly and fully created in accordance with state law so that a "de jure corporation" has been created in the fullest sense of that phrase. The basic question discussed in this Chapter is whether and to what extent the separate existence of such a corporation should be ignored in order to do basic justice or avoid the frustration of some clearly articulated public policy. At first blush, the basic concept that a corporation is a fictitious person or separate legal entity seems to dictate the answer that the separate existence of such a duly formed corporation should never be ignored. The law has not taken this extreme position, however, and the courts in a large number of cases have refused to recognize the separate existence of a duly formed corporation. To put the matter into perspective, however, it should be added that in an even larger number of cases courts have recognized the separate existence of corporations despite arguments that they should not do so. In a literal sense, the corporate fiction is a basic assumption that underlies many commercial transactions; there must be compelling reasons before a court will ignore such a basic assumption.

When the separate existence of the corporation is ignored, courts often use the colorful metaphor of "piercing the corporate veil."

§ 6.2 Shareholder Responsibility for Corporate Indebtedness: Introduction

The question of the status of a corporation usually arises when a liability has been incurred in the name of a corporation, but the corporation has become insolvent. The creditor, seeking to find a solvent defendant, may sue some or all of the shareholders, arguing that for some reason they should be called upon to pay the corporation's debts. [Indeed, such a creditor may also sue directors, officers, and anyone else in any way connected with the corporation. The possible liabilities of directors, officers, or employees are discussed in later chapters (see particularly § 14.1); this Chapter is limited to the possible liability of shareholders.] When the corporation is insolvent and recovery is sought from shareholders, the court is faced with deciding whether a loss should be imposed on third persons or on shareholders; there is a loss and someone must pay. A blind application of the "artificial entity" approach would mean that the creditor always suffers the loss; certainly that result is often reasonable but it is not inevitable.

Most opinions by courts shed little light on the considerations governing when corporate obligations should be imposed on the shareholders. The traditional statement in Bartle v. Home Owners Cooperative, 127 N.E.2d 832 (N.Y.Ct.App.1955) is that:

> "The law permits the incorporation of a business for the very purpose of escaping personal liability. Generally speaking, the doctrine of 'piercing the corporate veil' is invoked 'to prevent fraud or to achieve equity.' But in the instant case there has been neither fraud, misrepresentation nor illegality."

Such statements essentially restate the issue in different terms —fraud, equity, misrepresentation or illegality. Other cases suggest that the test should be whether the corporation has been so "dominated" by an individual or another corporation that it may be considered as the other's "alter ego." Still other cases utilize a variety of metaphors (*e. g.,* "shell," "dummy" or "fiction") rather than analysis; all such name-calling obviously asserts the conclusion without giving any clue as to the reasons underlying it. As early as 1926, Mr. Justice Cardozo commented that the whole problem "is still enveloped in the mists of metaphor" and that the appropriate tests are "honesty and justice." Berkey v. Third Avenue R. Co., 155 N.E. 58 (N.Y.Ct.App.1926).

§ 6.3 Shareholder Responsibility for Corporate Indebtedness: Contract and Tort Claims

In considering cases involving shareholder responsibility for corporate indebtedness, there should first be put to one side cases where liability is imposed upon shareholders under conventional theories of agency or tort law. To argue that the corporate veil is "pierced" in such cases is both unnecessary and confusing. Where the shareholder is actually acting as a principal in his own name, he is clearly liable on the obligation. Moreover, if the corporation is his agent under accepted principles of agency law, the shareholder-principal is still liable on a contract because he is a principal, and it is unnecessary to consider whether he is a shareholder in a corporation whose "veil has been pierced." Similarly, if the shareholder himself commits a tort while acting as an agent for his corporation, he is personally liable for the tort because of the general rule that tortfeasors are personally liable even though they are acting as agents.

In the great bulk of the remaining cases, a major consideration in determining whether the shareholder or the third party should bear the loss is whether the third party dealt voluntarily with the corporation or whether he is an involuntary creditor, typically a tort claimant. In a contract case, the third party has usually dealt in some way with the corporation and should be aware that the corporation lacks substance. In the absence of some sort of deception, the creditor thus more or less assumed the risk of loss; if he was concerned, he should have insisted that some solvent third person guarantee the performance by the corporation. Hence in the absence of deception the loss should be placed on the third person in contract cases—a result actually reached in the great bulk of the contract cases by not "piercing the corporate veil." In tort cases, on the other hand, there is usually no element of voluntary dealing, and the question is whether it is reasonable for businessmen to transfer a risk of loss or injury to members of the general public through the device of conducting business in the name of a corporation that is marginally financed. The issues of public policy raised by tort claims thus bear little relationship to the issues raised by contract claims and it is not surprising that the "corporate veil" is more likely to be "pierced" in a tort case than in a contract case. This fundamental distinction, however, has not always been perceived by courts, which sometimes indiscriminately cite, and purport to apply, tort precedents in contract cases and vice versa.

The distinction between contract and tort claims is particularly important in considering whether "inadequate capitalization" should be a factor in "piercing the corporate veil." Opinions in many cases rely on this factor in holding shareholders liable for corporate obligations; other cases expressly disavow the relevance of the amount of capitalization in determining whether or not to pierce the corporate veil. Unfortunately, the phrase "inadequate capitalization" has more than one possible meaning. Many corporation acts require every corporation, before commencing business, to have received some minimum amount of capital, usually $1,000, for the issuance of shares. In a sense, a corporation beginning business with less than the required amount of capital is inadequately capitalized, but that is not the meaning used here. "Inadequate capitalization" usually means a capitalization that is very small in relation to the nature of the business of the corporation and the risks the business necessarily entails. Inadequate capitalization is measured at the time of formation of the corporation; a corporation that was adequately capitalized when formed but has suffered unavoidable losses is not normally considered undercapitalized. Whether a corporation is undercapitalized obviously presents a question of fact that turns on the nature of the business of the particular corporation.

Comments that inadequate capitalization is irrelevant appear most commonly in contract cases. In those cases the separate existence of an inadequately capitalized corporation (often called a "shell" corporation) should usually be recognized, since, as indicated above, if a person knowingly deals with an under-capitalized corporation he is, in effect, assuming the risk of loss if the transaction does not work out. Indeed, shell corporations are often created to enter into transactions precisely because the shareholders do not wish to assume personal liability. A re-fusal by a shareholder to assume personal liability when re-quested to do so presents the strongest case against judicial imposition of that liability, since when the parties themselves are apportioning the risk of loss through their relative bargaining power, there is no reason for a court to disturb this alloca-tion of risk. There are some contract cases, however, in which inadequate capitalization should result in the shareholders being held personally responsible. If the shareholder misleads a third person regarding the financial status of the corporation so that the third person believes the corporation has more capital than it actually has, then the element of voluntary risk allocation disappears, and shareholder liability should be im-posed. Depending on the nature of the misrepresentation, the person making the representation may also be independently liable for fraud or deceit, though many cases exist in which the shell corporation was substituted—without overt misrepresenta-tion—at the last minute. Mere silence or an oral promise by a shareholder to guarantee the payment of the corporation's debt, which itself is unenforceable under the statute of frauds, should not normally be grounds for piercing the corporate veil. There may also be other extreme contract situations in which inade-quate capitalization may lead to the separate existence of a corporation being ignored. Perhaps a person might be tricked into dealing with the corporation. Situations involving manifest unfairness arising from unequal bargaining power not reaching the level of unconscionability may also be envisioned. These situations gradually shade over into those involving duress, coercion, or other independent grounds for setting aside a contract.

In tort cases there is usually no element of prior dealing between the corporation and the plaintiff. As a result, inadequate capitalization is usually given considerable importance in determining whether shareholders should be held liable for the tort liabilities of the corporation, though not all cases are in agreement. The underlying policy argument may be stated as follows: an inadequately capitalized corporation in a risky business in effect transfers the risk of loss to innocent members of the general public. While the corporation need not be capitalized to ensure that all conceivable liabilities will be discharged, a corporation should be reasonably capitalized in light of the nature and risks of the business. This argument was accepted in the leading California case of Minton v. Cavaney, 364 P.2d 473 (Cal.1961), and traces of it appear in opinions in a minority of other jurisdictions. Minton v. Cavaney like many other cases in this area, also involved another factor: a failure to complete the formation of the corporation, and the court may have been partially influenced by that factor as well.

The importance of inadequate capitalization in tort cases is increased if the corporate affairs are not conducted in a reasonable manner in the light of business risks. If assets that might be used for the purchase of insurance or retained in the business to increase the creditor's cushion are siphoned off through dividends, salaries or similar payments, the risk of shareholder liability is increased. Corporate affairs should not be conducted so as to minimize the assets available for tort claimants. The bounds of this rather appealing policy argument are totally undefined, and as a result it seldom appears in court opinions. Indeed, it was apparently rejected in the majority opinion in the leading New York case of Walkovsky v. Carlton, 223 N.E.2d 6 (N.Y.1966). Its influence, however, should not be underestimated: courts are much more likely to "pierce the corporate veil" and hold shareholders liable in tort cases when the elements of inadequate capitalization and dispersal of assets are present. Conversely adequate capitalization and clear evidence that the corporation "did the best it could" are likely to protect shareholders against tort claims based on the corporation's acts.

The taxicab industry has been an important source of new cases concerning shareholder responsibility for tort liabilities of the corporation. Particularly in New York City the practice has developed of separately incorporating one or two taxicabs in a large fleet and establishing a separate corporation to operate the central garage. Each operating taxicab company has the minimum required capitalization (usually invested in the taxicab itself) and carries the minimum insurance required by state law. The drivers themselves are usually judgment proof, so that seriously injured victims of taxicab accidents go largely uncompensated unless they can look to the assets of the shareholders. The theory of "enterprise entity" discussed in section 6.6 dictates that the separate existence of each minimally capitalized taxicab corporation should be ignored and the entire fleet of taxicabs treated as a single entity; the more difficult question is whether a claim may also be made against the shareholders individually. The leading New York decision is Walkovsky v. Carlton, 223 N.E.2d 6 (N.Y.1966) in which the Court refused to hold the shareholder liable in the absence of allegations that he was conducting business in his individual capacity, and "shuttling . . . personal funds in and out of the corporations 'without regard to formality and to suit their immediate convenience.' " However, thereafter the complaint was amended to make this specific allegation; this complaint was upheld on a motion to dismiss and the case was thereafter settled. The reluctance of the defendants to go to a jury in cases of this character is understandable; most of the litigation arises on a motion to dismiss, and the cases are settled if the complaint survives.

§ 6.4 Shareholder Responsibility for Corporate Indebtedness: Failure To Follow Corporate Formalities

Anyone reading cases dealing with shareholder liability for corporate obligations will be struck by the emphasis placed by the courts on the failure to follow the requisite corporate formalities as a ground for imposing shareholder liability in both contract and tort cases. In many opinions, the court describes the failure to follow normal corporate routine and then concludes that the corporation is the "alter ego" or "instrumentality" of the shareholder or that the "corporate veil should be pierced." While a complete catalogue of dangerous acts is probably impossible to prepare, there appears to be a substantial risk that the separate corporate existence will be ignored when business is commenced without completing the organization of the corporation or without issuing shares and receiving the consideration therefor, when shareholder meetings or directors' meetings are not held (or consents are not signed), when decisions are made by shareholders as though they were partners, when shareholders do not sharply distinguish between corporate property and personal property, when corporate funds are used to pay personal expenses, when personal funds are used for corporate expenses without proper accounting, or when complete corporate and financial records are not maintained.

It is difficult to see, as a matter of logic, why corporate confusion and informality have been given the importance that they have. In most cases, the confusion and informality are not related to the claim advanced by either tort or contract plaintiffs. As a matter of fact, evidence of informality or comingling of affairs is first found long after the transaction giving rise to the particular litigation took place. To hold shareholders personally liable because of activities which are almost always unrelated to the plaintiff's claim, creates a windfall. For this reason, some courts have refused to "pierce the corporate veil" despite considerable evidence of confusion. One possible explanation for "piercing the corporate veil" in these cases is that the shareholder should not be permitted first to ignore the rules of corporate behavior and then later to claim the advantage of the corporate shield. In the absence of harm to anyone or to the State, however, it is difficult to see why the shareholder should so be punished.

The importance given to corporate formalities as the test for determining whether the corporation's separate existence will be recognized tends to create a trap for unwary shareholders in closely held corporations. Shareholders in a small corporation often find managing the business a full-time occupation; formal corporate affairs such as meetings and the like are put off or ignored because there is full agreement in fact by all interested parties regarding what should be done and who should do it. The play-acting aspects of corporate meetings, elections, and the like in a closely held corporation may also strike businessmen as rather silly. Insistence by an attorney that formal corporate procedures be followed may be dismissed as a subtle attempt at an additional fee. This attitude invites disaster.

When failure to follow appropriate corporate procedures tends to injure third persons, there is little objection to holding the shareholder liable. Procedures within the corporation may be so undifferentiated that a person may believe he is dealing with a shareholder individually rather than with the corporation. Similarly, intermingled personal and corporate assets may disappear into the personal coffers of the shareholder to the detriment of corporate creditors. These factors, however, are present in only a small minority of the confusion cases.

§ 6.5 Shareholder Responsibility for Corporate Indebtedness: Parent-Subsidiary Cases

Many cases in which shareholder liability has been found concern shareholders that are themselves corporations. In these cases, a parent corporation is being held liable for the debts of a subsidiary. They have quite a different flavor than cases in which the shareholder defendant is an individual, and some cases even suggest that different tests are being applied depending on whether the shareholder-defendant is an individual or a corporation. When a corporation is the defendant, only a larger corporate entity is being held responsible for the debt; when an individual is the defendant, however, personal liability extending to non-business assets is being imposed. Whatever the merits of this suggestion as a basis for decision, courts seem to be more willing to "pierce the corporate veil" when the defendant is a corporation rather than an individual. Courts are particularly likely to find the parent business entity liable under the following circumstances:

(a) When the subsidiary is being operated in an "unfair manner," *e. g.,* the terms of transactions between parent and subsidiary are set so that profits accumulate in the parent and losses in the subsidiary;

(b) When the subsidiary is consistently represented as being a part of the parent, *e. g.,* as a "division" or "local office" rather than as a subsidiary;

(c) When the separate corporate formalities of the subsidiary are not followed;

(d) When the subsidiary and parent are operating essentially parts of the same business, and the subsidiary is undercapitalized; or

(e) When there is no consistent clear delineation of which transactions are the parent's and which are the subsidiary's.

The lack of a consistent clear delineation between the parent's affairs and the subsidiary's affairs is often virtually determinative of liability. These cases often phrase the test in terms of agency. Often the individual acting for the subsidiary is also an agent of the parent; unless the "hat he is wearing" when he acts is clear, the argument may be made that he was actually acting on behalf of the parent rather than the subsidiary or on behalf of both. Thus the probability of parental liability increases significantly when there are close relationships, informality of operation, and overlapping of personnel employed by the corporations.

Of course, in some cases the failure to delineate between operations of the parent and the subsidiary may actually mislead third persons into believing they are dealing with the parent corporate entity. Most cases, however, do not limit liability to situations where people are misled but simply impose liability whenever intermingling is present on a wide scale. The flavor of these parent-subsidiary cases was well captured in a law review article by Mr. Justice Douglas (published before he was appointed to the United States Supreme Court) which was written in the form of suggestions to avoid inter-corporate liability:

"The observance of the following four standards will keep the business units from being treated as assimilated: (1) A separate financial unit should be set up and maintained. That unit should be sufficiently financed so as to carry the normal strains upon it. The risks attendant on the conduct of a business of that type can roughly be averaged and that average met. (2) The day to day business of the two units should be kept separate. Normally each process can be tagged so as to identify it with the activity of one unit or with that of the other. Occasionally such tagging will be difficult in a case where the two businesses are merely units in a line of production. But such separation as the technology of the business permits should be sufficient. And in addition, the financial and business records of the two units should be separately kept. (3) The formal barriers between the two management structures should be maintained. The ritual of separate meetings should be religiously observed. The activities of the individuals serving on the two boards can be tagged so that the individuals *qua* directors of the subsidiary can always be distinguished from the same individuals *qua* directors of the parent. . . .

"The same problem arises in connection with the officers. And the same solution suggests itself. A man may not be indiscriminately one officer or another. The observance of the niceties of business efficiency are normally sufficient. Such demands are not exacting. They merely suffice to keep the record of the business affairs of the two units from becoming hopelessly intermingled. (4) The two units should not be represented as being one unit. Those with whom they come in contact should be kept sufficiently informed of their separate identities."

If such a basic separation is maintained, no difficulty should be created even though in other respects the ties are very close: the parent owns all the shares of the subsidiary, they have common officers, they have common auditors or attorneys, they file consolidated returns for federal income tax purposes, and they report their income on a consolidated basis. All of these close ties are basically consistent with the separate existence of the subsidiary.

A number of parent-subsidiary cases involve intermingling of assets. Often separate accounts are maintained, but informal transfers or "loans" are made from time to time to meet the day-to-day needs of the business. Such conduct increases the risk of parental liability. If funds owned by the parent are needed by the subsidiary, the proper procedure is to establish a formal loan, preferably using a promissory note, and then to transfer the funds to the subsidiary's bank account. The corporate books of both parent and subsidiary then reflect the transaction accurately and there is no risk that the intermingling of assets will result in the two corporations being treated as one.

§ 6.6 The Concept of "Enterprise Entity"

"Enterprise entity" is a phrase coined by Professor Berle to refer to the economic unity that is a single business enterprise. Courts are often suspicious of attempts to divide a single economic enterprise among several different corporations with the intention of minimizing the assets subject to claims of creditors of each enterprise. Perhaps this is because it is not "playing fair" with creditors who may believe that the entire enterprise is a single unit; in any event, courts may well put the enterprise back together despite the shareholders' attempt to segregate it into separate corporate entities. In this kind of case, a "brother-sister" corporate relationship may be ignored as readily as a parent-subsidiary relationship.

§ 6.7 "Piercing the Corporate Veil" To Further Public Policy

A second class of piercing the corporate veil cases involves the claim that a separate corporate existence should not be recognized because to do so would violate a clearly defined statutory policy.

To take an illustrative case, the statutes of several states prohibit branch banking. In other words in these states a banking corporation must stick to a single location and cannot open branches around the state. Accepting this statutory policy, may a banking corporation own the voting stock of another bank? Or, may a single holding corporation own a majority of, or all, the voting stock of several banks? Answers to questions such as these must be based on an evaluation of the strength of the state policy against branch banking rather than on policies underlying the separate existence of corporations. If the policy is a strong one, the recognition of a separate corporate existence may provide an unacceptable method of circumvention, and the separate corporate fiction must yield to the state policy. On the other hand, if the policy against branch banking does not appear to be a strong one, or if the policy is based on historical rather than modern banking requirements, there is no need for courts to find a fundamental conflict between the statute and the corporate form and hold invalid relationships that conform with the notion of separate corporate existence.

Public policy is also the critical question in the series of cases involving family corporations organized to obtain social security or unemployment benefits for owners who would not be eligible for such benefits if the business had continued to be conducted in noncorporate form. Several federal decisions have held that social security benefits may not be denied to a person who "incorporates" his assets for the sole purpose of qualifying for the benefits, but decisions at the state level concerning temporary disability insurance, workmen's compensation, and unemployment compensation, are split. A clearer example involves the unemployment compensation statutes which provide for an exemption from the tax for employers having fewer than some designated number of employees, *e. g.,* four. May a single business be divided into several separate corporate units each employing less than the statutory minimum to obtain the exemption for each? Courts have held, not surprisingly, that the state unemployment commissions may disregard the separate corporations, treat the business as a single unit, and impose the tax on it.

Generalization is difficult in such cases. Sometimes, assistance may be gained from statutory language that indicates that the policy should be applied to "direct or indirect" relationships. Nevertheless, delicate judgments are required in these cases, for the policies underlying regulatory statutes must be weighed against the policies supporting the concept of the corporate entity.

§ 6.8 "Piercing the Corporate Veil" in Taxation and Bankruptcy

Given the broad social and governmental policies involved in the federal income tax laws and the federal bankruptcy act, it is understandable that specialized tests have evolved under these statutes for determining when the separate corporate existence will be disregarded.

Under the Internal Revenue Code of 1954 there is a need to preserve tax revenue and to be able to set aside fictional transactions which have as their sole purpose the minimization of taxes. A corporation's separate existence generally will be recognized for tax purposes if it is in fact carrying on a bona fide business and is not merely a device created for the purpose of avoiding taxes. The taxpayer, however, must accept any tax disadvantages of the corporate form if he has elected to choose that form. Further, even if the corporate form is adopted and carefully followed, the Commissioner has broad powers to disallow deductions or exemptions, or reallocate items of income to clearly reflect income.

Entirely different policies are involved in the bankruptcy area. Bankruptcy courts have considerable flexibility in dealing with controlling or dominant shareholders of bankrupt corporations. The bankruptcy court may:

(1) "disregard the corporate entity" and hold the shareholder personally liable for the corporation's debts if the shareholder's conduct bring him within the rather vague tests of "piercing the corporate veil." The effect of this conclusion is that the controlling shareholder may be responsible for all corporate obligations; all payments made by the corporation to the shareholder before bankruptcy may also be recovered by the trustee since

essentially the corporation and shareholder are treated as a single unit.

(2) Refuse to recognize claims by shareholders against the corporation as bona fide debts provable in bankruptcy and consider them instead as contributions to capital. This treatment of shareholder debt is limited to loans made at or shortly after the formation of the corporation when the corporation is inadequately or thinly capitalized, and simply reflects that what in fact is equity capital may have to be treated as equity capital in bankruptcy proceedings. A number of decisions follow this approach and there are analogous holdings in the tax field. Yet the application of this principle is elusive: there is no easy way to determine when a corporation is in fact undercapitalized, and while most courts have treated the issue on an "all or none" basis and reclassified all the debt as equity, it is arguable that it should reclassify only that portion necessary to make the capitalization adequate. As a general test, where the corporation commences business with sufficient capital so that it can borrow the balance of the needed capital from a bank or other independent source of funds, the original capitalization is adequate; if the shareholder rather than the third party makes the loan under such circumstances, that transaction should be accepted by the bankruptcy court as a bona fide loan.

(3) Under the "Deep Rock" doctrine (so named from the Deep Rock Oil Corp., the subsidiary involved in the leading case of Taylor v. Standard Gas & Electric Co., 306 U.S. 307 (1939)), the court may subordinate claims presented by controlling shareholders to the claims of other creditors or preferred shareholders on the ground that the shareholder acted inequitably or unfairly. Examples of inequitable claims include taking unreasonable amounts as salary, manipulation of the affairs of the corporation in disregard of standards of honesty, or selling assets to the corporation at inflated prices. The type of conduct that will result in subordination under the Deep

Rock doctrine can only be stated in general terms: the doctrine is based on general principles of equity and fair dealing. It is not necessary to show that the indebtedness was a sham or fiction, since technically what is involved is the order of payment of debts rather than total rejection of the claim. The theory is that a person who has acted unfairly in his management of the corporation should step aside so that other creditors may be first satisfied. Of course if the assets of the bankrupt estate are inadequate to satisfy all claims, subordination will usually result in the shareholder's receiving nothing on his claim. Despite this underlying theory, in at least one case the Deep Rock doctrine was applied when the controversy was between innocent creditors of the bankrupt subsidiary and the equally innocent creditors of the bankrupt parent.

The type of conduct that triggers the doctrine of "piercing the corporate veil" often differs only in degree rather than kind from the kind of conduct that gives rise to subordination under the Deep Rock doctrine. In a sense these are alternative weapons in the bankruptcy court's arsenal.

§ 6.9   Other Generalizations About Piercing the Corporate Veil

Three final observations should be made about the confusing and inconsistent doctrines lying behind the "piercing the corporate veil" metaphor. First, there is no inherent reason to assume that ignoring the separate corporate existence must be an all-or-nothing affair. Particularly if the dominant question does not involve public statutory policies but merely liability for corporate obligations, a corporation should be deemed to exist for some purposes and possibly not for others. There is some case authority, for example, for piercing the corporate veil to hold shareholders active in the business personally liable, but recognizing the same corporation's separate existence to protect passive investors from the same liabilities. Second, there is a strong judicial feeling that when a person elects to do business in corporate form he must take the bitter with the sweet, and cannot later argue that the separate corporate existence should be ignored when it is of benefit to him. The doctrine of piercing the corporate veil, in other words, is not available for the benefit of shareholders, but only *against* shareholders. This view is particularly strongly developed in the tax cases. Finally, where the considerations are not strongly weighted one way or the other, a presumption of separate existence of the corporation should be recognized so that in close cases the separate existence of the corporation should be recognized. The fiction of separate corporate existence, in other words, should be the rule not the exception.

[For unfamiliar terms see the Glossary]

CHAPTER SEVEN

FINANCING THE CORPORATION

§ 7.1 Introduction

Perhaps no other area of corporation law is more confusing to law students without prior business backgrounds than corporate securities such as shares of stock, bonds and debentures. The language is new and unfamiliar, the concepts seem mysterious and sometimes illogical, and everything seems to build on what went immediately before.

The basic purpose of this chapter is to dispel the mystery by proceeding one simple step at a time. It begins with the issuance of shares of common stock by a newly formed corporation. It then briefly considers other classes of stock that corporations may issue, the use of borrowed capital—that is, debt—as a substitute for contributed capital, and finally, the issuance and reacquisition of shares of stock by an ongoing corporation. Reserved for later chapters are issues related to the payment of dividends or other distributions to shareholders and the relative rights of holders of different classes of shares.

§ 7.2 Authorized vs. Issued Shares of Common Stock

Shares of common stock are the fundamental units into which the proprietary interest of the corporation is divided. The articles of incorporation of a new corporation must state the number of shares of common stock the corporation is authorized to issue and in most states the "par value" of the shares or a statement that the shares are "without par value." (The limited significance of "par value" is discussed in the following sections.) Under modern corporation statutes there is no limitation on the number of shares that may be authorized and no requirement that all or any specific fraction of the authorized shares be actually issued. There may be practical constraints, however. Some states impose franchise or stock taxes on the basis of authorized shares; in these states to authorize many more shares than there is an intention to issue simply increases taxes with no offsetting benefit. Also, authorizing a large number of shares may create concern on the part of investors since authorized shares may be later issued merely by the board of directors without shareholder approval. On the other hand, it is generally believed desirable to authorize some additional shares over and above what is presently planned to be issued for unexpected contingencies and to avoid the need for amending articles of incorporation if more capital is needed.

The actual capitalization of a corporation is based on the issued shares and the capital received therefor, not on the number or par value of authorized shares. Capital received in exchange for issued shares is usually referred to as "contributed capital" and is viewed as being invested in the corporation permanently or indefinitely.

§ 7.3   The Price of Common Shares

Let us assume that a new corporation is authorized to issue 1,000 shares of common stock and it has been agreed that the two investors, A and B, will each contribute $5,000 for 50 percent of the stock. How many shares should be issued and for what price?

Within a broad range, the number of shares and price per share in such a situation can be set at any level. For example A and B might purchase one share each for $5,000, or 10 shares each for $500 per share, or 100 shares each for $50 per share. It is important, of course, that A and B each pay the same amount for each share and receive the same number of shares; however, as between themselves it makes no difference what that amount is per share. It would be undesirable, however, to issue 500 shares each at $10 per share, since that would exhaust the entire authorized capital and would require an amendment to the articles of incorporation if more capital was needed at a later date.

If only common sense were involved, the pricing of common shares would end at this point. However, most state statutes have an elaborate system of rules relating to the issuance of common shares which have substantive as well as accounting implications. These rules dealing with par value are the subject of the following four sections.

§ 7.4   Par Value, Stated Capital and Related Concepts

Most state statutes assume that shares will have a "par value" or "stated value" (which is the same thing). The possibility that a corporation may issue "no par" shares or shares "without par value" should be put to one side for the moment since in most states the treatment of such shares is based on the treatment of par value shares. Par value of a share of common stock is simply the dollar amount designated as par value by the draftsman of the articles of incorporation. It may be one mill, one cent, one dollar, ten dollars, whatever the draftsman designates. At one time par value had considerable importance because it was widely viewed as the amount for which the shares would be issued: shares with a par value of one hundred dollars could be subscribed for at one hundred dollars per share with confidence that all other identical shares would also be issued for $100. This practice, however, long ago fell into disuse. Today, par value serves only a minor function and is in no way an indication of the price at which the shares are issued, with this one exception: *The one basic rule about setting the price for shares of common stock with a par value is that the price must be equal to or greater than par value.* If this rule is violated and shares are issued for less than par value, the recipient shareholder in most states is automatically liable to the corporation for the difference. To summarize: the creator of a corporation may set both the par value and the issuance price as he wishes so long as the issuance price is equal to or greater than the par value. For several reasons the current practice in issuing common shares runs strongly in the direction of using a "nominal" par value, that is one cent, ten cents, or one dollar per share when the shares are issued for several dollars or more per share.

Several factors caused the gradual movement away from par value as a representation of the purchase price of shares and the development of nominal par value shares. One factor was the loss of flexibility of pricing shares. When a secondary market for shares develops, a corporation raising capital by selling shares with a par value of $100 for $100 per share competes with that market and would have to stop selling shares if the market price of the previously-issued shares dropped below $100 per share. At that point potential investors could get a better price in the secondary market than they could from the corporation which was locked into the $100 price by the par value. A second factor was the federal documentary stamp tax on issuance of corporate securities (since repealed) which, until 1958, was based on the par or stated value rather than actual value. A nominal par value thus reduced taxes. Similarly, state franchise and stock transfer taxes also were (and to a limited extent may still be) based on par or stated value. Another factor arose in the situation where property of uncertain value was being contributed; if high par value shares are given in exchange for such property, arguments may later arise that the property was not worth the par value of the shares received and the recipients might be sued for the difference. These various reasons provide adequate practical justification for abandoning high par value shares in every instance. Further, there is very little to be gained from using high par value shares; the principal advantage is possibly a psychological benefit to investors. Since such an advantage is not very persuasive, the result was a gradual shift away from the use of high par value shares.

Par value serves an important function in addition to establishing a price floor below which shares may not be issued: it is an essential ingredient in determining the "stated capital" and "capital surplus" of the corporation.

In order to understand "stated capital" and "capital surplus" and the issues that evolve from them, a brief excursion into fundamental accounting concepts is useful. The basic syllogism or truism on which financial statements are based is that *net worth* equals *assets* minus *liabilities*. That syllogism is obviously true for an individual such as you or me; it is equally applicable to a corporation that is treated as an entity or fictitious person. By simple arithmetical manipulation of the basic syllogism, *assets* also equal *liabilities* plus *net worth*. This is the formula used in a "balance sheet" where one side of the equation is placed on the left side and the balance on the right side of a ledger.

Assets	Liabilities + Net Worth _____
_____	

A balance sheet balances because it is simply a restatement of the basic equation.

Let us examine a balance sheet for a new corporation immediately after it has sold 100 shares of stock for 1,000 dollars in cash. The balance sheet shows:

Assets		Liabilities -0-
Cash	$1000	
	_____	Net Worth
	$1000	Common Stock 1,000

The concepts of stated capital and capital surplus relate to how the common stock item is shown on the right hand side of the balance sheet. Stated capital is defined to be the aggregate par value of all issued shares (plus or minus certain adjustments not relevant for present purposes). Any excess of capital contributed over the par value is allocated to capital surplus. Thus, if in our hypothetical the 100 shares of common stock had a par value of $1 per share and were sold at $10.00 per share the balance sheet would be as follows:

Assets		Liabilities	–0–
Cash	$1,000	Capital Accounts	
		Stated Capital	$100
		Capital Surplus	900

In this balance sheet, the phrase "capital accounts" has been substituted for "net worth" to somewhat more closely reflect modern accounting terminology but its meaning is the same. Under modern statutes, there is no requirement that any specific amount be put in in the form of stated capital; even states that establish a minimum capitalization of $1,000 (or some other amount) require only an aggregate capital of the specified amount without differentiating between how much is stated capital and how much is capital surplus.

Now, a logical question that may be asked is what difference does it make if the capital contribution is recorded as stated capital or capital surplus. Rather surprisingly it does make a difference, which can best be appreciated if we first draw up a balance sheet after the corporation (1) has borrowed $1,000 from a bank and (2) has had two years of operations during which it has earned and accumulated an aggregate of $2,000 over-and-above all costs, taxes, etc. Further, for simplicity we will continue to assume that all of the assets are held by the corporation in the form of cash. The balance sheet looks like this:

Assets		Liabilities	$1,000
Cash	$4,000	Capital Accounts	
		Earned Surplus	$2,000
		Stated Capital	100
		Capital Surplus	900
	$4,000		$4,000

At this point the shareholders decide they want to distribute to themselves some or all of the $4,000. If the balance sheet is to continue to balance, every dollar taken from the left-hand column must obviously be reflected by the reduction of a right-hand column entry. The right-hand entries thus in effect limit or monitor the distribution of assets from the left-hand column. For example, as described in a later chapter dividends may be lawfully paid "out of" earned surplus. This means that amounts may be paid from the cash of the corporation as dividends up to the maximum amount shown in the right-hand column under "earned surplus," or $2,000 in the above example. Of course, a dividend of, say, $500 paid out of earned surplus would in the above example result in the reduction of cash by $500 to $3500, offset by a reduction of earned surplus to $1,500, and the balance sheet will still balance.

Under most state statutes, corporations have greater freedom to make distributions from capital surplus than from stated capital. In most states stated capital is "locked in" the corporation and cannot be distributed except upon the liquidation of the corporation; however, assets may be distributed to the extent of capital surplus simply with the approval of the holders of a specified fraction of the common shares. Such a distribution is not a dividend in the normal sense of the word but is called by various names, *e. g.,* "liquidating dividend," "distribution in partial liquidation," or the like. (See § 16.4). Also capital surplus but not stated capital may be used to repurchase or redeem outstanding shares previously issued by the corporation. (See § 16.13).

If all the capital is put in the form of stated capital (*i. e.*, the par value of the issued shares equals the consideration received) all the capital is "locked in;" if the bulk of the capital contributed is recorded as capital surplus rather than stated capital there is greater flexibility to distribute unneeded capital to shareholders or reacquire outstanding shares at a later date. In other words, there is greater flexibility in a corporation with this balance sheet:

Cash	$1,000	Liabilities	
		Capital Accounts	
		Stated Capital	$100
		Capital Surplus	900

than there is in a corporation with this balance sheet:

Cash	$1,000	Liabilities	-0-
		Capital Accounts	
		Stated Capital	$1,000
		Capital Surplus	-0-

Such flexibility is viewed by corporate organizers as a mildly positive feature and is an additional reason for the wide-spread use of nominal par value which leads to low stated capital and high capital surplus. Of course, a bank that lends money to a corporation might be unhappy if large amounts of capital surplus are available for distribution to shareholders since the capital of the corporation forms a "cushion" for the creditor and increases the possibility that the corporation will have the liquid assets to repay the loan when it comes due. As a result, lenders very commonly insist on contractual restrictions on the freedom of corporations to distribute their contributed capital that modern corporation statutes provide. Such restrictions are required so routinely by most lenders that they have almost totally replaced the corporation statutes as the operative restriction on the freedom of corporations to distribute their capital to their shareholders.

§ 7.5 No Par Shares

In the early period of corporate history, corporations apparently only issued shares with par value. No par shares are a relatively recent wrinkle, and the rules relating to such shares were developed in the context of the established rules for accounting for par value shares. Obviously, the consideration for which no par shares are issued may be set without any reference to a minimum imposed by a par value. However, the capital received is still allocated between stated capital and capital surplus. When no par shares are issued under most state statutes the entire consideration fixed by the corporation for the shares constitutes stated capital. However, statutes generally permit the directors to allocate some portion or all of the consideration to capital surplus. Some states limit this power to 25 per cent or some other fraction of the consideration received (as did the Model Act before 1969). Such a restriction on creating capital surplus obviously reduces the attractiveness of no par shares to some extent. However, most states today permit allocation of consideration from no par shares to either stated capital or capital surplus without limitation. Apparently under such a provision it is possible to create a corporation with as little stated capital using no par shares as with nominal par value shares.

For many years no par shares suffered from a tax disadvantage in that federal stamp taxes were computed on no par shares based on the issue price while par value shares were valued at par value for tax purposes. Where this valuation structure is in effect (and it may continue to be in effect in some states) nominal par value shares obviously continue to offer a tax saving over no par shares. Perhaps this historical pragmatic reason explains why no par shares have never become more widely used. No par shares are also sometimes created where it is contemplated that the shares will be issued for property or for services which may be difficult to value. For the reasons discussed in the following two sections it is unlikely that no par shares provide any real advantage over nominal par shares in this regard.

Some state statutes provide that the board of directors has the power to fix the consideration for which no par shares are issued but the articles of incorporation may expressly reserve this power to the shareholders. It is always simpler and more convenient for the board of directors to exercise this power than the shareholders. This option is apparently a lingering vestige of the long since discredited idea that par value ensures equality of shareholders while no par shares do not. In the modern context, it is unlikely that the option for shareholders to set the issuance price is ever elected.

§ 7.6 Shares Issued for Property or Services

If shares are issued for cash on the barrelhead, the cash price of each share is readily established, subject only to the limitation that the price must equal or exceed the share's par value, if any. If the shareholder-to-be is contributing property or services, however, the situation is more complicated.

In the first place, under state statutes not all types of property or services may serve as acceptable consideration for the issuance of shares. Some state constitutions and many state statutes provide that shares may be issued only "in whole or in part, in cash, in other property, tangible or intangible, or in labor or services actually performed for the corporation." (MBCA § 19). In addition, many state statutes specifically provide that promissory notes or the promise of future services do not constitute permissible consideration. Shares issued for ineligible consideration under these statutes are not validly issued and may be cancelled or suit brought by other shareholders; or alternatively, persons receiving such shares may be compelled in a suit by creditors to pay in additional consideration on the theory the shares are "watered." See § 7.7.

The case law provides additional gloss on what is eligible consideration: preincorporation services are "services actually performed;" patents for inventions, "good will" of a going and profitable business, contract rights, or computer "software" constitute "intangible property" if they appear to have real value. On the other hand, a lease or contract right that is subject to a substantial condition may not constitute "property," as least if it is likely that the condition will not be fulfilled. Secret formulae, processes or plans that lack novelty or substantial value have also been held not to constitute "property." A note secured by a mortgage on real estate is usually considered to be eligible "property" rather than an ineligible "promissory note" in states that prohibit shares to be issued in exchange for promissory notes. Further, if shares are issued partially for services previously rendered and partially for services to be rendered in the future, the entire issue of shares is invalid since the court will not apportion it if the directors do not. Thus, shares to be issued to employees for services may be validly issued only at the end of the employment period.

Secondly, the value of the property or services must be determined. Many statutes are based on the Model Act provisions that require the board of directors to "fix" the "consideration, expressed in dollars" that the corporation is to receive (§ 18), and that "in the absence of fraud in the transaction," the judgment of the board of directors as to the value of the consideration "shall be conclusive." (MBCA § 20.) These provisions are equally applicable to par and no par value shares. Under these provisions, the resolution of the Board of Directors accepting property for shares must do two things: it must specify the specific property involved, and it must express or fix the value of the property in dollars. Of course, the value so expressed must exceed the par value of any shares being issued. Presumably, something close to actual fraudulent intent must be shown before the decision of a board of directors as to the value of property received can be overturned.

§ 7.7 Liability of Shareholders for Watered Stock

The term "watered stock" is a colorful common law phrase describing the situation where shareholders receive shares without paying as much for them as the law requires. The common law defines three classes of such shares—"bonus" shares, "discount" shares, and "watered" shares. "Bonus" shares are par value shares issued free when the shareholder fully paid for shares of another class; "discount" shares are par value shares issued for cash for less than par value; "watered" shares are par value shares issued for property that is worth less than the par value of the shares. All three of these types of shares are often indiscriminately referred to as "watered shares," a convenient generic phrase to describe these transactions.

Much of the early law relating to watered shares concerned the liability of shareholders receiving watered shares to pay the additional consideration needed to "squeeze out the water." Two alternative theories by which creditors might hold shareholders liable appear in the early cases. The "trust fund" theory in effect treated the stated capital of the corporation as being a trust fund available for the payment of creditors, and failure to pay in the proper amount was actionable by any creditor. As pointed out in Hospes v. Northwestern Mfg. & Car Co., 50 N.W. 1117 (Minn.1892), this theory is to a large extent a fiction since corporate capital lacks virtually all the elements of a true trust. The "holding out" theory in effect presumed (usually contrary to fact) that creditors relied on the stated capital in extending credit. On this theory, creditors with claims arising prior to the wrongful issuance, or subsequent creditors who were aware of the wrongful issuance, could not share in any additional payments by the shareholders. Early courts wavered between these two theories, often referring to a trust fund theory, but reaching decisions more consistent with the holding out theory.

Modern corporation acts now define the liability of shareholders in connection with the issuance of shares in precise though not always unambiguous terms. A widely adopted provision of the Model Business Corporation Act states that "a holder of . . . shares of a corporation shall be under no obligation to the corporation or to its creditors with respect to such shares other than the obligation to pay to the corporation *the full consideration for which such shares were issued or to be issued*." (MBCA § 25.) In effect, this article (1) substitutes a statutory obligation running both to the corporation and its creditors for the obligation based on the trust fund or holding out theories of common law, and (2) measures the extent of the liability on the basis of "the consideration for which such shares were issued or to be issued" rather than par value. This section must be read along with section 18 of the Model Business Corporation Act which authorizes par value shares to be issued "for such consideration expressed in dollars, not less than the par value thereof, as shall be fixed from time to time" by the directors. The similar provision for no par shares is essentially the same with the omission of the phrase "not less than the par value thereof."

Under these statutes it is clear that a shareholder is liable to the corporation if he pays less for the shares than the consideration fixed by the directors, and his liability is measured by the difference between the fixed consideration and the amount actually paid. Further, if the consideration is improperly fixed by the directors at less than the par value of the shares to be issued, the shareholder is liable for the difference between whatever he pays and the par value of the shares. If nominal par value shares are used, it is unlikely that a shareholder will end up actually paying less than the par value of the shares; however, even if he pays more than par value he will still be liable to the corporation if he pays less than the consideration fixed by the directors. Virtually the same risk of liability exists if no par shares are used: there is no possibility that a shareholder will pay less than par, but he still is liable if he pays less than the consideration fixed by the directors for the issuance of the shares. Under these statutes there is thus little, if any, difference in potential liability between par and no par shares.

Some ambiguity may exist under these modern statutory provisions where property at an excessive valuation is contributed in exchange for either par value or no par value shares. Under the Model Act, for example, when issuing shares for property, section 18 provides that the directors set "the consideration expressed in dollars" or the "consideration expressed in dollars, not less than the par value thereof " for no par and par shares respectively. Under section 25, shareholders have no liability to the corporation with respect to shares "other than the obligation to pay to the corporation the full consideration for which shares were issued or to be issued." The key phrase in this section, the "full consideration" for which shares were issued may conceivably refer either to the designated property itself or to the dollar value placed on the property by the directors when it expressed the consideration "in dollars." This question arises whenever a previously unincorporated business is incorporated, and is present where either nominal par or no par shares are used. To take an example, assume that the directors authorize the issuance of 1,000 shares of $1.00 par value stock for specified property which they value at $10,000. Assume further the valuation of $10,000 is fraudulent and the property is actually worth only $5,000. After the shares are issued, the balance sheet of the corporation looks like this:

Assets		Liabilities	
Property	$10,000	Capital Accounts	
		Stated Capital	$1,000
		Capital Surplus	9,000

At common law the rule in this kind of situation appeared to be that the shares were not watered at all since the value of the property received exceeded the stated capital of the corporation. If the shareholder in such a case did not expressly promise to pay $10,000 but only to contribute the specified property there appeared to be no way to hold the shareholder liable for more than the property itself. Of course, there is something peculiar about this balance sheet because the value of the assets are greatly overstated and the "capital surplus" account contains $5,000 of "water." It may be that a representation that the assets are worth $10,000 to a creditor would be fraudulent in and of itself; however, there is no basis for recovery against the *shareholder* unless he actually makes such a representation.

A final answer may depend on the precise language of the state statute involved. If the statute, unlike the Model Act, allows directors to establish the consideration for which shares are to be issued as simply specific property without setting a value "in dollars," it would seem that the shareholders would not be liable for watered shares since the "full consideration" required by law is only the property itself, and that has been contributed. However, if the statute, like the Model Act, requires the directors to express the value of the consideration "in dollars," as most statutes do, it is likely that the shareholder in the above example is liable for an additional $5,000 since the "full amount of the consideration fixed as provided by law" was $10,000 and he has only contributed property with a value of $5,000.

At common law the issuance of watered, bonus or discount shares gave rise to liability on the shareholders receiving the shares, not liability on the directors authorizing such shares.

It is possible, however, to devise common law theories of liability by which directors might be held liable for authorizing watered shares, particularly in suits brought by other shareholders or creditors who relied on the financial statements thereby created.

§ 7.8   Current Trends Regarding Par Value

When all is said and done, the concepts of par value and stated capital have relatively little to commend them in the modern era. At best they are historical oddities that provide little real protection to creditors and have been twisted by sophisticated attorneys to squeeze out the maximum flexibility for their corporate creations. At worst, they are confusing if not misleading.

In 1979 the committee that is charged with reviewing and updating the Model Business Corporation Act approved a proposal to amend that Act by deleting all references to par value and all consequences that flow from a distinction between stated capital and capital surplus. Under this amendment, the validity of corporate distributions to shareholders is measured by the test whether the corporation is insolvent in either the bankruptcy or the equity sense immediately after the distribution. While the adequacy of the protection to creditors thus provided is still under consideration, the elegance and simplicity thereby created has much to commend it. At least one major state has adopted this approach and many more will probably follow it in the future.

§ 7.9   "Equity" and "Debt" Securities

Securities issued by a corporation may be broadly classified into "equity securities" and "debt securities." "Equity" in this sense is roughly synonymous with "ownership" and is derived from the following, quite common usage: if one subtracts a business's liabilities from its assets, what remains is the owners' "equity" in the business. Equity securities therefore refer to all securities that represent ownership interests in the corporation, while debt securities, such as bonds or debentures, represent interests that must ultimately be repaid. Common shares, of course, are the quintessence of an equity security since they represent the basic residual ownership of the corporation.

The distinction between "equity" and "debt" underlies much of the modern law and practice relating to corporation finance. At the simplest level the distinction is easy to grasp. A "debt" is something that must be repaid: it is the result of a "loan," the person making the loan is a "creditor," and if periodic payments are made, they are "interest." On the other hand, "equity" represents an ownership interest in the business itself. One thinks in terms of "shareholders," shares of "capital stock," voting, and "dividends" rather than "interest." It is sometimes not realized, however, that as a matter of economics, the distinction between debt and equity may not be at all clear in many situations. For example, a 100 year "debenture" with interest payable solely from income if and when earned, and repayment subordinate to other debts of the business is more like an equity security than a debt security. Corporations may create mixed or "hybrid" securities which have some of the characteristics of debt and some of equity. Despite the lack of clear distinction between debt and equity in these situations, legal consequences vary substantially depending on how a particular hybrid security is classified. A hybrid security may be treated as a debt security for some purposes and as an equity security for other purposes, *e. g.*, for income taxation purposes, rights on bankruptcy or insolvency, and the right to participate in management. The classification of hybrid securities for tax purposes, in particular, has given rise to some litigation.

§ 7.10 Characteristics of Debt Securities

Debt securities are important sources of capital for publicly held corporations. Typical debt securities are *notes, debentures* and *bonds*. Technically a "debenture" is an unsecured corporate obligation while a "bond" is secured by a lien or mortgage on corporate property. However, the word "bond" is often used indiscriminately to cover both bonds and debentures and is so used hereafter. A "bond" is a long term debt security while a "note" is a shorter term obligation. Bonds are traditionally *bearer* instruments, negotiable by delivery, with interest payments represented by *coupons* that are periodically clipped and submitted for payment. Notes are usually payable to the order of a person and interest payments are merely obligations not evidenced by a coupon. However, bonds may also be *registered* with the issuer and transferable only by endorsement. Article 8 of the Uniform Commercial Code makes registered bonds negotiable.

Interest payments on debt securities are usually fixed obligations, due in any event, and expressed as a percentage of the face amount of the security. However, so-called income bonds, in which the obligation to pay interest is conditioned on adequate corporate earnings, are also known. Somewhat rarer are so-called participating bonds, where the amount of interest payable on the bonds increases with corporate earnings.

Debt securities are usually subject to *redemption*, which means that the corporation has reserved the power to call in and pay off the obligation before it is due, often at a slight premium over the face value. Securities chosen for redemption may be chosen by lot or by some other system. Many debt securities require the corporation to set aside cash, usually called *sinking fund* provisions, to redeem a part of the issue each year or to accumulate to pay off the entire issue when it matures.

Debt securities may be *convertible* into equity securities, particularly common stock, on some predetermined ratio. This ratio is often adjusted for stock splits, dividends, etc. The protection given by such adjustments is often referred to as protecting the conversion privilege from *dilution*. When convertible debentures are converted, they, and the debt they represent, disappear and the new equity securities (often called the conversion securities) are issued in their place. Convertible debentures themselves are treated as equity securities for many purposes.

Some states authorize holders of bonds to participate in the selection of the board of directors upon specified contingencies, such as default in payment of interest. The inclusion of such powers, of course, blurs the distinction between debt and equity securities.

§ 7.11   Classes of Equity Securities

Common shares are, of course, the basic equity security reflecting the underlying ownership of the corporation. Another well-known class of equity security are preferred shares, described below. State corporation statutes give corporations broad power to create novel types of securities or specially tailored classes of common or preferred securities; this flexibility is often utilized to effectuate intracorporate agreements in closely held corporations. The emphasis in this section, like the preceding one, is essentially descriptive, concentrating on broad classes of equity securities including those issued by large publicly held corporations to raise capital.

(1) *Preferred shares.*   Preferred shares differ from common shares in that they have preference over common shares in the payment of dividends and/or preference in the assets of the corporation upon the voluntary or involuntary liquidation of the corporation. "Preference" simply means that the preferred shares are entitled to receive some specified payment (either a dividend or a liquidating distribution, or both) before the common shares are entitled to anything. Most preferred shares contain preferences both as to dividends and liquidation.

The dividend preference may be described either in terms of dollars per share (the "$3.20 preferred") or as a percentage of par or stated value (the "five per cent preferred"). A dividend preference does not mean that the preferred is entitled to the payment in the same way that a creditor is entitled to payment from his debtor. A preferred dividend is still a dividend, and the directors may decide to omit all dividends, common or preferred, and this decision is in no way dependent on whether or not there is current income. Shares preferred as to dividends may be *cumulative, noncumulative,* or *partially cumulative.* If cumulative dividends are not paid in some years, they are carried forward and both they and the current year's preferred dividends must be paid in full before any common dividends may be declared. Noncumulative dividends disappear each year if they are not paid. Partially cumulative dividends are usually of the "cumulative to the extent of earnings" type so that such preferred shares continue to have first claim to actual earnings if not paid out as dividends. Unpaid cumulative dividends are not debts of the corporation, but a continued right to priority in future distributions. Since directors (who are elected by the common shareholders) may defer preferred dividends indefinitely if the directors are willing to forego dividends on the common shares as well, it is customary to provide that preferred shares may elect a specified number of directors if preferred dividends have been omitted for a specified period.

Preferred shares may also be *participating*, though typically they are not. Nonparticipating shares are entitled to a specified dividend before anything is paid on the common but no more, irrespective of the earnings of the corporation. Participating preferred shares are entitled to the original dividend, and after the common receives a specified amount, they may share with the common in any additional distributions. Such shares are sometimes referred to as "Class A common" or a similar designation reflecting that their right to participate is open-ended.

Like debt securities, preferred shares are often made *convertible* into common shares at a specified price or specified ratio and redeemable by the corporation at a fixed price. Typically, the original conversion ratio is established so that the common must appreciate substantially before it is profitable to convert the preferred. When the price of the common rises above this level, the preferred shares will fluctuate in price as the price of the common fluctuates. The redemption privilege usually does not limit the price of the convertible preferred since the privilege to convert customarily continues for a limited period of time after a call for redemption. A conversion is described as *forced* when shares are called for redemption at a time when the value of the shares obtainable on conversion exceeds the redemption price. Also like convertible debt securities, convertible preferred usually contain elaborate provisions protecting the conversion privilege from *dilution* in case of stock dividends, stock splits or the issuance of additional common shares. The statutes of some states prohibit the creation of a security which is convertible into shares having superior rights and preferences as to dividends or upon liquidation—in other words, a common may not be made convertible into preferred. State statutes also may limit the redemption privilege to securities that have a liquidation preference. These limitations are virtually the only substantive statutory restrictions on the issuance of classes of shares in most states.

Articles of incorporation may also authorize preferred shares to be issued in *series*. Such articles in effect authorize the board of directors to vary any of the substantive terms of the preferred from time to time. Where preferred shares in substantial amounts are to be sold by a corporation from time to time to raise capital, the privilege of issuing preferred in series simplifies financing since the price, dividend, liquidation preference, sinking fund provision, voting rights, and other terms of each series may be tailored to then-current market conditions. Shares of different series have identical rights except for the specified business terms which may be varied. Before a series of preferred shares is created, a public filing with the Secretary of State describing the terms of the new series is required. As a practical matter, these provisions are of considerably less importance today than they once were because of the decline in preferred share financing.

The various provisions defining the rights of preferred shareholders appear in the corporation's articles of incorporation bylaws, or directors resolutions. Collectively they are often referred to as the preferred shareholders' "contract" with the corporation and with other classes of shareholders.

(2) *Classes of common stock.* State statutes also give corporations broad power to create classes of common stock with different rights or privileges. Such classes are usually designated by alphabetical notations: "Class A common," "Class B common" and so forth. In closely held corporations, classes of common stock are primarily used to effectuate control, voting, or financial arrangements. The following examples illustrate the variety and flexibility that classes of common stock may provide:

(a) A Class A common may be created that is entitled to twice the dividend per share of Class B common, but in all other respects the two classes are identical.

(b) A Class A common may be created that has two votes per share while Class B common has one vote per share (this is permitted in some but not all states; some state statutes still have a "one vote per share" principle).

(c) A Class A common may be created that has the power to elect two directors; the holders of Class B common may have the power to elect one, two, or more directors, irrespective of the number of shares of each class outstanding.

(d) It may be required that the president of the corporation be a holder of Class A shares and the vice-president and treasurer be holders of Class B shares.

Classes of common stock may also be used to solve financial control, or dividend problems in publicly held corporations, though such use is less common. When the Ford Motor Company went public in 1946, it created a special class of common shares to be held by the Ford Foundation. The shares were convertible into common when sold by the Foundation. These shares were nonvoting so they permitted control of the corporation to be vested in the public without requiring the Foundation to abruptly liquidate its huge interest in the corporation. When Max Factor & Co. went public in 1948, it issued a new class of common stock, "Class A shares" to members of the Factor family. Class A was identical to the regular voting common except that the board was authorized to declare smaller dividends on the Class A than on the publicly held voting common. For many years the board did so, thereby permitting maximum dividends to be paid to the public shareholders, preserving the funds of the corporation, and reducing the income tax liability of members of the Factor family, who obviously did not need the income. The Class A shares were convertible into common, a privilege which the Factor family exercised shortly before selling the shares.

(3) *Non-voting shares.* In most states, the articles of incorporation may limit or deny the right to vote to classes of shares. Preferred shares are usually non-voting shares, but the privilege to vote may be extended to such shares, either with the common shares or as a separate class. In the closely held corporation, non-voting shares may serve a planning role similar to classes of common shares. For example, the right to vote may be limited or denied to classes of common shares in the election of directors, on other subjects normally submitted to shareholders, or both. In such corporations there seems to be little objection to the theory that a specific limitation on voting is part of the shareholder's overall "contract" with the corporation.

In publicly held corporations, non-voting shares have been treated with greater suspicion. Such shares are somewhat analogous to perpetual voting trusts, and have been criticized on policy grounds for this reason. (See § 9.7). Corporations with non-voting shares which are held by the public are ineligible for listing on the New York Stock Exchange, and may suffer market and other disadvantages as well.

In the early years of this century, many corporations were capitalized by the issuance of non-voting shares to the public while the voting shares were held by the members of the family which founded or controlled the corporation. This practice has declined in importance in recent years. Further, several corporations that had issued non-voting shares for this reason have later converted the shares into voting shares. This decision creates subtle issues as to the relative value of the right to vote and the fairness of the terms on which the privilege to vote is granted.

Under most state statutes, even non-voting shares are entitled to vote in connection with certain mergers, consolidations, and other extraordinary events that may affect the class of non-voting shares as a class.

(4) *Options.* Options to purchase shares may be used as a capital raising device, to provide employee incentives, and to a lesser extent as part of control devices. Of course, shares under option are not deemed issued and may not be voted until the options are exercised and the purchase price paid, or in some states, a firm commitment to pay the purchase price in the form of a promissory note has been delivered to the corporation.

Employee stock purchase or stock option plans are largely governed by the Internal Revenue Code, since favorable tax treatment is usually an essential part of the success of such plans. Many state corporation statutes contain provisions that authorize the issuance of shares in connection with such plans by the board of directors and provide that in the absence of fraud the determination by the board of the consideration for such shares shall be conclusive. (MBCA § 20).

Warrants are transferable options to acquire shares from the corporation at a specified price. Warrants have many of the qualities of an equity security since their price is a function of the market price of the underlying shares and the specified issuance price. Warrants frequently are issued as a "sweetener" in connection with the distribution of a debt or preferred stock issue; they may be issued in connection with a public exchange offer, or as compensation for handling the public distribution of other shares. Sometimes they are issued in a reorganization to holders of a class of security not otherwise recognized in the reorganization. Warrants are often publicly traded; warrants issued by a number of corporations are listed from time to time on the New York Stock Exchange or other exchanges. *Rights* are in effect short term warrants. They may also be publicly traded and listed on securities exchanges. Rights are often issued in lieu of a dividend, or in an effort to raise capital from existing shareholders. The exercise price of both warrants and rights must of course be below the market price of the optioned shares if the warrants or rights are to have value.

§ 7.12   The Advantages of Debt Financing

It is usually advantageous for a corporation to engage to some extent in debt financing. The notion that the best business is a debt-free business, while sounding attractive, is not consistent either with the minimization of income taxes or with the maximization of profits.

(1) *Tax advantages of debt.* There are usually tax advantages for shareholders to lend to the corporation a portion of their investment in the corporation rather than to contribute it outright. Such debt reduces the double taxation problem of corporations discussed earlier. (See § 2.3.) Interest payments on debt are deductible by the corporation whereas dividend payments on

equity securities are not. Further, repayment of a debt may be a non-taxable return of capital, while a purchase or redemption of equity securities from a shareholder by the corporation is often a taxable event leading to ordinary income. When a shareholder lends a portion of his investment to the corporation he is hopefully reserving the option of recovering this portion tax free at some later date if the corporation is successful.

There is no tax advantage in debt owed to persons other than shareholders.

The tax advantages of debt financing are so substantial that a substantial amount of case law has developed dealing with the question when debt in the corporate structure is excessive so that the Internal Revenue Service may treat the debt as a kind of equity, and disallow interest deductions or treat its repayment as a taxable dividend. (See § 7.13.) These cases are closely related to the doctrine of "piercing the corporate veil," discussed earlier (see Chapter Six).

(2) *Non-tax advantages of debt.* In the tax area, the advantage of debt lies basically in debt owed to shareholders which may be used to lessen the impact of the double taxation of corporations and shareholders. In the non-tax area debt owed both to third persons and to shareholders may be advantageous to a corporation, for entirely different reasons.

(a) Debt owed to third persons is desirable because of the factor of *leverage*. Leverage arises when the corporation is able to earn more on the borrowed capital than the cost of the borrowing. The entire excess is allocable to the equity accounts of the corporation, thereby increasing the rate of return on the equity invested in the corporation. An example should help to make this clear. Let us assume that a person is considering the purchase of a business which will yield $25,000 per year over and above all taxes and expenses. The purchase price is $200,000. If the person simply buys the business using only his own   capital,   the   annual   return   is $\frac{25,000}{200,000}$ or   12½   per   cent.

Let us assume that the same person can borrow 80 per cent of the purchase price at an interest cost of 10 per cent per year. The person will then invest $40,000 of his own capital (20 per cent of $200,000), and borrow the remaining $160,000 (80 per cent of $200,000). The interest cost of the loan is $16,000 per year (10% of $160,000). Since the business still makes $25,000 per year, the net profit after interest costs is $9,000 on a net investment of $40,000, and the return on the investment is

$\frac{9,000}{40,000}$ or 22.5%. In other words, by borrowing 80 per cent of the purchase price, the return per equity dollar invested is increased from 12.5 per cent to 22.5 per cent. If there were five such simultaneous opportunities, a rational investor would take his initial $200,000 and invest $40,000 in each of the five rather than buying only one business free debt. By buying five businesses with 80 per cent loans, he will make $9,000 × 5 = $45,000 rather than $25,000 × 1 = $25,000. This is leverage, a device well understood by real estate syndicates and promoters who seek to obtain the largest possible mortgage and the smallest possible equity investment of their own. The reason that it is desirable to leverage in the hypothetical is that each dollar invested earns 12½ per cent but the cost of borrowing is only 10 per cent. The 2½ per cent difference on every borrowed dollar is allocable to the equity investment—the 20 per cent —thereby increasing the overall return on the equity. The risk, of course, is that the income from the project may not be sufficient to cover the fixed interest charges. The investor would quickly see his return reduced to zero; it is possible that a "negative cash flow" would result and the investor would have to invest additional amounts to cover the shortfall of income over expenses. Certainly, the investor may be wiped out much more quickly in a leveraged investment than if no part of the purchase price were borrowed.

Since World War II, the United States has suffered an inflationary spiral which, at the time this is written, at least, shows no sign of abating. If inflation continues, debt financing is also attractive because the loans will ultimately be repaid with inflated dollars. Of course, the competition for loans in such circumstances may cause high interest charges which will offset, either wholly or partially, this advantage of debt financing.

(b) Leverage can be obtained only by the use of other people's money. Nevertheless, it is often advantageous for business reasons for shareholders to advance a portion of their investment in the business in the form of loans rather than capital contributions. (The tax advantages of doing this have previously been discussed.) As a creditor, a shareholder may have greater rights upon bankruptcy or insolvency than he would as a mere shareholder. However, if the loans are made as part of the original capitalization of the company, there is a substantial risk that such loans will be subordinated to the claims of general creditors in a bankruptcy proceeding. (See § 6.8). The basic test is whether the capitalization is such that a third person would have made an arms length loan. If so the loan by the shareholder should be treated as a loan, for bankruptcy purposes. Loans for subsequent business needs also may fare better and stand a good chance of being recognized as bona fide loans.

§ 7.13   Tax Consequences of Excessive Debt Capitalization

The substantial tax advantages of shareholder debt financing have led to a large amount of tax litigation as to whether ostensible debt should be reclassified as equity for tax purposes. The judicial decisions in this area do not establish a simple, easily understood test as to when a reclassification from debt to equity is proper. The diversity of possible factual situations is substantial, and there is less than total agreement in the cases as to the applicable legal principles. Perhaps Judge John R.

Brown was being somewhat ironic when, in the leading Fifth Circuit case on the question, he stated: "Although the results are diverse, sometimes favoring the taxpayer, sometimes the Government, the cases are in accord in applying with an even hand the controlling legal principles for determining the outcome . . . ." Tomlinson v. 1661 Corp., 377 F.2d 291 (5th Cir. 1967).

Two interrelated ideas appear to underlie the judicial reasoning in the numerous cases in this area: first, are the legal incidents of the relationship between corporation and shareholder more similar to an equity investment or to a debt relationship? And second, even where the principal incidents of debt exist, is there some paramount policy of federal tax law which requires that particular debt interests be treated as equity investments?

Certainly, many cases may be explained on the ground that despite the label "debt" attached to an interest, the shareholder really created an equity interest. Some of these cases adopt a test of the "intention" of the shareholder in making the investment, but state that this "intention" may be inferred from the provisions of the debenture itself or from surrounding circumstances The following factors tend to indicate an "intention" to make an equity or capital contribution: (a) use of initial payments, both capital and "loans," to acquire capital assets; (b) proceeds used to start up the corporate life; (c) subordination to other indebtedness; (d) an "inordinately postponed due date;" (e) provision for payment of "interest" only out of earnings; and (f) an express or implied agreement not to enforce collection of the "debt."

At one time it was thought that the talismanic test was the ratio between debt and equity. It was intimated in the Supreme Court decision in John Kelley Co. v. Commissioner, 326 U.S. 521 (1946), that a ratio of 4:1 (debt equal to four times equity) or more automatically led to the reclassification of the debt as equity. A corporation with a high debt/equity ratio is often called a "thin" corporation. Later cases, however, have rejected the suggestion that the test is a mechanical one based on an arithmetic calculation. In other words, courts have rejected in strong terms the argument by the government that a high ratio of debt to equity automatically indicated an objectionable avoidance of taxes, and therefore grounds for treating the debt as equity. However, high debt/equity ratios are relevant and it is not surprising that most cases in which debt has been reclassified as equity involve debt/equity ratios higher than 4:1, and often higher than 10:1.

§ 7.14   The Deep Rock Doctrine Revisited

The so-called Deep Rock doctrine has been discussed in a previous chapter (see § 6.8). The doctrine, evolved in bankruptcy cases, permits subordination of shareholder-owned debt to the claims of general creditors when the Court believes it is fair to do so. It is therefore the bankruptcy analogue to the "thin corporation" problem in tax law described in the last section. The shareholder claims which are subordinated may be either secured or unsecured: under this doctrine the court may treat secured shareholder claims either as on a parity with general unsecured claims or as inferior to all other such claims. Obviously, this doctrine, when applied, has the effect of eliminating one major advantage of shareholder indebtedness.

The doctrine has generally been applied in Federal bankruptcy cases, and it has also been recognized in some state insolvency proceedings.

Some cases have held that a mere showing of inadequate capitalization is not enough for disallowance or subordination in the bankruptcy area and that there must be some additional showing of unfairness, fraud. or misrepresentation. The shareholder involved may have the burden of showing "the inherent fairness and good faith of the transactions involved."

One court has suggested that "[i]t is only where the conduct of a stockholder or officer toward his corporation can be challenged as being detrimental to the creditors that there is any duty on behalf of the referee or the courts to recast the voluntary acts of the corporation into something different from what they have in good faith undertaken to engage in." As a practical matter, however, if the initial capitalization is grossly inadequate, some other element of unfairness can usually be found which under this test will permit the court to subordinate the shareholder indebtedness. Also the case law is in disagreement as to whether the adequacy of the initial capital is to be judged in the light of the needs of the particular business, or on an abstract basis of substantiality.

As in the case of tax controversies, subsequent loans needed to keep the business afloat are likely to be accepted by the courts as true loans for bankruptcy purposes, though unfair attempts to obtain security for such loans may still be attacked under the Deep Rock doctrine.

§ 7.15 Equalizing Capital and Services When Forming a Corporation

A recurring problem in financing a close corporation that utilizes the various concepts developed earlier in this Chapter involves the situation where investors have agreed to contribute capital or provide services in varying amounts, and shares are to be issued in some different agreed ratio. Assume, for example, that A and B have agreed to go into business with A providing the necessary capital of $100,000 with B to work exclusively for the new venture for at least three years. The parties have also agreed that A is to receive 60 per cent and B 40 per cent of the voting shares. How can the arrangement be worked out?

(1) In most states, B cannot be issued shares immediately upon the execution of a long-term employment contract, since "future services" are not valid consideration in most states.

(2) There is no obstacle, however, to issuing shares for *past* services. Hence the arrangement may be worked out by issuing A 60 shares for his $100,000 immediately, and issuing B 40 shares when the period of employment ends three years from now. Possible disadvantages are (i) until B has completed his services A is the sole shareholder with total power over the corporation and he may exclude B at any time (though such an exclusion may constitute a breach of contract); and (ii) B may have to provide services for an extended period without receiving dividends or a salary to live on. There is also a tax problem: If A's 60 shares are worth $100,000 after three years, the 40 shares issued to B for past services will be valued at about $66,667, and B will have to pay Federal income taxes on this amount finding the money to pay these additional taxes somewhere else.

(3) In some states B may sign a promissory note for the $66,667, have the 40 shares issued to him immediately, and pay off the note by rendering services under an employment contract. Again, Federal income taxes are a serious problem.

(4) Another solution is to issue shares at different prices. A may be issued 60 shares for $100,000 and B 40 shares for $40.00. Assuming that $1.00 par value shares are used, the capital accounts would be as follows:

(a) Stated capital $100,

(b) Capital surplus $99,900.

There is no statutory requirement that all shares of the same class be issued for the same consideration. However, this suggestion is manifestly unfair to A if the business does not do well and the parties desire to liquidate since B in effect has an immediate 40 per cent interest in A's capital. The Internal Revenue Service would take the position that the bargain sale to B constituted compensation for services and was taxable income to B to the extent of 40 per cent of $100,000.

(5) A more reasonable solution is to create two classes of common stock with identical rights on dissolution:

(a) Class A common, par value $1.00 per share, one vote per share; 6,000 shares issued to A for $100,000 in cash (or $16.67 per share).

(b) Class B common, par value $1.00 per share, one hundred votes per share, 40 shares issued to B for $667.00 (or $16.67 per share). If dividends are to be paid on a 60–40 ratio, the dividends on each share of class B stock would have to be set at one hundred times the dividend on each share of class A stock.

This solves the premature liquidation and watered stock problems, and minimizes the federal income tax problem since the Class B common would not be valued at a high price in view of its limited rights. However, multiple votes per share are not permitted in some states. Essentially the same pattern could be created by giving A shares with a fraction of a vote per share, if that is permitted under the specific state statute.

(6) An even better solution is to issue A 60 common shares for $60 and B 40 common shares for $40, and have A lend the corporation $99,940. This creates a "thin" corporation for tax purposes, and an attempt by the corporation to deduct interest payments on the $99,940 "debt" would certainly be disallowed. A also would probably not be able to maintain creditor status in a bankruptcy proceeding under the "Deep Rock" doctrine. B might also object that A should not have a creditor's claim to all his capital while B is contributing services for which he has no claim at all.

(7) Perhaps the best solution is this: A receives 60 common shares, par value .01, for $60.00 ($1 per share) and B receives 40 common shares, par value .01, for $40.00 ($1 per share). A also receives 500 preferred shares, par value $10.00, for $50,000 ($100 per share) and "lends" the corporation the remaining $50,000. Since the aggregate capitalization is now

$50,100 (combining all the consideration received for the common and preferred), debt is less than 50 per cent and the debt/equity ratio is about 1:1. The chances of applying the "thin" corporation or "Deep Rock" doctrines are therefore greatly reduced. This pattern was essentially upheld in the Maryland case of Obre v. Alban Tractor Co., 179 A.2d 861 (Md.1962), involving a state insolvency proceeding. It may be noted that the dividend preference of the preferred is not specified. Under the circumstances, that is a matter of negotiation between A and B.

§ 7.16　Issuance of Shares by a Going Concern:　Preemptive Rights

The issuance of shares by a going concern must meet the same requirements as to kind and amount of consideration as on the original formation and capitalization of the corporation. The number of shares to be sold and the consideration therefor is set by the board of directors. In addition, however, the issuance of new shares may affect the financial and voting rights of existing shareholders, and as a result additional legal requirements may be applicable. If shares are issued to the current shareholders in strict proportion to their shareholdings, the relative position of each shareholder is obviously unaffected though the aggregate capital invested in the corporation has increased. However, if shares are issued to third persons or to existing shareholders not in strictly proportional amounts, the voting power of some shareholders will necessarily be reduced. Further, if the shares are issued disproportionately and for less than current value (a term that need not here be precisely defined), the financial interest of some shareholders in the corporation will necessarily be diluted.

A "preemptive right" is a common law concept that permits an existing shareholder, subject to several important exceptions, to subscribe—in preference to strangers and pro rata with other existing shareholders—for his relative share of new shares to be issued by the corporation. Ideally, the preemptive right of each existing shareholder protects him from injury resulting from the issue of shares. However, in practice it often does not work out that way. For one thing, preemptive rights under modern statutes are permissive rather than mandatory and corporations may limit or deny such rights by provisions in the articles of incorporation. However, even if preemptive rights are excluded, equitable principles may limit the power of corporations to dispose of new shares on an unfair basis.

Shares sold by a going corporation may come from three sources. They may be shares which are newly authorized by the corporation by an amendment to the articles of incorporation. Or, they may be shares which were previously authorized in the articles but never previously issued. Or they may be "treasury shares," that is, shares that have been issued and subsequently reacquired by the corporation. Even though the issuance of any additional shares, no matter what the source, has the same dilutive effect, different legal principles may be applicable depending on the source of the shares.

At common law, it was generally held that a shareholder's preemptive right was an integral part of the ownership of shares. However, the common law preemptive right did not extend to the following types of transactions:

(1) Shares which were originally authorized but unissued. The rationale for this exception was that an implied understanding existed between the original subscribers that sale of the remaining authorized shares to obtain necessary capital may be completed. However, this rationale is not persuasive in light of the modern practice of authorizing additional shares which are not planned to be sold as part of the original capitalization. As a result some modern courts have refused to recognize this exception.

(2) Treasury shares. The rationale for this exception is that shareholders are not injured since the shares had previously

been issued and their reissuance simply restores a dilution that had existed previously.

(3) Shares issued for property or services rather than cash or shares issued in connection with a merger. The theory underlying these exceptions is that preemptive rights in such situations would frustrate or render impractical desirable transactions, or are impossible to work out since existing shareholders may not own, and therefore cannot contribute, property on a proportional basis.

(4) Shares issued to satisfy conversion or option rights.

(5) Shares issued pursuant to a plan of reorganization or recapitalization under court supervision.

Some recent decisions have refused to apply these exceptions mechanically and have looked to the realities of the particular situation. One court, for example, held that preemptive rights should not be denied when property is the consideration for shares except where because of peculiar circumstances the corporation has great need for the particular property, and issuance of shares therefor is the only practical and feasible method by which the corporation can acquire it. In many situations, the corporation may pay cash to acquire the needed property; to allow the corporation to acquire it with shares defeats the preemptive right that would exist if shares were issued for cash and the cash used to acquire the property.

Modern state statutes change the common law preemptive right in several respects:

(1) They give corporations the privilege of dispensing entirely with preemptive rights if they so choose. The choice must be made by a specific provision in the corporation's articles of incorporation. Statutes may grant preemptive rights unless they are specifically negated in the articles, or preclude preemptive rights except to the extent specifically granted in the articles.

(2) They sometimes give preemptive rights more broadly than the common law, *e. g.,* they may extend the right to "authorized but unissued shares," "treasury shares," and securities convertible into common shares, all types of shares to which the common law preemptive right did not extend.

(3) They provide specifically that preemptive rights do not exist between different classes of shares, *e. g.,* holders of preferred do not have a preemptive right to acquire common.

(4) They provide that shares issued pursuant to employee incentive or compensation plans are not subject to preemptive rights if the plan was originally approved by the shareholders.

What considerations enter into the decision to limit or deny preemptive rights? The argument in favor of preserving preemptive rights is that the shareholder who subscribes for a given percentage of the original issue of the shares of a corporation should be entitled to maintain his percentage interest provided he is willing to subscribe for his proportion of additional issues of shares. This sounds like a democratic principle and undoubtedly it is in many cases. There are situations, however, in which preemptive rights are more a nuisance than anything else. Suppose for example that a corporation with a fairly large number of shareholders is in need of immediate funds and can obtain them only by a prompt sale of additional shares to bankers or underwriters. It may well find that compliance with and satisfaction of the preemptive rights of its existing shareholders will be expensive, time-consuming and only partially successful. The result may be that the corporation will lose its financing.

If it is anticipated that the corporation will for some time remain a close corporation preemptive rights are often retained so as to give each shareholder the maximum protection against dilution. But, if it is anticipated that the corporation will in the near future engage in public financing or will seek to acquire other companies or properties by the issuance of its shares, preemptive rights are often eliminated to avoid legal complications when the time arrives for the sale of additional shares or the acquisition of other companies or properties. In any event, preemptive rights serve little purpose where shares are publicly traded, since additional shares can usually be bought on the open market if desired. Where preemptive rights have been excluded, the directors may always later decide to offer additional shares pro rata to existing shareholders. In fact, existing shareholders are often the most logical market, and one likely to be pursued.

§ 7.17   Oppressive Issuance of Shares

Additional shares of stock may often be issued oppressively to dilute the interests of other shareholders in the corporation. Misuse of this power is often referred to as a *squeeze out* or *freeze out*.

A number of cases attest that corporate management has a fiduciary duty of taking corporate action according to the best interests of the corporation rather than for personal advantage. This principle amply covers situations where, in the absence of preemptive rights, management dilutes the interests of shareholders simply by issuing additional shares to itself at a bargain price. This principle may also cover situations where management issues shares to itself at a fair price to ensure retention of control without offering the shares more broadly. In the first situation there is dilution of both financial and voting interests; in the second there is only dilution of the voting power.

Much more difficult are cases involving a combination of legitimate and self-serving purposes. Shares may be issued to friendly persons for apparently worthwhile purposes and entirely in accordance with statutory requirements, but the minority shareholders complain that the real purpose and principal effect of the transaction is to freeze them out or dilute their interest.

Most cases have permitted such transactions to stand, at least where the ostensible purpose does seem to have substance. Courts are naturally reluctant to second guess decisions by directors and interfere in intracorporate disputes, but will do so if they feel that the ostensible purpose is a sham, and the real purpose of the transaction is simply to benefit management.

Preemptive rights give shareholders considerably less protection against such tactics than is often thought. Indeed, as a practical matter, the protection provided by preemptive rights is often illusory. A minority shareholder may be frozen out if he lacks the financial ability to exercise his preemptive right and purchase the additional shares in order to protect his proportionate interest. Often, the majority or dominant shareholders may purchase their allotment by offsetting indebtedness owed to them by the corporation (thereby exercising their preemptive rights without further financial investment) while other shareholders have to invest substantial amounts of cash just to stay even. In one case, for example, the court refused to intervene when a shareholder was given the choice of investing an additional $136,000 to preserve his twenty per cent interest or permitting his interest in the corporation to be diluted to less than one per cent. Hyman v. Velsicol Corp., 97 N.E.2d 122 (Ill.App.1951). In another case, where the reduction was from about 32 per cent to less than one per cent, the court applied the test whether the issuance of shares seemed to serve a substantial corporate purpose or whether it was designed simply to benefit management, and over one dissent, concluded that the issuance of shares should be set aside. Browning v. C. & C. Plywood Corp., 434 P.2d 339 (Or.1967). The issue in these cases usually comes down to an evaluation of the need of the corporation for the additional capital, or where indebtedness is cancelled and the corporation receives no additional cash, whether the improvement in the balance sheet caused by the cancellation of indebtedness is a bona fide purpose.

§ 7.18 Treasury Shares

Treasury shares are shares of a corporation which have been issued but subsequently reacquired by and belong to the corporation. Treasury shares have an intermediate status—they are usually treated as issued but not outstanding in the corporate financial statements—and may not be voted or be counted in determining the number of shares outstanding. Of course, they are not entitled to dividends.

While not technically treasury shares, shares owned by a wholly- or majority-owned subsidiary of the issuing corporation also may not usually be voted or considered as outstanding. In other words, circular control is prohibited under most statutes. On a similar theory, shares held by the issuing corporation in a fiduciary capacity also may be barred from being voted or counted in determining the number of shares outstanding.

Treasury shares differ in kind, not degree, from shares of other corporations which the corporation may own. Shares of other corporations are investments; on the other hand, it is incorrect to argue that treasury shares of a corporation are also an investment. When a corporation acquires some of its own shares, the assets of the corporation are reduced by the amount of the purchase price and all the other owners of shares have a somewhat increased proportional interest in the reduced assets. Treasury shares are economically indistinguishable from authorized but unissued shares. Thus, it is not meaningful to treat the acquisition of treasury shares as anything but a disproportionate distribution of corporate assets to the selling shareholders, or better, a disproportionate dividend. See § 16.11.

§ 7.19 A Cautionary Postscript: The Risk of Violating Securities Acts While Raising Capital

The Federal Securities Act of 1933 and state statutes, called "blue sky laws," require corporations to register issues of securities with governmental agencies before they are sold publicly. (The picturesque name, "blue sky laws" is reputedly derived from the practice of certain turn-of-the-century promoters of selling "lots in the blue sky in fee simple absolute.") Registration under these statutes, considered at length in advanced courses on securities regulation, is expensive, difficult, and time-consuming. Further, selling shares without registration when required gives rise to substantial civil liabilities and may lead to criminal prosecution as well.

When corporations raise capital by selling shares, it is important that the offering not become inadvertently a public one, thereby triggering the registration requirements of these statutes, or that some other exemption from registration under these statutes is available. The definition of a "public offering" and the scope of exemptions from registration are often complex legal issues. As a result the risk of an inadvertent violation of these statutes is often a real one.

When a corporation first registers securities under these statutes it is often said to "go public."

[For unfamiliar terms see the Glossary]

CHAPTER EIGHT

THE DISTRIBUTION OF POWERS WITHIN A CORPORATION: THE SPECIAL PROBLEMS OF THE CLOSELY HELD CORPORATION

§ 8.1 The "Statutory Scheme"

Each state business corporation act envisions a particular model or norm of management and control within the corporation. This model is often referred to as the "statutory scheme." The statute assumes that every corporation has certain characteristics, even though manifestly not all corporations in the real world possess these characteristics. For example, the statute assumes that shareholders will hold meetings to select directors who in turn elect or appoint officers. A corporation with only a single shareholder does not fit this scheme very well. Rather surprisingly, a large, publicly-held corporation also may not fit this scheme very well either since shareholders in a public corporation may be so diverse and poorly organized that their principal function is ratifying the selection of directors by "management," a group of persons who control the corporate destiny with a small financial investment in the corporation. It is probable, however, that the statutory scheme more or less accurately describes the control relationships in many intermediate corporations in the continuum between the very small and the very large.

A question that is often critically important is the extent to which the statutory requirements relating to management and control may be varied by agreement between the parties. This question usually arises in the context of small, closely held corporations which in practice more closely resemble partnerships than publicly held corporations. A person not versed in corporation law might well conclude that in the absence of harm to some class of persons, businessmen should be permitted to vary the statutory norms to fit the needs of their particular business relationship. Such freedom is generally available in partnerships, and there seems to be no reason why it should not be equally available in corporations. The reason it is not is the survival of the theory that the granting of the privilege of limited liability and permission to conduct business in the name of a fictitious entity is a concession by the State: in order to gain the concession one must follow the procedures and rules set forth in the business corporation statutes. (See generally Chapter 1, § 1.2.) Despite criticism of this theory, it appears to be firmly embedded in the jurisprudence of most states, and it is therefore unsafe to attempt by agreement substantial variations from the statutory norm. Legislation is the ultimate solution if greater freedom is felt to be necessary, and indeed, as described in a later chapter (Chapter 12), an increasing number of states have adopted special statutes to relieve closely held corporations from the strictures of the statutory scheme.

§ 8.2   The Statutory Scheme—Shareholders

The shareholders in the statutory scheme are the ultimate owners of the corporation, but have only limited powers to participate in management and control. The statutes contemplate that they may act through four main channels:

(1) Election and removal of directors;

(2) Approval or disapproval of corporate operations which are void or voidable unless ratified;

(3) Approval or disapproval of amendments to articles of incorporation or bylaws constituting the "contract" between the corporation and its shareholders; and

(4) Approval or disapproval of fundamental changes not in the regular course of business (mergers, consolidations, dissolution, or disposition of substantially all the corporate assets).

This list, however, does not fully exhaust the shareholders' powers in fact. For example, statutes also grant shareholders miscellaneous incidental powers, which include, *e. g.*, a veto power over repurchases of corporate shares out of capital surplus, the power to enjoin ultra vires acts, a veto power over dividends payable in the shares of the corporation, and the power to approve the consideration for which no par shares are issued. It is also well established that shareholders may adopt resolutions making recommendations to the board of directors, and because of the power to select and remove directors, it is probable that the directors will listen carefully to the views of a majority of the shareholders. (See § 8.6.) Further, some matters such as the selection of independent accountants have been either by tradition or because of regulations by the Securities and Exchange Commission vested in the shareholders. Nevertheless, the fact remains that the shareholders have only limited powers to participate in management and control: their principal function is to select other persons—the directors—to manage the business of the corporation for them.

§ 8.3   The Statutory Scheme: Power of Shareholders to Remove Directors

At common law, a director has considerable security of office for the period of his election. He can be removed only for cause, a procedure technically known as "amotion." Further, a director, threatened with removal for cause, is entitled to some minimal elements of due process including notice of charges, an opportunity to be heard, and a hearing. Of course, in a corporation with shares widely held by the general public, a "trial" of a director by the shareholders at a meeting is unwieldy and impractical. Decision is made in fact by the granting or withholding of a proxy, a fact that has been recognized by courts which insist that the imperiled director be given access to the proxy machinery to conduct his defense. There is also some case law questioning the power of a court to remove a director even for cause if a majority of the shareholders refuse to do so. Statutes in some states specifically authorize such a court order. These various rules are basically consistent with the principle that directors' independence of judgment cannot be restricted or interfered with by shareholders.

Modern corporation statutes permit shareholders to remove directors with or without cause, though in some states, a power to remove directors without cause exists only if the specific power is reserved to the shareholders in the bylaws. These statutes relaxing the common law rule and permitting the removal of directors without cause subtly change the relation between shareholders and directors. They may be important in at least two areas:

(1) Where a person has recently acquired a majority of the outstanding shares (or at least working control) and desires to put "his own people" in control of the corporation;

(2) In closely held corporations where a majority shareholder may wish to elect friends as directors but ensure their continued loyalty. An unlimited power of removal without cause goes a long way to ensuring that loyalty.

A question exists as to whether an amendment to bylaws granting an unlimited power of removal may be made effective against incumbent directors who were elected under bylaws that guaranteed them greater security of office. A court may be tempted to argue in this situation that a change in the bylaws during the term of a director is an invalid deprivation of a vested right.

§ 8.4 The Statutory Scheme—Directors

The business corporation acts of many states include a general provision that "the business and affairs of a corporation shall be managed by board of directors." The word "shall" has a mandatory ring, and it is pursuant to this article that courts have often struck down, as against public policy, agreements between businessmen which purport to dictate how persons shall vote as directors.

In the very large corporation with billions of dollars of assets, it is not realistic to expect the directors actually to manage the day-to-day affairs of the business. That is management's responsibility. In recognition of this the Model Business Corporation Act and the statutes of some states have modified the basic obligation of directors to read: "all corporate powers shall be exercised by *or under authority of*, and the business and affairs of a corporation shall be *managed under the direction of*, a board of directors . . .." (MBCA § 35).

The scope of the phrase "business and affairs" is not defined in the statutes. Generally, directors are expected to formulate the policy of the corporation, and authorize the making of important contracts. They may delegate details of the actual daily operation of the corporation to officers and agents, but must retain some responsibility for general supervision. Presumably, the powers of the directors begin where the powers of the shareholders stop.

Directors also have specific statutory authority in numerous areas. For example, the decision to declare dividends is specifically a directoral function, as is the determination of the consideration for which shares are to be issued. Even in the case of important corporate changes which require shareholder approval, the directors have the responsibility to formulate the proposed change, approve it, and submit it to the shareholders for approval or disapproval. Thus, decisions on such basic matters in most states are shared between shareholders and directors, and both must concur in the proposal. In a handful of states, including Massachusetts, shareholders have power to effectuate basic corporate changes without the concurrence of the directors.

The power of directors to manage the business and affairs of the corporation in a sense flows from the statute rather than from the shareholders who elected them. Directors may, if they wish, disregard the expressed desires of a majority of the shareholders and act as they think best—subject of course, to the ultimate power of the shareholders to select different directors next time. However, there are only a few recorded illustrations of the exercise of this independent power. As a practical matter, the power of selection and removal of directors is a powerful brake on boards of directors acting independently of the wishes of a majority of the shareholders. In addition, there is perhaps a partially articulated notion that such independence of action is inconsistent with shareholder democracy in publicly held corporations. This problem occasionally arises immediately after a successful corporate takeover where the shareholders do not possess the power to remove sitting directors.

The relationships between directors, shareholders and the corporation are *sui generis*. The shareholders elect directors who are granted broad powers of management with respect to the corporation and its property, which in the last analysis is owned by the shareholders. Further, responsibility accompanies power. The directors owe a fiduciary duty to the corporation and to the shareholders. Such duties include specified statutory liabilities for director misconduct plus broader common law duties —due care, loyalty, corporate opportunity, and the like. A director may be liable for misconduct even though he is following the wishes of a majority of the shareholders of a corporation. Because of this risk of directoral liability, cases involving the role of directors place great importance on their unimpaired independence of decision. Shareholder agreements on matters that are reserved to the discretion of directors are against public policy. They "fetter" the discretion of directors, or in extreme cases, "sterilize" the board.

§ 8.5 The Statutory Scheme—Officers

Corporation statutes generally do not attempt to define the authority and role of officers. A typical statutory provision merely states that officers and agents of the corporation "shall have such authority and perform such duties in the management of the corporation as may be provided in the bylaws, or as may be determined by resolution of the board of directors not inconsistent with the bylaws." (MBCA § 50). In theory, corporate officers administer the day-to-day affairs of the corporation subject to the direction and control of the board of directors. The precise scope of the implied authority of officers vis a vis third persons—particularly the President—is somewhat broader, but varies from state to state. (For a discussion see Chapter 11, § 11.4. The basic point for present purposes, however, is that corporate officers are supposed to be agents carrying out policies established by the board of directors.

§ 8.6 Shared Responsibility With Respect to Corporate Operations

As indicated previously, the directors have responsibility for the management of the business and affairs of the corporation. Shareholders also may have a limited role on business matters, including the following:

(1) Shareholders may be called upon to review and approve the selection of accountants, auditors or attorneys who are to evaluate the stewardship of the directors. For example, the Investment Company Act of 1940 requires the selection of independent accountants for registered investment companies to be ratified by the shareholders.

(2) Shareholders are sometimes called upon to approve or refuse to approve corporate operations or corporate transactions. Shareholder ratification usually involves transactions in which management is personally interested. It has become almost standard operating procedure, for example, for publicly held corporations to submit incentive compensation plans (profit sharing plans, stock option plans, "phantom stock" plans, and the like) to the shareholders for approval. Such approval does

not totally immunize the plan from attack since a court may subsequently decide that such a plan involves waste or a gift of corporate assets. Approval by shareholders, however, probably prevents shareholders who voted to approve the plan from later attacking it; approval may also shift the burden of proof from management to the attacking shareholders. Ratification or approval of transactions, however, does not validate fraudulent, oppressive or manifestly unfair transactions involving officers or directors.

(3) Shareholders are sometimes asked to approve a blanket resolution covering all business and other transactions by management during the period since the last meeting. Such resolutions probably do not validate improper transactions of which the shareholders have no knowledge.

(4) Shareholders also may make recommendations to the board of directors on corporate matters. While without legal effect, such resolutions expess the views of the ultimate owners of the corporation, and are usually followed. For example, in one leading case, Auer v. Dressel, 118 N.E.2d 590 (N.Y.1954), it was held proper for shareholders to vote upon a resolution approving the administration of an ousted president and demanding his reinstatement. The Court said, "The stockholders, by expressing their approval of Mr. Auer's conduct as president and their demand that he be put back in that office, will not be able, directly, to effect that change in officers, but there is nothing invalid in their so expressing themselves and thus putting on notice the directors who will stand for election at the annual meeting."

§ 8.7 Shared Responsibility: Approval of Fundamental Corporate Changes

Shareholders have the specific statutory power to approve or disapprove fundamental changes in the corporation's structure proposed by the board of directors. In a few states shareholders have the power both to propose and to adopt such changes, but in most states the responsibility is shared by shareholders and directors. While changes subject to shareholder approval vary to some extent from state to state, most states require shareholder approval of the following:

(1) Amendments of articles of incorporation.

(2) Mergers and consolidations.

(3) Dissolution.

(4) Sale of substantially all its business not in the ordinary course of business.

In most states, two-thirds of the outstanding shares must approve the proposed transaction, though several states have adopted a simple majority principle. Also, many states allow the articles or bylaws to vary the needed vote within specified limits. Class voting by classes of shares is also often authorized. In addition to these fundamental changes, state statutes may provide for shareholder approval of less substantial transactions, including distributions in partial liquidation out of capital, reductions of stated capital, or the purchase of corporate shares out of capital surplus.

§ 8.8　Shared Responsibility: Bylaw Amendments

In most states, the initial bylaws of a corporation are adopted by the board of directors or incorporators, typically at the initial meeting of the board. Thereafter, the power to amend or repeal bylaws may be vested in either the shareholders or the directors. The Model Act provides that the power to amend is vested in the board of directors "unless reserved to the shareholders by the articles;" further the shareholders may "repeal or change" bylaws adopted by the directors. (MBCA § 27). States vary widely in the vesting of power to amend or repeal the bylaws as between shareholders and directors. Generally, the primacy of shareholders in this regard is recognized. For example, in many states directors may not repeal or amend bylaws adopted by shareholders. However, one can also argue under the statutes of some states that the directors' power over bylaws is granted directly by the statute and, therefore, that the power to amend is an original, not a delegated, one.

§ 8.9 May the Statutory Scheme be Varied? The Problem of the Close Corporation

The greatest strain on the statutory scheme occurs in corporations with relatively few shareholders—"close corporations" or "incorporated partnerships." If two or three persons own a business which is being conducted in corporate form each person active in the business usually will be simultaneously a shareholder, a director, and an officer. While it is possible for each businessman to indicate which hat he is wearing at any particular time, the rigid tripartite separation of levels of control and ownership required by the stautory scheme is apt to be considered formalistic nonsense.

Further, a person in a close corporation may wish to have protection against abuse of power by his "partners" which are difficult to fit into the statutory scheme. For example, a shareholder in a closely held corporation may desire to retain a veto over the corporation borrowing money in excess of some stated amount. In one case the shareholders agreed that two corporations would not borrow more than $10,000 and $40,000 respectively except by unanimous approval of the shareholders. The agreement also stated that each party "binds himself to vote as stockholders and directors in such a manner as to carry out bona fide the purposes and intent of this agreement." This provision obviously fettered to some extent the discretion of a majority of the directors, and thereby departed from the statutory scheme. The court invalidated the portion of the agreement relating to the directors: "An agreement by which directors abdicate or bargain away in advance the judgment the law contemplates they shall exercise over the corporation is void. The agreement of the parties to bind themselves *as direc-*

tors is void." Burnett v. Word, Inc., 412 S.W.2d 792 (Tex.Civ.App.1967). Cases such as this, whether or not correctly decided, illustrate the pervasive impact of the statutory scheme on judicial thought and the danger of assuming that simply because all parties in interest agree to a variation in the statutory scheme, the variation is valid. It may be noted in passing that the agreement was upheld to the extent it constituted an agreement by shareholders to vote as shareholders in a specified manner. In other words, the rule about directors' agreements is not applicable to agreements between shareholders as to how shareholders will vote as shareholders.

Some courts have upheld some variations on the statutory scheme, and the modern trend distinctly appears to be running in the direction of upholding such agreements and away from the strict position of Burnett v. Word, Inc. The leading line of cases arose in New York. In McQuade v. Stoneham, 189 N.E. 234 (N.Y.1934) the Court invalidated an agreement between the majority shareholders that they would maintain themselves as officers at specified salaries. The Court said, "We are constrained by authority to hold that a contract is illegal and void so far as it precludes the board of directors, at the risk of incurring legal liability, from changing officers, salaries or policies or retaining individuals in office, except by consent of the contracting parties. On the whole, such a holding is probably preferable to one which would open the courts to pass on the motives of directors in lawful exercise of their trust." (An independent ground for this decision also existed.) Two years later the same problem again came before the highest New York court in the case of Clark v. Dodge, 199 N.E. 641 (N.Y.1936). Clark owned 25 per cent and Dodge owned 75 per cent of the stock of two corporations manufacturing medicinal preparations by secret formulae. Dodge did not actively participate in the management of the business; the secret formulae were known only to Clark, who actively managed the business. In 1921, Dodge and Clark entered into an agreement by which

Dodge agreed to retain Clark as general manager of the business and to pay him one-fourth of the income either in the form of salary or dividends. The agreement was to continue so long as Clark remained "faithful, efficient and competent to so manage and control the said business." Clark, in turn, agreed to disclose the secret formulae to Dodge's son and upon Clark's death without issue to bequeath his 25 per cent interest in the corporation to the wife and children of Dodge.

This entirely sensible business arrangement appears to run afoul of the *McQuade* principle, since Dodge was in effect agreeing to vote as director to retain Clark as general manager and to pay twenty-five per cent of the earnings to him in the form of salary or dividends. The Court nevertheless upheld the agreement:

> "Are we committed by the McQuade case to the doctrine that there may be no variation, however slight or innocuous, from [the statutory] norm, where salaries or policies or the retention of individuals in office are concerned? There is ample authority supporting that doctrine . . . . [S]omething may be said for it, since it furnishes a simple, if arbitrary test. Apart from its practical administrative convenience, the reasons upon which it is said to rest are more or less nebulous. Public policy, the intention of the Legislature, detriment to the corporation, are phrases which in this connection mean little. Possible harm to bona fide purchasers of stock or to creditors or to stockholding minorities have more substance; but such harms are absent in many instances. If the enforcement of a particular contract damages nobody—not even, in any perceptible degree, the public—one sees no reason for holding it illegal, even though it impinges slightly upon the broad provision [vesting directors with the powers of management]. Damage suffered or threatened is a logical and practical test and has come to be the one generally adopted.

"Where the directors are the sole stockholders, there seems to be no objection to enforcing an agreement among them to vote for certain people as officers. . . .

"If there was any invasion of the powers of the directorate under that agreement it is so slight as to be negligible; and certainly there is no damage suffered by or threatened to anybody. The broad statements in the McQuade opinion, applicable to the facts there, should be confined to those facts."

The *Clark* opinion arguably rests on two different grounds:

(1) The Court emphasized that in *Clark* all the shareholders were parties to the agreement. In *McQuade*, there were shareholders who were not parties to the agreement. Certainly, non-consenting shareholders may be injured if directors fail to exercise their "honest and unfettered" judgment, and hence it seems reasonable to reconcile the two cases on this ground. On the other hand, the agreement in *McQuade* was not being attacked by a non-consenting shareholder, but by a person who was a party to the agreement and was not living up to it. No emphasis was placed on the presence of non-consenting shareholders in the *McQuade* decision.

(2) The *Clark* opinion stresses that the arrangement harmed no one, and that "damage suffered or threatened" is a logical and practical test. If this were the sole test adopted in Clark v. Dodge, the courts might accept very substantial variations from the statutory norm—possibly to the extent of permitting the total abolishment of the board of directors. However, subsequent cases in New York indicate that this is too-expansive a reading of Clark v. Dodge and that as much stress should be placed on the statement that the impingement in that case was "slight" or "innocuous" as on the language that no damage was "suffered or threatened." Hence the common law rule in New York, and probably in most other states as well, is that only "slight impingements" that damage no one will be accepted.

The leading case that rejects this rather narrow view is Galler v. Galler, 203 N.E.2d 577 (Ill.1964), a decision which enforced a complex shareholders agreement containing numerous "impingements" of varying degrees of seriousness on the statutory scheme. After drawing sharply the distinction between closely held and publicly held corporations, the Court called for statutory recognition of the special problems of the closely held corporation, and concluded that "any arrangements concerning the management of the corporation which are agreeable to all" should be enforced if (1) no complaining minority interest appears, (2) no fraud or apparent injury to the public or creditors is present, and (3) no clearly prohibitory statutory language is violated. While this decision has generally been approved and applauded, a subsequent Illinois case refused to extend *Galler* to validate a shareholders' agreement that more or less squarely contradicted a specific statutory provision. The increasing enactment of special statutory provisions relating to the close corporation (see Chapter 12, § 12.7) ensures that the principle of *Galler* will be broadly applied in the future.

§ 8.10　Delegation of Management Powers and the Statutory Scheme

Interference with the discretion of directors has also been used to attack broad management agreements between the corporation and outsiders by which the sole power of management appears to be taken from the board and vested in the managers. Similar arguments have been applied to invalidate agreements between shareholders which provided that the sole power to manage a portion of the corporation's assets is vested in one shareholder. Potentially overbroad delegation to an executive or other committee of the board may also be attacked on this ground though that question is now usually dealt with by statute. (See Chapter 10, § 10.10.) The test in all these cases is whether the agreement "sterilizes" the board so that it has no managerial role at all or whether reasonable powers of oversight are preserved to the board.

[For unfamiliar terms see the Glossary]

CHAPTER NINE
SHARES AND SHAREHOLDERS

§ 9.1 Annual and Special Meetings of Shareholders

Every state statute contains more or less routine provisions about meetings of shareholders. The Model Business Corporation Act, for example, provides that an annual meeting shall be held "at such time as may be stated in or fixed in accordance with the bylaws," (MBCA § 28), that notice of an annual or special meeting shall be given not less than ten nor more than fifty days before the meeting (MBCA § 29), and so forth. The failure to hold an annual meeting does not work a dissolution of the corporation, though any shareholder may obtain a summary court order to hold an annual meeting if one is not held within any thirteen-month period. So far as notice is concerned, statutes permit written waivers that may be executed before, at, or after the meeting in question (MBCA § 144).

The principal purpose of an annual meeting is the annual election of directors, but the annual meeting may act on any relevant matter and is not limited to the purposes set forth in the notice. Indeed, under the Model Act (MBCA § 29), no statement of purposes at all need appear in the notice of annual meeting.

A special meeting is any meeting other than the annual meeting. It may be called by the persons specified in the statute or in the bylaws of the corporation. Typically, such a meeting may be called by the directors, the holders of some specified percentage of the outstanding shares of the corporation, or by certain officers. Unlike the annual meeting, the only subjects that may be considered at a special meeting are matters described in the notice of meeting.

A quorum at any annual or special meeting consists of a majority of the outstanding shares, except that the quorum requirement may be increased or decreased by provisions in the articles or bylaws. Statutes often prescribe a minimum (one-third in the Model Act and in many other statutes) below which the quorum may not be reduced (MBCA § 32). Statutes, however, do not prescribe a maximum, and it is therefore possible to require the presence of all outstanding shares to constitute a quorum. Such a provision may be adopted in close corporations as a planning device, even though it increases the risk of a deadlock since a single shareholder, no matter how small his holding, may prevent the existence of a quorum.

Where a quorum is present, a majority may act to bind the corporation. Where a quorum is present a disgruntled faction may sometimes lose a vote, and leave the meeting seeking to "break" the quorum and prevent the victorious faction from conducting further business. The general rule is that a quorum, once present, continues, and the withdrawal of a faction does not disable the remaining shareholders from continuing. For this reason, a minority faction usually stays away to prevent a quorum from ever being present rather than appearing and later withdrawing in an attempt to break the quorum.

A number of states authorize shareholders to conduct business by unanimous written consent without a meeting. Such a provision is particularly helpful in closely held corporations, where most shareholders' decisions are unanimous, and the formality of a meeting may be dispensed with. A few states, including Delaware, have gone a step further and authorized holders of the number of shares needed to act on a matter to act by written consent without a meeting. (Del.Gen.Corp.Law, Del.Code Ann.Tit. 8, § 228.) As discussed in the chapter on proxy voting in publicly held corporations, this rejection of the unanimity requirment is not as radical a proposal as might first be thought since most shareholder votes in such a corporation are cast by written proxy in any event. (See Chapter 13, § 13.6.)

§ 9.2   Eligibility to Vote: Record and Beneficial Ownership

Every corporation retains records of the persons in whose name shares have been issued and every share certificate that is issued refers by name to that person. This person is called the "record owner" and generally the corporation may deal with him as though he were the sole owner of the shares. When the record owner sells his shares, he normally hands over the certificate to the purchaser with the endorsement on the reverse side of the certificate properly executed; the purchaser may then submit the endorsed certificate to the corporation with a request that a new certificate be issued in his name. The old certificate is cancelled and a new certificate is issued in the name of the purchaser who then becomes the new record owner. The corporate records of the names and addresses of record owners are usually called the stock transfer books though they may consist simply of stubs formerly attached to share certificates. A purchaser who does not obtain the issuance of a new certificate is still the "beneficial owner" of those shares; while corporations deal only with record owners, it is clear that the beneficial owner is the equitable owner and can compel the record owner to turn over any dividend received by him or to execute appropriate documents to permit the beneficial owner to exercise the power to vote.

Obviously every publicly held corporation with active trading in its shares must not only have available a large number of new certificates to issue to transferees but also must take steps to ensure that transfers are properly recorded, that new certificates refer to the same number of shares as old certificates, and so forth. These mechanical functions of registering share transfers are handled by "transfer agents" who keep exact records of all shareholders, their names, address and number of shares owned. Publicly held corporations also use "registrars," whose function is to make sure the corporation does not inadvertently overissue shares.

When shares are actively transferred, some rule must be established to determine the point in time that eligibility to vote is determined. Statutes usually provide two alternatives:

(1) The board of directors may order the stock transfer books closed for a stated period, which the Model Act sets as at least ten days but not more than fifty days before the meeting (MBCA § 30). If the stock transfer books are closed, the corporation refuses thereafter to register transfers of shares and eligibility to vote is determined by the closed books. In effect the corporate records are frozen, though, of course, individual shareholders may endorse and deliver certificates to purchasers during the period.

(2) Alternatively, the bylaws may establish, or in the absence of a bylaw the directors in advance may establish, a record date, which usually must be at least ten but not more than fifty days before the meeting. If a record date is established, the corporation continues to register transfers and issue new certificates to transferees, but the persons eligible to vote are those in whose name the shares were registered on the record date.

If a corporation fails to do either, the corporation is deemed to set a record date as of the date the notice of the meeting is mailed, and eligibility to vote is determined as of that date.

These provisions are obviously for the benefit of the corporation. They permit the corporation to give proper notice of the meeting, to prepare a voting list, and to establish precisely who is entitled to vote. They also permit management and other shareholders to solicit votes before the meeting. As a practical matter, as between the various alternatives, most corporations of any size use a record date rather than closing the transfer books, since closing the transfer books for any period of time would cause an impossible backup of transfers awaiting processing. The record date is usually specified in the resolution of the board directors establishing the dividend.

Analogous provisions determine who is entitled to receive corporate dividends as between transferor and transferee (§ 16.2).

§ 9.3 Preparation of Voting List

A voting list of shareholders eligible to vote must be prepared before each shareholder meeting. Section 31 of the Model Business Corporation uses the term "voting record" rather than voting list. The list must be prepared by "the officer or agent having charge of the stock transfer books" and must be available for inspection by any shareholder at the registered office of the corporation for at least ten days before the meeting, and must also be available at the meeting. Every shareholder has an absolute right to inspect this list, and this right is not subject to the qualifications imposed upon a shareholder's right to inspect other books and records of the corporation. (See Chapter 15). While the failure to prepare the voting list does not affect the validity of any action taken at the meeting, it may create personal liability on the person charged with this responsibility.

At the meeting, the share transfer books (rather than the voting list) determines "who are the shareholders entitled . . . to vote at any meeting of the shareholders." (MBCA § 30).

§ 9.4 Election of Directors: Cumulative or Straight Voting

Directors are elected each year at the annual meeting of shareholders by a vote of a majority of the shares (1) present at the meeting and (2) entitled to vote, assuming that a quorum is present. In many states the articles of incorporation or bylaws may increase, but may not decrease, the percentage of the shares required for election. In close corporations it is not uncommon to exercise this privilege and require unanimity as a planning device, even though the possibility of a deadlock is thereby increased.

The most important question relating to the election of directors is whether shares may be voted "cumulatively" or must be voted "straight." In several states cumulative voting is mandatory by state constitution or provisions in the state corporation statute. Most states, however, give a corporation an option to exclude cumulative voting; usually this option requires a specific exclusion in the articles of incorporation though in some states, cumulative voting is permitted only if specific provision for it is made in the articles.

The workings of cumulative voting can be most simply described by an illustration. Let us assume a corporation with two shareholders, A with 26 shares, and B with 74 shares. Further, let us assume that there are three directors and each shareholder nominates three candidates.

A critical point is that candidates do not run for specific places. The three candidates with the most votes in this election are the winners. If only straight voting is permitted, A may cast 26 votes for each of any three candidates, and B may cast 74 votes for each of any three candidates. The result, of course, is that if they do not agree on any candidates, all three of B's candidates are elected. If cumulative voting is permitted, the total number of votes that each shareholder may cast is first computed and each shareholder is permitted to distribute these votes as he sees fit over one or more candidates. In the example above, A is entitled to cast a total of 78 votes (26×3) and B is entitled to cast 222 votes (74×3). If A casts all 78 votes for himself, he is assured of election because B cannot divide 222 votes among three candidates in such a way as to give each candidate 79 or more votes and preclude A's election. (If B gives 79 votes to himself and 79 votes to B_1, he will only have 64 votes left for B_2.) Obviously, the effect of cumulative voting is that it increases minority participation on the board of directors. In straight voting, the shareholder with 51 per cent of the vote elects the entire board; in cumulative voting, a relatively small faction (26 per cent in the above example) obtains representation on the board.

The difference between cumulative and straight voting may be vividly illustrated by the deadlock situation where all shares are owned equally by two shareholders—say fifty shares each. If only straight voting is permitted and each shareholder votes only for his own candidates a deadlocked election is inevitable. If there are two places to be filled A will vote 50 shares for himself, and 50 shares for A_2; B will vote 50 shares for himself, and 50 shares for B_2. Thus, four candidates will each have 50 votes for two positions, and the result is that no one is elected. If cumulative voting is permitted on the other hand, A may cast 100 votes for himself and he will be guaranteed election (since B obviously cannot give two candidates more than 100 votes each.) If there are an odd number of directors to be elected (say 3) straight voting still leads to deadlock: A_1–50, A_2–50, A_3–50, B_1–50, B_2–50, B_3–50. If cumulative voting is permitted, A and B may each elect one director but the situation is unstable: a deadlock will be created if each tries to elect the tie-breaking director and the other votes rationally. However, the strategy and counterstrategy can become complex. If A gives A_1 76 votes, A_1 will be guaranteed of election since B has only 150 votes and obviously cannot prevent A_1's election; similarly, if B gives B_1 76 votes, A cannot prevent B_1's election. If both shareholders follow this conservative strategy, the result will be A_1–76, A_2–74, B_1–76, B_2–74, with A_1 and B_1 each being elected and a tie existing between A_2 and B_2. However, if B knows that A will follow this strategy in voting, B might be tempted to divide his vote equally between two candidates in order to elect two of the three directors: A_1–76, A_2–74, B_1–75, B_2–75, with A_1, B_1, and B_2 all being elected. A may counter this strategy by also giving his two candidates 75 votes each, thereby creating a four way tie and electing no one. Indeed, it is disastrous if either shareholder deviates from these very precise voting patterns. If B decides to vote only slightly illogically, for example, B_1-77, B_2-73, he delivers control of the corporation over to A even if A follows the conservative strategy of guaranteeing the election of one director: B_1-77, A_1-76, A_2-74, B_2-73, with B_1, A_1 and A_2 elected. In these and the following illustrations it is assumed that A or B, once they have adopted a strategy and cast their votes, cannot thereafter change them. This is true only to a limited extent in the real world. Balloting for directors is by written ballot rather than voice vote so that each shareholder must establish his voting strategy without being sure of his opponent's strategy; however, until the vote is announced, a shareholder may recast his votes and thereby correct mistakes in his voting pattern.

As the preceding discussion illustrates, one undesirable aspect of cumulative voting is that it tends to be a little tricky. If a shareholder casts votes in an irrational or inefficient way, he may not get the directorships his position entitles him to; when voting cumulatively it is relatively easy to make a mistake in spreading votes around. Another graphic illustration of this are the cases where a majority shareholder votes in such a way that he elects only a minority of the directors. This is most likely to occur when one shareholder votes "straight" and another cumulates. For example, if A has 60 shares and B only 40, with five directors to be elected, B may nevertheless elect a majority of the board if A votes "straight," and B knows that A is doing so. The result might look like this:

A_1-60, A_2-60, A_3-60, A_4-60, A_5-60, B_1-67, B_2-66, B_3-65, B_4-1, B_5-1.

B should not create tie votes among his own candidates. If he does so, and the tie candidates come in fifth and sixth in an election for five directorships, the tie may be broken by a new election for only the fifth seat; A may be able to vote his shares in the new election for his own candidate, thereby causing B to lose a seat. This strategy is daring of B because he is spreading his vote over three persons when he can be sure only of electing two. If A knows that B will try to elect three persons, A, by properly cumulating his votes, can elect four directors, in effect "stealing" one of B's. The results of such an election might be as follows:

A$_1$–73, A$_2$–74, A$_3$–75, A$_4$–76, A$_5$–2, B$_1$–67, B$_2$–66, B$_3$–65, B$_4$–1, B$_5$–1.

The statutes of a few states, including California, require shareholders to give advance notice before the meeting if they plan to vote cumulatively. Such a requirement seems plainly desirable because the last illustration graphically demonstrates that election results are illogical if some shareholders vote cumulatively while others do not.

The following formula is useful in determining the number of shares needed to elect one director:

$$\frac{S}{D + 1} + 1.$$

Where S equals the total number of shares voting, and D equals the number of directors to be elected. The analogous formula to elect n directors is:

$$\frac{nS}{D + 1} + 1.$$

A minor modification may sometimes be necessary. The first portion of the formula, $\frac{S}{D + 1}$, establishes the maximum number of shares voted for a single person which are insufficient to elect that person as a director. Any share, or fraction thereof, in excess of that amount will be sufficient to elect a director. The formula in the text ignores fractional shares which sometimes may lead to a one share-error. For example, where there are 100 shares voting and five directors to be elected, the first portion of the formula is $\frac{100}{5 + 1}$, or $\frac{100}{6}$.

In this example, 16 shares will not elect a director, but 17 shares will, since the first part of the formula yields 16⅔. The above formula mechanically yields an answer of 17⅔.

The reason that several states have mandatory constitutional or statutory cumulative voting is that it is believed to be democratic in that persons with large (but minority) holding should have a voice in the conduct of the corporation. Also, arguably, it may be desirable to have as many viewpoints as possible represented on the board of directors; and the presence of a minority director may discourage conflicts of interest by management since discovery is considerably more likely. Arguments in opposition include: (1) The introduction of a partisan on the board is inconsistent with the notion that the board should represent all interests in the corporation; (2) a partisan director may cause disharmony which reduces the efficiency of the board; (3) a partisan director may criticize management unreasonably so as to make it less willing to take risky (but desirable) action; (4) a partisan director may leak confidential information; and (5) in practice cumulative voting is usually used to further narrow partisan goals, particularly to give an insurgent group a toehold in the corporation in an effort to obtain control.

As a practical matter, cumulative voting in a close corporation may be of considerable importance. In the large, publicly held corporation, it is likely to be considered more of a nuisance than anything else because it complicates proxy voting. It should be observed, however, that where large boards are involved cumulative voting simplifies the task of "public interest" or other groups whose only goal is to elect a single director rather than take over control of the corporation. For this reason, some groups have advocated that public corporations adopt cumulative voting.

In states where cumulative voting is mandatory, and sometimes in corporations formed in other states as well, it is not uncommon to employ devices that minimize the effects of cumulative voting. One device that reduces the impact of cumulative voting is the "classification" (or "staggering") of the board of directors if the board consists of nine or more members. Under most statutes, the directors of a large board may be divided into two or three classes of as nearly equal numbers as possible, and one class may be elected each year. In a classified board, each director serves for two years (if there are two classes) or three years (if there are three classes). The theoretical justification for classification is that it ensures "experience of service" on the board, since only one-half or one-third of the board may be replaced each year. However, experience of service is usually not a major motivating factor for classifying a board, since as a practical matter, experience of service is usually provided by the simple process of reelecting the same persons as directors year after year. Even where a take-over attempt has been successful, or where a controlling interest in a corporation has been sold to outsiders, there is often a period during which some directors are continued in office to provide the necessary continuity and experience. Staggering has two basic effects:

(1) It makes it more difficult for a minority faction to elect a director when there is cumulative voting. For example, if there are nine directors elected each year, ten per cent of the stock can elect a director; if the nine directors are classified and three are elected each year, it takes twenty-five per cent of the stock to elect a director. (If you do not believe these percentages, try them out on the formula set forth above.)

(2) It makes take-over attempts more difficult. Where the board consists of three classes, a person becoming a majority shareholder cannot be ensured of electing a majority on the board for more than two full years. In some instances classification has been proposed in publicly held corporations prima-

rily for this reason even though the corporation does not have cumulative voting.

Other devices also limit the impact of cumulative voting. Reduction of the size of the board of directors has much the same effect as staggering the election of directors. Shares may sometimes be tied up in voting trusts or voting agreements; in many states non-voting shares also may be used consistently with a cumulative voting requirement. The influence of minority directors may be minimized by having informal director discussion in advance of meetings, scheduling board meetings at inconvenient times or places, and delegating functions to committees composed entirely of management directors. Also, it may be possible to remove the minority director without cause and replace him with a more congenial person, at least until the next election. The Model Act, however, and the statutes of many states, prohibit the removal of a minority director elected by cumulative voting unless the votes to remove him would have been enough to prevent his original election in an election for directors. (MBCA § 39, 2d ¶.)

Of course, in states where cumulative voting is permissive it may be eliminated by an amendment to the articles of incorporation in the same way as any other attribute of shares. (See § 18.1).

§ 9.5 Proxies and Proxy Voting

A proxy is the grant of authority by a shareholder to someone else to vote his shares. The relationship is one of principal and agent. Some confusion may arise in terminology since the single word "proxy" may interchangeably be used to designate the document, the grant of authority itself, and the person granted the power to vote the shares (the proxyholder).

The law of proxy regulation rather neatly divides itself into two areas. On the one hand is the skimpy—almost nonexistent —state law dealing with the legal requirements and duration of a proxy. Under state law, perhaps the most lively issue is whether a proxy that is stated to be irrevocable is in fact irrevocable. That this is not an earthshaking issue is attested to by the fact that there is very little reported litigation on this question. On the other hand is the burgeoning law of federal proxy regulation in publicly held corporations subject to the reporting requirements of the Securities Exchange Act of 1934. This is discussed in a later chapter (see Chapter 13, § 13.5).

The standard state statutory provision relating to proxies merely states that a shareholder may vote "either in person or by proxy executed in writing by the shareholder or by his duly authorized attorney-in-fact." (MBCA § 33, 3d ¶.) No particular form of proxy is required under this section. Proxies have been ruled valid despite omission of the name of the proxyholder, the date of the meeting, or the date of the proxy. However, the proxy must be in writing, a provision of obvious benefit to the inspector of elections and the corporation. A proxyholder need not be a shareholder.

The usual state statutory provision relating to duration of a proxy provides that "no proxy shall be valid after eleven (11) months from the date of its execution, unless otherwise provided in the proxy." (MBCA § 33, 3d ¶.) The theory of the eleven-month provision is that a new proxy should be executed before each annual meeting. However, there is nothing to prevent the parties from agreeing that a much longer period shall be applicable to a specific proxy.

A proxy, being the appointment of an agent, is normally revocable at the pleasure of the person executing it. Thus, even if a long period is designated as the duration of the proxy, it still may be revoked. A proxy may also be revoked by implication. For example, the execution of a later proxy constitutes a revocation of an earlier, inconsistent proxy. Personal attendance at a meeting may also constitute revocation of an earlier proxy, though this depends on the intention of the shareholder.

Since later proxies revoke earlier ones, it is important that proxies be dated as of the time of execution. Inspectors of election, where there is a contest, must determine which is the latest proxy executed by a specific shareholder in order to determine how the shares are to be voted.

Certain proxies may be irrevocable. Generally a mere recitation that a proxy is irrevocable does not make it so; such a proxy is usually as revocable as any other proxy. The general rubric for determining whether a proxy is truly irrevocable is whether it is "coupled with an interest." This phrase, which has its origin in the agency case of Hunt v. Rousmanier's Adm'rs, 8 Wheat. (21 U.S.) 174 (1823), of course, has no inherent meaning of itself and must be fleshed out with examples and further analysis. It is not enough that the proxy merely be supported by consideration. The clearest example of this is a purchase of a proxy for cash. Such a purchased vote almost certainly would be held to be against public policy and unenforceable; rather than being irrevocable, such a proxy might not be enforceable at all. On the other hand, if a person lends a shareholder money and takes a lien on the shares as security, an irrevocable proxy granted to the creditor almost certainly would be enforced against the shareholder. What is the difference between these two situations? A person who purchases a vote presumably intends to recoup his investment in the vote by exercising the power to vote in some way. This power may very well be exercised in a manner adverse to the corporation: the proxyholder's interest is in recouping a personal payment, and in a sense he is antagonistic to the corporation. The creditor's interest, on the other hand, is to preserve or increase the value of the shares which constitute his security. Thus he has a financial interest consistent with that of the corporation which the vote purchaser does not.

An irrevocable proxy separates the ownership from the voting power. Because of the possibility of injury to the owners by the abuse of a naked voting power unconnected with a financial interest in the corporation, the courts have generally refused to recognize the irrevocability of a proxy except where there appears to be little likelihood that the power to vote will be abused. This is the nub of the notion of "coupled with an interest." The following types of proxies have been held to be proxies "coupled with an interest:"

(1) A proxy given to a pledgee under a valid pledge of the shares;

(2) A proxy given to a person who has agreed to purchase the shares under an executory contract of sale;

(3) A proxy given to a person who has lent money or contributed valuable property to the corporation;

(4) A proxy given to a person who has contracted to perform services for the corporation as an officer; and

(5) A proxy given in order to effectuate the provisions of a valid pooling agreement (described in the following section).

Some courts have upheld irrevocable proxies which do not squarely fall within any of the above categories. On the other hand, New York and California have statutes which define the five situations described above as those in which an irrevocable proxy should be recognized (N.Y.Bus.Corp.Law, § 609(F); Cal.Corp.Code, § 705). Such a statute resolves possible future disputes very simply, but there may be a slight danger that a reasonable proxy might be invalidated because it does not fit squarely into any of the above categories.

§ 9.6 Shareholder Voting Agreements

A shareholder voting agreement is a contract among the shareholders, or some of them, to vote their shares in a specified manner on certain matters. Such an agreement is usually called a "pooling agreement" because it results in the shares of the participants being voted as a block. The purpose may be to maintain control, or to maximize the voting power of the shares where cumulative voting is permitted, or to ensure that some specific object is obtained. The manner in which the shares are to be voted, that is for or against a specified proposal or motion, may be specified in the agreement itself, or be the subject of subsequent negotiation and decision of the shareholders with some method of determining how the shares are to be voted in the event of a failure to agree. The shareholders pooling agreement extends only to voting on matters that are within the province of shareholders, such as the election of directors, and should be sharply distinguished from agreements that attempt to resolve matters that are vested in the discretion of directors. The latter type of agreement raises serious questions of validity (see § 8.9). The pooling agreement does not.

In a pooling agreement, the shareholders retain all the indicia of ownership of shares except the power to vote. In this respect, a pooling agreement differs from a voting trust (discussed in § 9.7) which contemplates that legal title to the shares be transferred to the trustees. Generally, the advantages of a pooling agreement over a voting trust are that it is less formal, easier to establish, and there is no disruption of other ownership attributes.

The pooling agreement is generally recognized as a valid contract, subject only to the rules applicable to the validity of contracts in general. A few states have adopted statutes regulating pooling agreements, often limiting the period during which a pooling agreement may continue (*e. g.*, to ten years), requiring that copies of the pooling be deposited at the principal office of the corporation, and so forth. However, in most states, the pooling agreement is essentially an unregulated contractual voting device that may continue for long periods of time.

A basic part of a pooling agreement is the manner of resolution of possible disagreements in the future. While the parties to the agreement are presumably in complete accord as to how their shares should be voted today, there is no assurance that there will be such accord tomorrow. Pooling agreements often specify that participants will consult in advance of the meeting as to how the pooled shares should be voted, and that the shares will be voted as a majority or some other percentage specify. For example, in an important Delaware case, the agreement provided that the six participants in the pool could select eight agents (most selecting one; some two) and the shares would be voted as any seven agents specified. Abercrombie v. Davies, 130 A.2d 338 (Del.Ch.1957). Arbitration was provided for in the event seven agents were unable to agree. While this agreement ultimately was held to constitute an invalid voting trust rather than a pooling agreement, the method of dispute resolution is interesting in that it required a high degree of consensus by the participants. Resolution of disagreements is usually by arbitration, an arbiter, or by a decision of some person mutually trusted by all the participants. However, if the pooling agreement covers enough shares to constitute working control of the corporation, arbitration may in fact vest control of the corporation in the hands of the arbiter, a person with no financial interest in the enterprise. A "runaway" arbiter is unlikely because the shareholders may, by agreeing between themselves, retake control over the voting of the pooled shares. Pooling agreements also often provide that the participants in the pool may substitute arbiters by mutual agreement. Instead of arbitration, a pooling agreement may give a participant the option of withdrawing his shares if disagreement continues over a period of time. Such a provision, of course, in a sense defeats the original purpose of a pooling agreement.

Enforcement of a pooling agreement creates special problems since the shares are registered in the names of the individual shareholders. Many courts will enforce a pooling agreement by decreeing specific performance. It is not always certain, however, that specific performance will be available. In Ringling Bros. Barnum & Bailey Combined Shows v. Ringling, 53 A.2d 441 (Del.1947), the leading Delaware case involving pooling agreements, the agreement itself did not specifically grant a proxy to anyone to vote the shares of an objecting shareholder who refused to follow the arbiter's instructions. Nevertheless, the Chancellor, 49 A.2d 603 (Del.Ch.1946), found by a process of implication that such a proxy existed. On appeal, the Supreme Court held that the proper remedy was simply not to count votes cast in contravention of the instructions of the arbiter. Under the circumstances, the result was to defeat utterly the purpose of the pooling agreement, since the minority shareholder who was not a party to the pooling agreement had a majority of the remaining shares after giving effect to the disqualification.

Some state statutes specifically address the enforcement issue by authorizing specific performance of pooling agreements. New York, for example, validates and makes irrevocable a proxy granted in connection with a pooling agreement (N.Y.Bus.Corp.Law §§ 609(e), 620). To take advantage of such a statute, the agreement probably must contain specific reference to the irrevocable proxy. Enforcement of pooling agreements creates practical problems for inspectors of corporate elections who must decide who is entitled to vote disputed shares. In such circumstances, an inspector may insist that a court decree be first obtained determining how the shares should be voted.

§ 9.7 Voting Trusts: Purpose, Operation and Legislative Policy

A voting trust differs from a pooling agreement primarily in that legal title to the shares is vested in trustees, and the shares are registered in the names of the trustees on the books of the corporation. Voting trust agreements usually provide that all dividends or other corporate distributions be passed through to the equitable owners of the shares. The trustees may also issue transferable voting trust certificates representing the beneficial interests in the shares and such certificates may be traded much as shares of stock are traded. While voting trust agreements may limit the power of trustees to vote on certain matters or to transfer the shares held by them to third parties without the consent of the beneficial owners, nevertheless, in a voting trust the legal title to the shares, and usually the entire power to vote, is separated from the equitable ownership of the shares.

At common law there was great suspicion of voting trusts. One commentator described a voting trust as "little more than a vehicle for corporate kidnapping." However, state statutes now uniformly recognize the validity of voting trusts. The Model Business Corporation Act states that a voting trust may be created subject to the following requirements:

(1) The agreement may not extend beyond ten years;

(2) The agreement must be in writing;

(3) A counterpart of the agreement must be deposited with the corporation at its registered office, to be subject to the same right of inspection by (a) shareholders or (b) holders of a beneficial interest in the trust that is provided a shareholder to inspect books and records of the corporation; and

(4) The shares subject to the trust must be transferred to the trustee or trustees (MBCA § 34).

A statement of the formal requisites of a voting trust may be misleading, however, since some states have imposed the further substantial requirement that the essential purpose of the trust must be a proper one. For example, a trust created solely for the purpose of securing control of or lucrative employment with the corporation would be invalidated in some states. Obviously, proof of such motives depends on subjective testimony; the cautious, close-mouthed creator of a voting trust in such states may create an enforceable voting trust despite wrongful motives, while a garrulous person with basically good motives may inadvertently make damaging statements about the underlying purpose of the trust. In a majority of the states, the purpose of a voting trust is not inquired into; a voting trust is valid if it complies with all statutory requirements.

A voting trust agreement that fails to comply with all statutory requirements is considered invalid in its entirety in most states. Even though these requirements are basically simple ones that may be easily complied with, a number of cases have arisen in which these requirements have been ignored.

§ 9.8 Voting Trusts: Use in Public Corporations

A voting trust, unlike most of the other control arrangements discussed in this Chapter, may be widely used in publicly held corporations as well as in closely held corporations. For example, a voting trust may be used in connection with the capitalization or reorganization of a corporation to provide for temporary stability of management. A temporary voting trust may be ordered where as a result of the reorganization the voting power is lodged in a large, unorganized group of bondholders who previously had no power to control the corporation. Another possible use is in connection with divestiture orders under the Federal antitrust laws, where the court desires to order an immediate termination of control, but where the financial details of the divestiture may take a long period to work out. A voting trust may also be used by creditors of a publicly held corporation to remove holders of large blocks of stock whom the creditors mistrust from the control of the corporation. An outstanding example of this use was a 1960 loan of $165,000,000 to Trans World Airlines by a consortium of banks. As a condition to the loan, Hughes Tool Co., wholly owned by

Howard Hughes, was required to place its shares of TWA (amounting to 75 per cent of the outstanding shares) into a voting trust with the banks designating the trustees. In this way, Mr. Hughes was isolated from the actual management of the debtor corporation.

§ 9.9   Voting Trusts: Powers and Duties of Trustees

Voting trusts usually contain precise provisions defining the powers and duties of the trustees. Voting trustees often have working control of the corporation for extended periods of time, but may have little or no financial interest in the corporation. Problem areas that have arisen include:

(1) May the trustees elect themselves as directors and/or officers? The wisdom of permitting dual offices is debatable since it is unlikely that a voting trustee would vote to remove himself as a director.

(2) May the trustees remaining in office fill a vacancy in the trustees? Trustees are often given this power, though it may also be vested in the holders of voting trust certificates.

(3) May the trustees vote on major corporate changes, such as mergers, dissolution, or the sale of substantially all of its assets? Arguably, consent of the holders of voting trust certificates should be obtained on such major matters, but voting trust agreements often provide that the trustees may vote on such matters as they see fit.

(4) May the trustees dispose of the shares subject to the voting trust? Voting trust agreements often provide that no sale of underlying shares may be effected without the prior consent of all, or a designated percentage, of the holders of voting trust certificates.

(5) Should the trustees be relieved of liability for errors in business judgment or nonfeasance? Trustees typically desire broad exculpatory clauses, but such clauses may be inconsistent

with the legitimate interest of depositing shareholders. Also, courts may decline to enforce broad exculpatory clauses applicable to fiduciaries or read such clauses very narrowly.

(6) What deductions, if any, may the trustees make from dividends received by them before paying them over to the equitable owners?

(7) What compensation are the trustees entitled to?

Generally, courts tend to construe voting trust agreements narrowly or to imply a broad fiduciary duty by which trustees' actions may be tested.

§ 9.10 Creation of Floating Voting Power Through Different Classes of Shares

The common law treats with some suspicion various devices that effectively divorce the privilege of shareholder voting from the ownership of shares: irrevocable proxies (§ 9.5), shareholder pooling agreements (§ 9.6), and voting trusts (§§ 9.7–9.9). While each of these devices are valid and enforceable within limited spheres, they are hedged with restrictions or limitations.

One device that apparently permits the effective divorce of voting power from ownership of significant financial interest in the corporation without restriction or limitation is the creation of classes of shares with disproportionate voting and financial rights. In most states, no limitation is placed on the creation of classes of shares without voting rights, with fractional or multiple votes per share, with power to select one or more directors, and with limited financial interests in the corporation. The leading case involving the use of special classes of stock to create a floating voting power without a significant financial interest in the corporation is Lehrman v. Cohen, 222 A.2d 800 (Del.Ch.1966). Two families, the Lehrmans and the Cohens, owned equal quantities of the voting stock of a major grocery chain. The shares were divided into two classes, denominated AL and AC, and each could elect two directors. Because of internal disputes and disagreements that could not be resolved because of the makeup of the board, both families agreed to the creation of a third class of voting stock, AD stock, consisting of one share with the power to elect one director. The par value of the one share of AD stock was $10; this stock was not entitled to receive dividends, and on liquidation was entitled to receive back only its par value. Further, it could be redeemed or called at any time upon the vote of four directors upon the payment of the par value to the holder.

For several years, this tie breaking mechanism worked well. The holder of the one share of AD stock was the attorney for the corporation; he elected himself director and participated actively in the meetings of the board. Eventually, the holder of the AD stock allied himself with the Cohen family and together they made the attorney the chief executive officer of the corporation pursuant to a long term employment contract.

Despite the fact that the AD stock was little more than a floating vote or tie breaking mechanism with only a nominal financial interest in the corporation, its validity was upheld against the contentions that it constituted a voting trust or an invalid voting arrangement. One plausible justification for the result upholding the validity of the Class AD stock is that it seems impossible to draw a line between permissible and impermissible classes of shares. The statute gives virtually total freedom to vary voting and financial interests; one cannot say that $10 is too little, but that some other financial interest is enough.

While there has not been very much litigation on this type of arrangement, what there is tends to support the basic conclusion of the Delaware Supreme Court.

§ 9.11   Share Transfer Restrictions: Purposes, Operation and Effect

In the absence of specific agreement, shares of stock are freely transferable. However, restrictions on free transferability of shares are often important in both closely held and publicly held corporations.

A. *Closely Held Corporations.* In the closely held corporation share transfer restrictions typically constitute contractual obligations to offer shares either to the corporation or to other shareholders, or to both successively, on the death of the shareholder or before selling or disposing of the shares to outsiders. The restriction may take the form of (1) an *option* in the corporation or shareholders to purchase at a designated price, or (2) a mandatory *buy-sell agreement* obligating the corporation or shareholders to purchase the shares, or (3) merely a *right of first refusal*, giving the corporation or the shareholders an opportunity to meet the best price the shareholder has been able to obtain from outsiders. The choice between these three forms of share transfer restrictions depends on the business needs of the shareholders. Obviously, an option or a right of first refusal does not guarantee the shareholder a specified price, whereas a buy-sell agreement does.

In closely held corporations, share transfer restrictions enable participants in the venture to decide who shall participate in the venture. In effect they achieve the corporate equivalent of the partnership notion of *delectus personae.* They also may ensure a stable management and protection against an unexpected change in the respective proportionate interests of the shareholders which might occur if one shareholder is able to quietly purchase shares of other shareholders. A further advantage of share transfer restrictions in a closely held corporation is that they may materially simplify the estate tax problems of a deceased shareholder. If the corporation or other shareholders are obligated to purchase the shares owned by the deceased shareholder (a buy-sell agreement) the estate is assured that a large, illiquid asset will be reduced to cash. Further, either an option or a buy-sell agreement, if established in good faith, will be accepted by the Internal Revenue Service as establishing the value of the shares for Federal estate tax purposes, thereby avoiding a serious dispute with the tax authorities. Since closely held shares have no market on which value can be based, the Internal Revenue Service is apt to take a very optimistic attitude as to the value of such shares unless there is an agreement establishing the value.

Share transfer restrictions in closely held corporations may also be imposed to ensure the continued availability of the subchapter S election (See § 2.3). Restrictions on transfer for this purpose may be necessary to ensure that the fifteen shareholder maximum is not exceeded and that shares are not transferred to an ineligible shareholder such as a corporation or trust which would cause the loss of the subchapter S election.

B. *Publicly Held Corporations.* In a publicly held corporation, share transfer restrictions are usually used to prevent violations of the Federal Securities Act where the corporation has issued unregistered shares, *e. g.,* in connection with the acquisition of another business. In order to prevent the unregistered shares from immediately being resold in the public market, share transfer restrictions are imposed on the unregistered shares and instructions may be placed with the transfer agent to refuse to accept unregistered shares for transfer unless accompanied by an appropriate attorney's opinion. Share transfer restrictions may also be used to ensure the continued availability of an exemption from registration which may be lost, for example, if the shares are offered for resale to nonresidents. The availability of several exemptions from registration under regulations adapted by the Securities and Exchange Commission are expressly conditioned upon the corporation imposing restrictions on the transfer of shares issued in reliance upon the exemption.

Share transfer restrictions in publicly held corporations differ in nature as well as purpose from share transfer restrictions in closely held corporations. In the latter, restraints usually are of the option or buy-sell variety which require the shareholder to offer or sell his shares to the corporation or other shareholders. In the publicly held corporation on the other hand, restrictions usually take the form of flat prohibitions on transfer unless the transferor can establish that the transfer is consistent with the securities laws or regulations. This may require an opinion of counsel, affidavits by the purchaser or transferee, and the acceptance of further restrictions on transfer by the purchaser or transferee. Such uses of share transfer restrictions are considered fully in courses on securities regulation.

§ 9.12   Share Transfer Restrictions: Scope and Validity

Most courts take the position that share transfer restrictions are restraints on alienation and should therefore be strictly construed. As a result it is important to specify clearly and unambiguously the essential attributes of the restrictions and the events that trigger the restraint. In option or buy/sell agreements for example, the death, divorce or bankruptcy of a shareholder may trigger the restriction. A desire to sell or donate the shares to a third person will also usually trigger the restriction but a transfer by gift to children or grandchildren may be excluded from the restriction. Careful drafting is essential. It has been held, for example, that a restriction against sales "to the public" does not prohibit a sale to another shareholder, or that a prohibition against sale to an "officer-stockholder" does not cover a corporation owned by an officer stockholder. Obviously, such holdings often tend to defeat rather than further the basic purpose of share transfer restrictions.

The legal test as to the validity of a share transfer restraint is that it "does not unreasonably restrain or prohibit transferability." In most states, this test involves application only of common law principles. An outright prohibition on transferability would certainly be held invalid. Also dangerous are restrictions which prohibit transfers unless consent of the directors or other shareholders is first obtained; the possibility that consent may be arbitrarily withheld may invalidate the restraint. Other questionable types of restrictions include restrictions barring transfers to competitors or to a distinct class, such as aliens; restrictions imposing a penalty, such as a loss of vote or loss of dividend as a consequence of the transfer; or the creation of callable common shares. (See § 7.11).

The niggardly common law view about the enforceability of share transfer restrictions reflected in the preceding paragraphs has caused several states to adopt legislation broadening the types of restrictions that may be enforced. Delaware, for example, provides that a restriction may validly require consent by the corporation or the holders of a class of securities to any proposed transfer, the approval of the proposed transferee, or the prohibition of a transfer to designated persons or classes of persons, unless such designation "is manifestly unreasonable." (Del.Code Ann.Tit. 8, § 202.) Several other states have adopted similar statutes.

§ 9.13 Share Transfer Restrictions: Duration of Restraints

Unlike voting trusts, which usually have a statutory duration of ten years or less, there is no express restriction on the duration of share transfer restrictions. So long as the type of restriction is limited to the traditional option or buy-and-sell agreement, it is probable that the restriction remains enforceable without regard to the rule against perpetuities or equitable notions of "reasonableness." Other types of valid restraints normally continue so long as the need or justification for them exists.

Share transfer restrictions may terminate prematurely in one of two ways: by express agreement of the shareholders involved (*e. g.*, when all decide to sell their shares to an outside purchaser despite a restriction against such sales), or by abandonment or disuse. If shares are sold or transferred without compliance with the restrictions and without objection by the various parties, a court may conclude that the restrictions have been abandoned and are no longer enforceable. Isolated sales in violation of the restriction may not be sufficient to support such a conclusion, though a person objecting to the current sale may be estopped if he participated in the earlier transaction.

§ 9.14   Share Transfer Restrictions: Procedural Requirements

In creating share transfer restrictions it is important that the proper formalities be followed and that the requirements of the relevant business corporation act be complied with. Most restrictions appear in the articles of incorporation or bylaws of the corporation, though some may be imposed by contracts between the corporation and shareholders or between the shareholders themselves. Statutes generally require that a reference to any restriction imposed in corporate documents must also be placed or "noted" on the face or back of each share certificate which is subject to the restriction; generally, however it is not necessary for the full text or a complete description of the restriction to appear on the certificate. Article Eight of the Uniform Commercial Code further requires that this reference or notation be "conspicuous," a term that is defined by the UCC as "so written that a reasonable person against whom it is to operate ought to have noticed it. A printed heading in capitals . . . is conspicuous. Language in the body of a form is 'conspicuous' if it is in larger or other contrasting type or color." [§ 1–201(10).] Unless these requirements are complied with, the restriction is unenforceable against a person who is unaware of the restriction; a person who knows of the restriction before he buys the shares is bound by the restriction whether or not these procedural requirements have been met.

§ 9.15   Option or Buy/Sell Agreements: Who Should Have the Right or Privilege to Buy?

Share transfer restrictions that constitute option or buy/sell agreements to purchase the shares may run either to the corporation or to some or all the other shareholders. The choice is a matter of convenience, though usually it is preferable for the restriction to run to the corporation. The advantages of this are two-fold: the corporation may be able to raise the necessary cash more easily than the shareholders individually, and the proportionate interests of the remaining shareholders are necessarily unaffected by a corporate purchase. On the other hand, unless the corporation has the necessary earned or capital surplus at the time the purchase is to be made, a purchase by the corporation may be unlawful (see § 16.13). In order to take care of this last possibility in buy/sell agreements, the agreement may require the shareholders or some of them to agree to buy the shares if the corporation is not legally permitted to do so.

If the share transfer restrictions run to the other shareholders, a problem arises if one or more of the shareholders are unable or unwilling to purchase their allotment of shares. Agreements usually provide that in that situation the shares not purchased should be reoffered proportionately to the remaining shareholders; indeed, otherwise such shares would probably be deemed totally free of all restrictions. The proportionate interests of the shareholders will necessarily be changed if one shareholder is unable or unwilling to purchase his allotment. However, the shareholders may not always desire that the shares be offered proportionately to the other shareholders. For example, a majority shareholder with a son and daughter may wish to provide that all shares be first offered to his son and then to his daughter (or vice versa) rather than be offered proportionately.

If the number of shareholders is large—more than four or five, say—the mechanics of having the restrictions run to the shareholders become complicated, and it usually is preferable for the restrictions to run to the corporation. Many share transfer restrictions provide for a successive offer, first to the corporation, and then proportionately to the other shareholders if the corporation elects not to purchase them. Finally, if life insurance is to be used to provide funds to purchase shares on the death of a shareholder, it is usually simplest to have the corporation pay the premiums and own the policies on the lives of each shareholder rather than having each shareholder attempt to insure the life of every other shareholder. If there were 25 shareholders, a complete cross-purchase arrangement with life insurance would require 600 policies!

§ 9.16 Option or Buy/Sell Agreements: Establishment of Purchase or Option Price

The price provisions of shareholder option or buy-and-sell agreements are often the most difficult and important problem in drafting such agreements. Since closely held shares by definition have no market or quoted price, one simply cannot refer to a "fair," "reasonable," or "market" price; some definite method of valuation must be provided. Further, since it usually is impossible to know whose shares will be first offered for sale under such an agreement, everyone's goal in establishing such a mechanism is usually to be as fair as possible.

The following methods are often used to establish a purchase price usually stated on a per share basis:

(1) A stated price;

(2) Book value;

(3) Capitalization of earnings;

(4) Best offer by an outsider;

(5) Appraisal or arbitration, either by trained, impartial appraisers or arbitrators, or by directors or other shareholders; or

(6) A percentage of net profits to be paid for a specified number of years following the event which triggers the sale.

It is impossible to state definitively which is the most desirable method, since it depends on the nature of the business and assets being valued. The simplest method is for the parties to fix a definite price in the agreement itself. This may be par value, original purchase price, or a price established by negotiation. In the absence of fraud or overreaching, courts have enforced agreements where the price is well below the value of the shares, though there is always a possibility that a court may deem a grossly inadequate price to constitute an unreasonable restraint on alienation or to be "unconscionable." Generally, it is desirable to provide for periodic reevaluation of the fixed price as the fortunes of the corporation rise or fall. One problem that may arise is what happens if the parties fail to agree on a new price, or if they fail to revise the price from time to time as contemplated by the agreement. A willful refusal by a younger shareholder to renegotiate the price under such an agreement might be considered fraudulent, as might be a convenient "forgetfulness" on the part of such a shareholder. It is also possible that a court might conclude that there is a sufficient fiduciary relationship between the shareholders to justify a court-ordered price reevaluation whether or not specific provision therefor was made.

By far the most popular method of valuation is "book value," which may be computed by a simple division of a balance sheet figure by the number of outstanding shares. Indeed, it is probable that book value is often used without serious consideration as to its advantages or disadvantages in connection with the specific business. Book value is based on the application of certain accounting conventions to corporate transactions and whether or not book value is a realistic estimate of value depends on the circumstances; it may be appropriate to require that book value be adjusted in certain ways before being used to establish a purchase price. For example, one accounting convention requires assets to be valued at cost and not be reappraised upwards to reflect current market values. Thus, a corporation which owns real estate acquired decades earlier at low prices often will have a book value that considerably understates the true value of the assets. Similarly investments in readily marketable securities may be shown on the books at cost even though current market values may be obtained from the financial tables of any newspaper. In these instances, a restatement of such assets in terms of current market or appraised values may be more appropriate than "pure" book value. Accounting conventions also allow corporations to include certain things as assets which may never be realized; for example, costs of initial formation or of "good will" acquired in connection with the purchase of another business. It may be appropriate to eliminate such "assets" from the balance sheet before computing book value.

A number of accounting techniques have been developed for federal income tax purposes, and it may be undesirable to have a shareholder's interest in a corporation valued on the basis of such accounting principles. For example, if the corporation utilizes accelerated depreciation schedules for tax purposes, it may be desirable to specify that straight line depreciation should be used to compute book value for valuation purposes. Or, if inventory is valued on a LIFO basis, it may be desirable to require the inventory to be valued at a more realistic figure before computing book value.

Appraisal of the value of closely held stock has its own difficulties. Appraisers often prefer capitalization of earnings or a direct appraisal of the market value of assets, or a combination of the two, to book value. Capitalization of earnings is a fairly complex method of estimating the value of a business, though the basic idea is simple enough: if a corporation has average earnings of, say, $50,000 a year, and it is reasonable to capitalize those earnings at ten per cent, the corporation should be valued at $500,000. If the reasonable capitalization ratio were eight per cent, the business would be valued at $625,000 (625,000 × .08 = 50,000); if it were fifteen per cent, it would be valued at $333,333 (333,333 × .15 = 50,000). One may quite legitimately ask where the ten per cent figure came from, particularly since different capitalization ratios have such a significant effect on the overall valuation. An appropriate capitalization ratio may be justified on the basis of earnings ratios of comparable publicly held businesses, the appraiser's general experience with valuing businesses in the particular industry, or simply the appraiser's intuitive "feel" as to how risky a specific business is. Valuation based on capitalization of earnings may also be affected by different assumptions about the level of average earnings in the future, and whether different assets should be capitalized at different rates.

Normally, an appraiser or arbitrator will take into account all the various possible methods of valuation, and in fact the price he sets may reflect an average of various possible values, for example, the average of book value, the capitalized value, and the estimated liquidation value if the assets were sold.

After the value of the overall business is obtained, the per share value is usually obtained by a simple division by the number of outstanding shares. However, complications may involve the basis on which senior securities are valued and whether a further discount from the per share value should be taken if the shares are an isolated minority block with no chance of sharing in control.

§ 9.17 Option or Buy/Sell Agreements: Life Insurance

The unexpected death of a shareholder may cause serious disruption in a close corporation. Two things are essential if the corporation is to pass smoothly through such difficult periods: planning and money. A properly drafted buy-and-sell agreement or option may provide the former; life insurance is often the simplest way of providing the latter. It is possible, of course, to provide that the estate of a deceased shareholder is to be paid out over a period of time from anticipated future earnings. This may not be satisfactory from the standpoint of an estate, faced with large tax liabilities and a desire to wind matters up promptly. Life insurance, usually owned by the corporation, may provide the necessary funds to allow the estate's interest to be retired promptly. Of course, this assumes that the shareholder is insurable and that his age is not such that the cost of premiums is prohibitive.

[For unfamiliar terms see the Glossary]

CHAPTER TEN
DIRECTORS

§ 10.1 Number and Qualifications of Directors

Historically, virtually all statutes required that there be at least three directors, and many statutes required that each director have certain qualifications, such as being a shareholder or a resident of the state. Qualification requirements have been almost universally eliminated and an increasing number of states now permit boards of directors to consist of one or two directors. The privilege of having a board of one or two directors is often limited to corporations with one or two shareholders, but under the Model Act and the statutes of some states, any corporation, no matter how many shareholders, may elect to have a board consisting of one or two members.

Under the Model Act the number of directors of a corporation is fixed in the bylaws, and if the bylaws fail to do so, the number is the same as the number of initial directors stated in the articles of incorporation (MBCA § 36). The number of directors may be increased or decreased by express amendments to the bylaws, but a decrease does not have the effect of eliminating or shortening the term of any sitting director. Some cases have recognized that bylaws setting the number of directors may be amended informally, as for example by the shareholders electing four directors when the bylaws specify that the board shall consist of only three directors. However, it seems clear that that is not a desirable practice, injecting future uncertainty as to the number of directors to be elected and reducing the value of the written bylaws.

§ 10.2 Directors Meetings: Notice, Quorum and Similar Matters

Detailed provisions relating to directors meetings appear in corporate bylaws and only skeletal provisions are set forth in business corporation statutes. Regular meetings of the board of directors may be held weekly, monthly, quarterly or at any regular interval. The bylaws usually specify when such meetings are to be held, or may authorize the directors themselves to specify, by resolution, when regular meetings are to be held. It is customary to hold a regular meeting of directors either immediately before or immediately after the annual meeting of shareholders. Special meetings are meetings other than regular meetings. The principal difference between regular and special meetings is that a regular meeting may be held without notice, while a special meeting may be held "upon such notice as is prescribed in the bylaws." However, unlike a shareholders meeting, any relevant business may be transacted at a special meeting of directors even though not referred to in the notice. As a result there is little practical difference between regular and special meetings of directors. Directors may waive notice in writing before, at, or after the meeting.

A quorum of directors consists of a majority of the number of directors fixed in the bylaws, or if the number is not fixed in the bylaws, a majority of the number stated in the articles of incorporation (MBCA § 40). The articles of incorporation or bylaws may specify that a greater number than a majority constitute a quorum; some states permit a quorum to be reduced to less than a majority (*e. g.*, N.Y.Bus.Corp.Law § 707 —one third), but in most states, by negative inference, a quorum may not be set at less than a majority. Provisions increasing a quorum to all the directors are permitted and sometimes appear as control provisions in closely held corporations. Where a quorum is present, the act of the majority of the directors present at the meeting is the act of the board, unless the articles of incorporation or bylaws require a greater number. Again, unanimity requirements sometimes appear as control provisions in closely held corporations.

With a single exception, if a quorum is not present the board of directors may not act. The only exception is where the

directors are filling a vacancy; the Model Business Corporation
Act provides that a vacancy "may be filled by the affirmative
vote of a majority of the remaining directors though less than a
quorum." An ambiguity hides in this language. Even though
there are vacancies, the number of directors *in office* may still
be greater than a quorum. However, if two factions are vying
for control, the smaller faction may stay away from a meeting
called by the larger faction to prevent a quorum from being
present. At such a meeting the directors *present* are less than a
quorum even though the directors are greater than a quorum.
The cases are split as to whether the faction present at such a
meeting, "though less than a quorum," may fill the vacancies.
In Tomlinson v. Loew's, Inc., 135 A.2d 136 (Del.Ch.1957)
bylaw language similar to the phrase "though less than a
quorum" was held to refer to the directors in office rather than
to the directors present at the meeting. Several other cases,
however, adopt the opposite construction.

§ 10.3 Compensation of Directors

The traditional view is that a director is not entitled to
compensation for his ordinary services as director unless specific
provision is made by the board. The theory is that either
directors are acting as trustees or that they are motivated by the
prospect of increasing the return on their shares. However, a
director may be entitled to compensation pursuant to contract
entered into in advance or for extraordinary services beyond
normal directoral functions, or for service as a corporate officer
or agent. These principles are based on tradition not legal
power. A number of state statutes, following the Model Business Corporation Act, provide that the "board of directors shall
have authority to fix the compensation of directors unless otherwise provided in the articles of incorporation." (MBCA § 35,
1st ¶.)

The traditional view is gradually changing particularly among
large public corporations. Rather than paying their directors

nothing or a small honoraria for attending meetings, an increasing number now pay substantial sums to outside persons to serve as directors. Many corporations believe such payments improve the quality and interest of directors.

§ 10.4 Filling of Vacancies on the Board

Many older statutes distinguish between an "old" and a "new" vacancy. An "old" vacancy is created by the death or resignation of a director and may be filled by remaining directors, "though less than a quorum." (See § 10.2 for a discussion of this phrase.) A successor director in an "old" vacancy serves only for the unexpired term of his predecessor. A "new" vacancy, on the other hand, is created by an increase in the number of directors by amendment of the bylaws or articles. A "new" vacancy may be filled only by the shareholders, not the directors. The distinction between "old" and "new" vacancies arose in decisions from the State of Delaware, and was reflected in the 1950 version of the Model Act. The Model Act was revised in 1962 to permit "new" vacancies to be filled by the directors in the same way as "old" vacancies. Many, but not all, statutes reflect this simpler and more sensible provision.

§ 10.5 Hold-Over Directors

Statutes provide that despite the expiration of a director's term, he continues to hold office until his successor has been "elected and qualified" (MBCA § 36). As a result, the failure to hold an annual meeting does not affect the power of a corporation to continue to transact its business since the directors presently in office continue in office with power to act.

The hold-over director provision is particularly important in situations where the shareholders are deadlocked in voting power and unable to elect successors to directors whose terms have expired. In this situation, those who are "in" remain as directors apparently forever; however, the ultimate solution is the involuntary dissolution of the corporation if the deadlock cannot be broken. See Chapter 12, § 12.5.

§ 10.6 Necessity for Meeting and Personal Attendance

Numerous early cases refer to the rule that the "power invested in directors to control and manage the affairs of a corporation is not joint and several, but joint only," and that therefore action by directors must be "as a body at a properly constituted meeting." The underlying theory was that the shareholders were entitled to a decision reached only after group discussion and deliberation. Views may be changed as a result of discussion, and the sharpening of minds as a result of joint deliberation improves the decisional process. Several corollaries arise from this theory: first, the independent, consecutive approval of an act by each of the individual directors is not effective directoral action; second, directors may not vote by proxy; and third, formalities as to notice, quorum, and similar matters must be fully adhered to.

These corollaries make very little sense when applied to a close corporation where all the shareholders are active in the business, and even the requirement of a formal meeting of the directors in that situation is likely to be considered a meaningless formality. Further, rigid application of the doctrine often permits a corporation to use its own internal procedural defects as a sword to undo undesired transactions. This basic injustice is heightened because persons dealing with the corporation usually have no way of verifying that the formalities were in fact followed.

As a result, the broad principle was vitiated by judicially created exceptions even as it was being articulated. The basic exceptions are "estoppel," "ratification," and "acquiescence." Even though informal directoral action may be ineffective to formally authorize a transaction, it may be considered acquiescence in and ratification of the transaction. "Ratification" is usually applied where the corporation accepts the benefit of the contract without objection or where all the shareholders are aware of the contract and voice no objection. "Estoppel" is usually applied where the secretary of a corporation certifies that a meeting took place when it in fact had not; the corporation is estopped from questioning whether the requisite formalities were followed.

While it is dangerous to assume that the historical principle that directors may act only at meetings is totally obsolete, it is probable that one or more of the exceptions will be found applicable in specific situations.

§ 10.7 Telephonic Meetings

The Model Business Corporation Act contains a provision, widely copied in state statutes, that allows a board of directors or committee to "participate in a meeting . . . by means of a conference telephone or similar communications equipment by means of which all persons participating in the meeting can hear each other at the same time." (MBCA § 43, last ¶.) Such participation, the statute adds, constitutes presence in person at a meeting. This provision may be of considerable practical usefulness where directors are widely scattered, or where one or more of them are distant from the location where regular meetings are held. However, the fact that specific statutory authorization was felt to be necessary for a common sense idea such as telephonic meetings illustrates the persistence of the common law notion that directors can act only in meetings.

§ 10.8 Action Without a Meeting

Most states now permit directors to act without a formal meeting "unless otherwise restricted by the articles of incorporation or bylaws." The Model Business Corporation Act provision, widely copied in state statutes, provides that "any action which may be taken at a meeting of directors or of a committee, may be taken without a meeting if a consent in writing, setting forth the action so taken, shall be signed by all of the directors or all of the members of the committee . . .." (MBCA § 44.) Further, such a consent has "the same effect as a unanimous vote." Del.Code Ann.Tit. 8, § 141(F). This modest and sensible provision solves most problems created by the rule requiring directors meetings. Problems still may arise, however. For one thing, obtaining a written consent signed by all the directors is itself a formality which may be overlooked by a careless attorney; while a consent signed after the transaction has been entered into is effective, it is always possible that by that time one or more directors may have changed their minds. And, of course, the procedure is inapplicable if one of the directors objects to the transaction in question and refuses to execute the consent; a formal meeting is then apparently necessary.

§ 10.9 Directors' Objections to Actions

Directors are sometimes faced with the difficult problem of what to do when a majority insists on authorizing the corporation to enter into transactions which the director feels to be precipitate, risky, or outright illegal. The concern of such a director is not entirely theoretical, since in some circumstances he may be held personally liable even though he objected to the transaction and voted against it. To avoid this result a director must make sure that his dissent appears in writing since otherwise he is presumed to have assented to the action. If his dissent is not recorded in the minutes he must, in the words of the Model Act, "file his written dissent to such action with the secretary of the meeting before the adjournment thereof or . . . forward such dissent by registered mail to the secretary of the corporation immediately after the adjournment of the meeting." (MBCA § 35, last ¶.) Filing of a dissent not only eliminates liability, but also obviates later questions of proof and may have a psychological effect upon the other directors who realize that at least one director considers the conduct sufficiently questionable as to seek legal protection. Also, it affords notice to shareholders or others examining the records that at least one director questioned the propriety of a specific transaction. Other steps a director might take include requesting the corporation to obtain an opinion of counsel as to the propriety of the proposed transaction. While directors may rely in good faith on the opinion of counsel (MBCA § 35, 2d ¶), as a practical matter, an unqualified, reliable opinion may be difficult to obtain if the transaction is questionable. Finally, the director may resign, though if the resignation occurs after the transaction is approved, liability may be avoided only if the director files the appropriate dissent.

Similarly, even though a meeting is called without proper notice, a director waives his objection if he attends the meeting, except where he attends for the sole purpose of objecting to the transaction of any business. Any participation by him in the business undertaken at the meeting is likely to be considered a waiver even if he prefaces his participation by objecting to the lack of notice. (MBCA § 43.)

§ 10.10 Executive and Other Committees

Where a board of directors is large, it may be convenient to appoint a smaller executive committee to perform the functions of the board of directors between meetings of the full board. Corporation acts usually specifically authorize an executive committee, and define the area in which it may or may not function with more or less specificity.

Under the Model Business Corporation Act, an executive committee may be created only if specific provision therefor appears in the articles of incorporation or bylaws. (MBCA § 42.) Many statutes provide that an executive committee must consist of at least two members; in some states the creation of such a committee also requires approval by more votes than is necessary for the adoption of resolution. For example, the Texas Business Corporation requires approval by "a majority of the number of directors fixed by the bylaws, or in the absence of a bylaw fixing the number of directors, a majority of the number stated in the articles of incorporation." (V.A.T.S. Bus.Corp.Act, Art. 2.36.) Since most acts of boards of directors are accomplished by the vote of a majority of a quorum of the board, this provision, by requiring an absolute majority of the entire board, establishes a super-voting requirement.

The power of an executive committee extends generally to all matters relating to the business and affairs of the corporation over which the board of directors has authority with specified exceptions:

(a) Exceptions set forth in the resolution creating the executive committee, the bylaws, or the articles of incorporation; and

(b) Important matters which the applicable business corporation act specifically vests in the board of directors. The Model Act lists eight such actions, including declaring a dividend, approving a merger, authorizing the sale of shares, and so forth. The basic distinction is between routine matters relating to the business of the corporation and decisions referred to in the business corporation act which affect the governance of the corporation or its basic structure. In this way, the possibility of a "run away" executive committee is largely obviated. Delegation of authority to an executive committee generally does not relieve the board of directors, or any member thereof, of any responsibility imposed upon it or them.

In older statutes, the executive committee is often the only committee specifically referred to, though authorization may be given in general terms to create other committees. During the decade of the 1970s, a strong trend developed toward creating additional committees within the boards of directors of publicly held corporations. The three most popular committees are the *audit* committee, the *compensation* committee, and the *nominating* committee; in many corporations they are composed primarily or exclusively of "outside" directors, that is, directors not affiliated with management. The trend toward the creation of these important committees has been given strong impetus during the decade by the Securities and Exchange Commission, the New York Stock Exchange, and committees of the American Bar Association. (See § 13.4).

In addition to committees of directors, many corporations create committees of management personnel to consider business-related problems. These committees form part of executive management rather than part of the management structure of the board of directors.

[For unfamiliar terms see the Glossary]

CHAPTER ELEVEN

OFFICERS

§ 11.1 Express Authority and Power to Act in General

The source of express authority of corporate officers should first be sought in the state's business corporation act, second in the corporation's articles of incorporation, third in the corporate bylaws and, fourth, in corporate resolutions adopted by the board. The first two sources rarely shed light on the authority of officers. A typical statutory provision simply creates the offices of president, one or more vice presidents, secretary, and treasurer, and then provides that each "shall have such authority and perform such duties in the management of the corporation as may be provided in the bylaws, or as may be determined by resolution of the board of directors not inconsistent with the bylaws." (MBCA § 50.) Modern articles of incorporation generally do not refer at all to corporate officers, so that one is remitted to the bylaws and express resolutions of the board. Bylaw provisions are usually so general as to give little specific or reliable practical guidance (see § 11.2.), so that as a practical matter express authority is apt to be found solely in authorizing resolutions of the board.

In addition to express authority, corporate officers may possess implied actual or apparent authority, either from the nature of the office held or the manner in which business was conducted in the past. Finally, amorphous doctrines of "ratifiation," "estoppel," or "unjust enrichment" may sometimes allow third persons to hold corporations liable despite the absence of express, implied, actual, or apparent authority when the transaction was entered into.

[185]

§ 11.2   Roles of Corporate Officers

The roles of corporate officers are usually outlined in corporate bylaws which may vary from corporation to corporation. The following descriptions are drawn from model bylaws and therefore represent normal "boilerplate" descriptions.

(1) The president is "the principal executive officer of the corporation" and, subject to the control of the board, "in general supervises and controls the business and affairs of the corporation." He is the proper officer to execute corporate contracts, certificates for securities, and other corporate instruments.

(2) The vice president performs the duties of the president in his absence or in the event of his death, inability or refusal to act. Vice presidents act in the order designated at the time of their election, or in the absence of designation, in the order of their election. Vice presidents may also execute share certificates or other corporate instruments.

(3) The secretary has several different functions: he keeps the minutes of the proceedings of shareholders and the board of directors, he sees that all notices are duly given as required by the bylaws, he is custodian of the corporate records and of the corporate seal and sees that the seal of the corporation is properly affixed on authorized documents, he keeps a register of the names and post office addresses of each shareholder, he signs, along with the president or vice president, certificates for shares of the corporation, and he has general charge of the stock transfer books of the corporation.

(4) The treasurer has "charge and custody of and is responsible for" all funds and securities of the corporation, and he receives, gives receipts for, and deposits, all moneys due and payable to the corporation. The treasurer may be required to give a bond to ensure the faithful performance of his duties.

The board of directors may assign additional duties to any corporate officer. The president may also assign additional duties to any vice president, the secretary or the treasurer.

In addition to the named officers, corporations may create assistant secretaries, assistant treasurers, and other officers not specifically referred to by statute. Such officers may have titles such as comptroller, general manager, cashier, loan officer, or other designation. The chief executive officer in publicly held corporations may hold an office with a designation other than president, for example, chairman of the board of directors. In such corporations, the president may be an intermediate rather than leading position.

§ 11.3 Express Authority Delegated by Board of Directors

When a person negotiates with a corporation, he deals with a flesh-and-blood human being who may represent, either expressly or by implication, that he is authorized to bind the corporation. How does one make certain that the corporation—a fictional entity—will in fact be bound by a transaction so negotiated? It is possible, of course, to trust to appearances, implied authority, general descriptions of authority set forth in the previous section, blind luck, and the like, but that is very dangerous since litigation may be necessary to prove that the person in fact had authority to bind the corporation, and, because the doctrines are vague and amorphous, it is always possible that one may lose.

The simple and foolproof way to ensure that the corporation is bound by transaction is to require the person purporting to act for the corporation to deliver, prior to the closing of the transaction, a certified copy of a resolution of the board of directors authorizing the transaction in question. The certificate should be executed by the secretary or an assistant secretary of the corporation, the corporate seal should be affixed, and the certificate should recite the date of the meeting (or a statement that the resolution was approved by unanimous written consent) and quote the resolution itself. There is no reason to go behind the certificate and attempt to ascertain whether or not the stated facts are true, since the corporation is estopped to deny the truthfulness of facts stated in the secretary's certificate relating to the records in his custody. Or to put the issue in a somewhat different way, keeping and certifying corporate records is within the actual authority of the secretary and the act of certification therefore binds the corporation. However, since the binding nature of the certificate rests on an estoppel, an inquiry into the background behind the certificate may possibly destroy the basis of the estoppel. Cautious attorneys have followed this procedure for many years. That it has not achieved universal acceptance probably is a result of two factors: ignorance, particularly on the part of laymen who may not realize that the inherent authority of a corporate president is very narrow in many states (see § 11.4), and the small size of many transactions, which may make any formality, no matter how simple, uneconomic.

§ 11.4   Inherent Power of the Corporate President

Most non-lawyers are apt to think that the president of a corporation is the most important single person within the corporation and that he therefore must have authority to enter into ordinary business transactions, and probably has authority to enter into extraordinary transactions as well. In fact, these widely held views are often erroneous: the present state of the law in many jurisdictions is that the president has only limited authority which may not extend beyond minor, ordinary, routine transactions. Essentially, the locus of power to approve more significant transactions is in the board of directors, not the president.

This narrow construction of the president's authority may lead to injustice. Persons relying on reasonable appearances may discover that their reliance was ill-advised, and that the corporation is not obligated on a relatively routine transaction authorized by the corporate president. Persons aware of the rule are forced virtually to insult the president by demanding an exhibit of his authority.

Some courts have broadened the implied authority of the president or chief executive officer, and there appears to be a general trend in this direction. Broader authority of the president is likely to be found in cases where the corporation later regrets the transaction and seeks to hide behind the lack of authority of its chief officer. Some courts have concluded that a president presumptively has any powers which the board could give him. Others give him authority to enter into transactions "arising in the usual and regular course of business," and construe that phrase broadly. This may include, for example, the power to hire or discharge all employees. However, the inherent authority test is at best uncertain in its application to specific facts so that all unusual or extraordinary contracts should be authorized by the directors—including such matters as lifetime or long-time employment contracts, contracts to sell, lease or mortgage real estate, and settlement of material litigation.

§ 11.5 Implied Authority, Apparent Authority, Ratification, Estoppel, and Unjust Enrichment

Even where the authority of the person purporting to act for a corporation has not been established by a previous action of the board, the doctrines of ratification, estoppel, implied actual authority, or apparent authority may be available to a third person seeking to hold the corporation. These various doctrines are closely interrelated.

The board of directors of a corporation may learn that an officer has entered into a transaction in the past without being specifically authorized to do so. If the board does not promptly attempt to rescind or revoke the actions previously taken by the officer, it is probable that the corporation will be bound on the transaction on a theory of "ratification." Ratification may arise merely from knowledge of the transaction and failure to disaffirm or rescind it; usually, however, there are also elements of retention of benefits by the corporation and/or known reliance by the third party on the existence of the contract. "Estoppel" or "unjust enrichment" might equally well be found in such cases. Estoppel differs from ratification mainly in that attention is placed on the reliance of the third person, and the inequitableness of permitting the corporation to pull the rug out from under a person who reasonably relied on the corporation's silence.

Most problems involving implied authority of corporate officers arise when the third person seeks to hold the corporation on a current transaction by showing that the directors accepted or ratified prior similar transactions in the past. The argument is that the acquiescence of the board of directors indicates that an actual grant of authority was informally made. The same facts which support a finding of ratification of transaction A_1 may be used to conclude that a later similar transaction, A_2, was impliedly authorized. This is, of course, implied actual authority.

Apparent authority bears somewhat the same relationship to the concept of estoppel as implied authority bears to ratification. To show apparent authority, one must prove such conduct on the part of the principal as would lead a reasonably prudent person, using diligence and discretion, to suppose that the agent has the authority he purports to exercise. A third person, knowing that an officer has exercised authority in the past with the consent of the board of directors, may continue to rely on the appearance of authority, and the doctrine of apparent authority may protect such reliance. For apparent authority to exist, there must be some conduct on the part of the *principal, i. e.,* the corporation, which creates the appearance of authority; a mere representation by an agent that he possesses the requisite authority is not sufficient. However, such conduct may consist of silence when the principal is aware that the agent represents that he has authority, or it may consist of acquiescence in, and ratification of, acts performed in the past.

The principal practical difference between apparent authority and implied actual authority is that for apparent authority, the third person must show that he was aware of the prior acts or holding out and that he relied on appearances, while implied actual authority may be found even in the absence of knowledge or reliance on the part of third persons. However, the same conduct may often be cited to prove either implied actual authority or apparent authority.

In view of the close interrelationship between the various doctrines referred to in this section, it is not surprising to find that courts sometimes slip from one doctrine to another, sometimes perhaps not being fully aware of the differences.

The various doctrines discussed in this Section may be applicable to situations other than silence and acquiescence. For example, a corporation may expressly ratify a transaction, or a corporation may be estopped to deny that a transaction was authorized if it expressly creates the appearance of authority but withholds actual authority. Similarly, implied authority or apparent authority may arise from a variety of affirmative circumstances as well as silence on the part of the directors.

Courts may be reluctant to find ratification of an unauthorized act by an officer where the act is fraudulent, unfair to minority shareholders, or against public policy. Often, in such situations, the court may conclude that the corporation lacked the requisite full knowledge to ratify the act. Of course, to avoid such an act the directors must offer to return any benefits obtained by the corporation.

§ 11.6   Fiduciary Duties of Officers and Agents

Corporate officers and agents owe a fiduciary duty to the corporation. The standard imposed involves a high degree of honesty, good faith, and diligence because corporate officers and agents render services for pay, and are often full-time employees. The officer or agent should act for the sole benefit of the corporation and give to it his best uncorrupt business judgment. Full disclosure of possibly conflicting transactions may be required, and the officer or agent may hold in trust for the corporation profits he made personally in competition with, or at the expense of, the corporation. When all is said and done, however, general statements about the scope of fiduciary duties rarely decide specific cases.

The scope of an officer's obligation to the corporation is determined in part by the nature of the performance required of him. The duty of subordinate officers or agents may be somewhat narrower than the analogous duty of a director. However, most of the litigation relating to fiduciary duties involve directors, see Chapter 14, and such cases are often relied on to establish the duties of high-level or managing corporate officers and agents.

A corporate officer or agent may also be liable to the corporation if he exceeds his actual authority and binds the corporation in a transaction with a third person. Such a transaction, of course, must be within the officer's or agent's apparent authority if the corporation is to be bound.

§ 11.7   Liability of Officers and Agents to Third Parties

A corporate officer or employee who acts within the scope of his authority as his corporation's representative in a consensual transaction is not personally liable on the transaction if he acted solely as an agent. This statement of basic principles of agency is little more than a truism; what is significant are ways in which a corporate officer or employee may, despite the general agency principle, make himself liable on a corporate obligation. There are several possibilities:

First, he may expressly guarantee the performance by the corporation, intending to be personally bound on the obligation. Such a guarantee may be written or oral, and may or may not be supported by consideration, depending on the sequence of events and what is requested. Of course, to be enforceable, a promise must be supported by consideration. Whether or not it must also be in writing usually depends on the proper scope of the provision of the statute of frauds dealing with promises to answer for the indebtedness of another. For example, an oral promise by the president of a corporation to a supplier of merchandise that he would assume the obligation of payment if goods were delivered might be enforced despite the statute of frauds on the theory that the president was the primary obligor. Similarly, the so-called "main purpose" or "leading object" exceptions to the suretyship provision of the statute of frauds may in some circumstances make an oral guarantee by a corporate officer enforceable.

Second, he may not intend to be personally bound, but may in fact bind himself if he creates the impression that he is negotiating on an individual rather than corporate basis, or if he executes the agreement in such a way as to indicate personal liability. If a person negotiates a transaction without disclosing he is acting on behalf of a corporation he is personally liable to the third person on general agency principles. Even if the existence of the corporation is disclosed, joint liability of the corporation and the officer may be created because of informality in the manner of execution. The proper manner for an officer to execute a document in the name of, and on behalf of, a corporation is as follows:

ABC Corporation

By_____

President

Any variation from this form is dangerous, since the mere designation of the corporate office may be deemed a description of the signing party rather than evidence that he signed as agent. For example, the following form of execution:

ABC Corporation

_____, President

is ambiguous since the corporation and the president may be either joint obligors or the president may have intended to sign only in his representational capacity. The word "president" does not resolve the ambiguity since it may be an identification of the individual obligor or an indication that he signed only as a representative. In cases involving ambiguous forms of execution courts appear to be more willing to allow corporate officers to testify about the "real intention of the parties" in executing general contracts than in executing promissory notes.

Third, if the agent is acting beyond the scope of authority, he may be personally liable on the transaction unless the corporation takes him off the hook by ratifying the transaction. A person acting as an agent generally warrants his own authority; this principle, of course, does not apply where the third person is aware the officer or agent lacks authority and the transaction must be submitted to the board of directors for approval.

Finally, liability may arise because imposed by statute. Failure to pay franchise taxes or to publish a notice upon incorporation may, in some circumstances, lead to individual as well as corporate liability on corporate obligations. The federal income tax statutes provide for a penalty of one hundred per cent of the tax for failing to pay over income taxes withheld from employees. This penalty tax may be imposed on "any person required to collect, truthfully account for, and pay over" the tax. (IRC § 6672.) There are perhaps other situations as well where personal liability is imposed by statute.

§ 11.8   Imputation of Knowledge to Corporation

In the foregoing discussion, there have been several references to "corporate knowledge" or understanding that appear to ignore the fictional nature of a corporation. Of course, a corporation can "know" or "have notice of" something only if one or more persons who represent the corporation know or have notice of the thing. Usually, knowledge acquired by a corporate officer or employee while acting in furtherance of the corporate business or in the course of his employment will be imputed to the corporation. Thus, if the president knows of a transaction, the corporation ratifies it if the corporation accepts the benefits of the transaction, even though one or more directors or other officers may not know all the details. Service of process on an authorized agent of the corporation will support a default judgment against the corporation even though the agent fails to forward the papers to the corporation's attorney.

Difficult problems arise when it is sought to impute knowledge of an agent to the corporation if the agent is acting adversely to the corporation. Generally information or knowledge may be imputed from an agent who has ultimate responsibility for the transaction to his corporation even if the agent is acting adversely to and in fraud of the corporation. Similarly, if a corporate officer learns that a low level employee is defrauding the corporation, the officer's knowledge may be imputed to the corporation even though the officer does not disclose his knowledge to other officers or directors.

Generally, an agent's wrongful intention may be imputed to a corporation so that a corporation is subject to civil or criminal prosecution, including prosecution for traditional crimes such as murder or rape. Of course, for the corporation to be prosecuted such acts must be connected with, or be in furtherance of, the corporation's business.

§ 11.9   Tenure of Officers and Agents

Corporate officers and agents generally serve at the will of the person or board having authority to elect or appoint the officers or agents. Corporate officers are elected by the board of directors, and corporation acts generally provide that they may be removed by the board of directors "whenever in its judgment the best interest of the corporation will be served thereby." So far as agents appointed by the president or general manager are concerned, the power to discharge is implicit in the power to employ. Corporate bylaws usually explicitly grant the power to remove or discharge as part of the power to appoint.

Of course, an officer or agent may be given an employment contract, and removal of such an officer or agent may give rise to a cause of action for breach of contract. However, the mere election or appointment of an officer or agent, even for a definite term, is not usually held of itself to give rise to a contract right. The validity of such contracts in light of corporate bylaws is discussed in the following section.

§ 11.10   Long-Term Employment Contracts

Long-term employment contracts have given rise to a substantial volume of litigation.

(1) *Validity.* Corporate bylaws usually provide that specified named officers, such as the president, vice president, secretary, and treasurer, are to be elected by the board of directors for a term of one year. Does such a bylaw restriction limit the power of a corporation to grant such an officer an employment contract extending beyond the term of his office? Generally, the answer is "no" since, despite the contract, the officer or employee may be relieved of his duties at any time. Of course, the corporation may be liable for breach of contract for the premature termination of the employment period. On a parity of reasoning, long-time contracts, *e. g.,* leases, have been upheld

despite the fact that they "bind" subsequent boards of directors. A second argument may also be made if the board has power, as most boards of directors do, to amend the bylaws. An employment contract for more than one year may be deemed to be an implied amendment of the bylaws by the board, since the board could first amend the bylaw and then enter into a long-term employment contract. While some courts have accepted this argument, there is a practical problem with implied amendments of bylaws since one cannot then rely on the written bylaws as being the current and complete rules governing the corporation's internal affairs.

(2) *Life Time Employment Contracts.* The claim that a person has been given a life time employment contract by a corporation has been treated with hostility by the courts. Such contracts are usually oral and arise within the context of a family-run business. While such a contract is not within the statute of frauds, courts may feel that the factual basis for such an open-ended commitment is inherently implausible. Also, such contracts may subject a corporation to a substantial liability which may run for a long and indefinite period during which circumstances may substantially change. Most cases which have refused to enforce such arrangements have done so on the ground the officer making the arrangement had neither actual nor apparent authority to enter into such an arrangement.

(3) *Discharge for Cause.* It is clear that an officer or employee with a valid employment contract may nevertheless be discharged for cause. "Cause" may consist of acts of dishonesty, negligence, refusal to obey reasonable orders, refusal to follow reasonable rules, or a variety of other acts such as engaging in an unprovoked fight. In effect, such conduct constitutes a breach of an implied—if not express—covenant in the employment contract. Of course, since officers usually do not have employment contracts, it is usually unnecessary to determine whether or not "cause" exists.

(4) *Basis of Compensation.* Employees sometimes request that they be compensated on the basis of a percentage of corporate earnings or profits rather than at a flat rate. No particular legal problem is raised by such contracts, though questions sometimes arise as to how earnings and profits are to be measured. The simple phrase "net profits" is often ambiguous and its meaning may be elusive.

(5) *Miscellaneous.* Employment contracts for highly paid personnel in publicly held corporations often provide for deferred compensation, options to purchase shares, reimbursement of business expenses, and other tax-related benefits. In the closely held corporation, an employment agreement may be an integral part of the basic planning arrangement between shareholders. Terms relating to employment are often placed in shareholder's agreements so that they will be binding on all the other shareholders as well as the corporation. There also may be a greater possibility of specific performance of a shareholders' agreement than of a simple employment contract; specific enforcement may be significant in a close corporation where the right to participate in management may be important and the salary derived from the arrangement is the only available financial benefit.

[For unfamiliar terms see the Glossary]

CHAPTER TWELVE
THE CLOSELY HELD CORPORATION

§ 12.1 Close Corporations in Perspective

A "close corporation" or "closely held corporation" may be defined preliminarily as a corporation with a few shareholders. (See § 1.5.) Most states do not provide any special treatment for such corporations and they must comply with the various provisions of the state corporation statute the same way as any other corporation. In recent years, however, an increasing number of states have enacted special statutes dealing with such corporations. Also, the legal literature has long recognized that such corporations have special problems and needs. As a result, a "jurisprudence" of closely held corporations is in the process of being developed.

A closely held corporation has certain unique attributes:

(1) Since it has only a relatively small number of shareholders, there is no public trading in, or public market for, its shares. Small blocks of shares may be totally unsalable; potential purchasers must be found among present shareholders, or rarely, among outsiders willing "to take a gamble." As a result, the market for small blocks of closely held shares is at worst non-existent and at best a buyer's market; there is usually no competition and therefore little incentive for buyers to offer reasonable prices for shares. On the other hand, if the shares offered for sale constitute a majority interest, they are often readily salable to outsiders interested in running the business in which the corporation is engaged.

(2) The management of the corporation is closely associated with the principal shareholders, or with all the shareholders. The majority shareholders may name the board of directors, and through them, the officers and employees. If there is a

disagreement between the majority and minority shareholders, the majority may exclude the minority totally from the corporation and its business, and without specific employment rights there is little that the minority shareholder can do about it.

(3) The majority shareholders usually have little interest in paying dividends. Rather, for tax reasons they usually prefer to distribute earnings in the form of salaries or other payments to the shareholders, or some of them, that are tax deductible by the corporation.

(4) The management may wish to operate the business in an informal manner, often as though it were a partnership rather than a corporation.

(5) Shareholders usually desire a voice in determining who their fellow shareholders are, and may wish to limit the shareholders to persons active in the management of the corporation.

Because shares in a close corporation are not readily salable and minority shareholders ordinarily have no power to force a dissolution of the corporation, a person may be "locked in" a minority position for long periods of time, receiving little or no return on his investment and being unable to dispose of it at a reasonable price. Indeed, over a period of time in which deaths, withdrawals, or fallings out are likely, the possibility that adverse and hostile interests will develop within a closely held corporation is fairly high.

This chapter considers control arrangements within the close corporation. Such arrangements may be made to ensure control by a working majority, or to give a minority a greater voice in corporate affairs than it naturally has, or to give a minority shareholder some protection against the possible tyranny of the majority referred to in the preceding paragraphs.

§ 12.2 Traditional Control Devices in Closely Held Corporations

In the absence of special statutory treatment of closely held corporations, such corporations must establish control devices through the use of traditional and accepted techniques. An earlier section has discussed the limited validity of shareholders' agreements that restrict the discretion of directors (§ 8.9); that rule of law of uncertain scope obviously limits the usefulness of the simple contract as a control device. Accepted voting control devices such as shareholders pooling agreements (§ 9.6), voting trusts (§§ 9.7–9.9) and irrevocable proxies (§ 9.5) have their place, but their inherent usefulness is often limited.

Of greater practical importance is the use of restrictions on the transfer of shares (§§ 9.11–9.17). Such restrictions not only ensure that shareholders have a voice in who is a shareholder in the corporate venture, but often of greater importance, a mandatory buy/sell agreement may be the best guarantee to a minority shareholder that he or his estate will be able to dispose of his interest in the corporation at a reasonable price (see § 9.11).

The most flexible and fool-proof device to establish desired control relationships involves the use of different classes of shares, usually different classes of common stock (see generally §§ 7.11, 9.10). The following examples illustrate the flexibility and variety of this device:

(1) A corporation is to have two shareholders, one putting in $100,000, the other $50,000. They desire to share equally in control but in the ratio of their contributions (2:1) for financial purposes. The attorney suggests that an equal number of shares of two classes of common stock, Class A common and Class B common, be authorized. Each class is entitled to elect two directors, but the dividend and liquidation rights of the Class A are twice those of Class B. The corporation then issues all the Class A common to one shareholder for 100,000 dollars and all the Class B common to the other shareholder for 50,000 dollars. Alternatively, if shares with multiple votes per share are authorized in the particular state, the shares may be identical in all financial respects, with the class received by the smaller contributor having two votes per share.

(2) A minority shareholder wishes to be assured of being treasurer of the corporation and to have a veto over all amendments to the articles of incorporation. The attorney suggests that a special class of common stock be issued to the minority shareholder, and the articles of incorporation provide that (1) the treasurer must be a holder of that class of stock, and (2) the articles may be amended only by an affirmative vote of two-thirds of each class of stock, voting by classes. In other respects the classes have equal rights.

(3) There are three shareholders, each contributing the same amount of capital, but C is also contributing the basic idea and wants the same voting power as A and B combined. One simple solution is to issue voting and non-voting common stock (with equal dividend and liquidation rights) in the following amounts:

	Voting	*Non-voting*
A	50	50
B	50	50
C	100	-0-

Somewhat the same result can be obtained by the use of nonvoting preferred stock or indebtedness rather than non-voting common stock.

(4) A, B, and C are each contributing the same amount of capital, but A wants to be sure that B and C will not combine to oust him and cut off his income. The attorney suggests that A execute a five-year employment contract with the corporation guaranteeing him the specified income, renewable for a second five years at the option of A. To assure that A will be assured of a right to participate in the board deliberations, the attorney suggests that three classes of stock be created, each with the power to elect one director.

There seems to be little doubt about the validity of such control arrangements based on different classes of stock. While there has been little litigation on the outer bounds of the power to create specialized classes of stock, recent decisions appear uniformly favorable. In perhaps the most startling case, Lehrman v. Cohen, 222 A.2d 800 (Del.Ch.1966), the Delaware Supreme Court upheld a class of common stock which consisted of one share having a par value of $10; the share (1) could elect one of the five directors (the other four elected by two equal factions), (2) was not entitled to receive dividends, (3) could share in the proceeds of dissolution only to the extent of the par value of the one share, and (4) could be redeemed by the corporation at any time by paying the shareholder the par value of the share, upon approval of four of the five directors. This share comes close to a naked vote completely divorced from ownership, yet was upheld. This one share class was designed to avoid a potential deadlock between the two principal shareholders and was issued to the attorney representing the corporation; after several years, the attorney and one of the other two shareholders combined forces to take over working control of the corporation, a situation which was cemented by a long term employment contract for the attorney. This arrangement was upheld in its entirety. (See § 9.10 for a discussion of the same case in a different context.)

§ 12.3 Increased Quorum and Voting Requirements

Another useful device in effectuating shareholder control devices is increased voting requirements in order to give minority interests a veto power. This veto power may be applicable at the shareholder level, at the board of directors level, or both. In most states, it is possible to increase the percentage needed to approve a measure to any desired number; usually unanimity is imposed, but in some circumstances a lesser percentage may be sufficient or have the same effect. While a requirement of unanimity was held invalid by a few courts, most notably Benintendi v. Kenton Hotel, Inc., 60 N.E.2d 829 (N.Y.1945), the language of modern statutes is broadly permissive, and there seems little doubt today about the validity of increased voting requirements.

It is usually important to increase both the quorum requirement and the minimum vote requirement in order to make sure that it is impossible for the corporation to act without the assent of the minority shareholder. Where the quorum requirement has not been increased it is sometimes possible for the minority shareholder to prevent action by staying away from the meeting if that makes it impossible to obtain a quorum. In one case, such conduct was held to constitute a breach of fiduciary duty. Gearing v. Kelly, 182 N.E.2d 391 (N.Y.1962). This decision seems questionable given the dynamics of the closely held corporation.

§ 12.4   Dangers of Dissension and Deadlock

A closely held corporation is often involved in dissension and deadlock. "Dissension" refers to internal squabbles, fights, or disagreements; "deadlock" to control arrangements that effectively prevent the corporation from acting. Many small corporations at one time or another in their history are wracked by such problems, and some advance planning may help to reduce or eliminate such disagreeable incidents.

In a typical close corporation, all the shareholders actively participate in the management of the business; it is easy to envision how disagreements may lead to distrust or friction. There may be good faith disagreement as to desirable business policies or a less than good faith suspicion that another shareholder is attempting a power grab or trying to obtain more than his "fair share" of the assets. The relationship of shareholders within a close corporation requires good faith and cooperation on all sides in much the same way as in a partnership; when this is lacking, serious disagreements are bound to arise.

Dissension within a close corporation creates more serious problems than in a partnership. If one faction has effective working control, the minority faction is in a weak if not help-less position. Typically, the minority has no power to force dissolution and no right to share in the fruits of management (except to the extent the majority permits). The minority may have the dubious recourse of trying to sell their shares to the majority. Where there is dissension a majority group is often willing to pay something to eliminate the nuisance of a minority block. However, the majority may well decide to "soften up" the minority by removing them from salaried positions with the corporation, cease paying dividends, and letting them sit for a year or so. In this situation, some attorneys have counseled minority shareholders to adopt obstructionist tactics, including litigation, in an effort to improve their bargaining position. Of course, such tactics are likely to increase the enmity and friction within the corporation.

Equally complex problems arise if neither faction has effective working control, since the corporation may become deadlocked. A corporation is potentially subject to deadlock if (1) two factions own exactly fifty per cent of the outstanding shares, (2) there are an even number of directors, and two factions each have the power to select the same number, or (3) a minority shareholder has retained a veto power in one of the ways previously described. In each of these situations, the corporation may in effect be on dead center and unable to function as a corporation.

A deadlock may occur either at the shareholders' level or at the directors' level. If the shareholders are deadlocked, the corporation may continue to operate, since the board of directors in office when the deadlock arose will presumably remain in office indefinitely. A deadlock at the directoral level may prevent the corporation from functioning, though it is possible that the president or general manager may continue to operate the business, often to the complete exclusion of the other faction of shareholders.

The most practical solution for the truly deadlocked corporation is usually for one faction to buy out the other. It is ordinarily preferable to preserve a going corporation rather than to dissolve it. The business assets of a corporation, including intangible good will, are ordinarily worth more as a unit than fragmented. While it sometimes may be possible for deadlocked parties to work out a sale after the deadlock has arisen, the more logical solution is to address the problem when the parties are in amity and to work out an agreement in advance by which one faction should buy out the other at a fair price in the event of a deadlock. Such buy-sell agreements are no different in principle than those discussed earlier relating to the death or retirement of a shareholder (see §§ 9.11–9.17). Some additional problems are created, however. For example, who is to buy out whom if both desire to continue the corporate business? Often the senior should buy out the junior, though if the age discrepancy is large, it may be more sensible to reverse the order and have the junior buy out the senior. Another variation, which somewhat resembles roulette, is to have one shareholder set a price at which he is willing to buy out the other shareholder or to sell his own shares, at the election of the other shareholder. Precisely what events trigger the power to buy? Some kind of objective standard is usually desirable, such as the failure to agree on a slate of directors for some specified period. Which of the various pricing formulas should be used and which should be avoided? In light of the possible deadlock it seems important to choose a formula that does not rely on a cooperative effort to set the price; it also seems desirable to use a formula that will yield as "fair" a price as possible rather than one that appears to create a bargain for one faction or the other.

In the event a buy-out cannot be worked out, the ultimate remedy in the event of dissension or deadlock is involuntary dissolution, and that is the remedy usually provided by statute (see § 12.5). It should be recognized, however, that the ultimate remedy of dissolution may very well benefit one faction of shareholders at the expense of another. If a single shareholder's personal abilities largely explain the corporation's success, he may well desire liquidation. By performing services for the corporation, the dominant shareholder is in effect sharing the fruits of his ability with other shareholders. If the corporation were dissolved, presumably the dominant shareholder could continue to operate the business without sharing the fruits with anyone. Serious problems may arise if the dominant shareholder simply abandons the corporation and starts a new business in competition with the corporation since such action might be deemed to constitute an usurpation of a corporate opportunity by the dominant shareholder. A classic example of the attempted use of dissolution by a dominant shareholder is In re Radom & Neidorff, Inc., 119 N.E.2d 563 (N.Y.1954). Whether or not dissolution unfairly benefits a shareholder in such a situation is debatable.

§ 12.5 Resolution of Deadlocks by Dissolution

If a corporation is truly deadlocked and unable to break the deadlock, business corporation acts provide the ultimate remedy of involuntary dissolution at the request of a shareholder. Generally, this remedy may not be available to a shareholder unless he can establish that the case comes within the precise language of the statute. There is no general common law right of dissolution. While statutory language as to the availability of the involuntary dissolution remedy varies from state to state, the following language taken from § 97 of the Model Business Corporation Act is typical:

The shareholder seeking dissolution must establish that—

(1) The directors are deadlocked in the management of the corporate affairs and the shareholders are unable to break the

deadlock and that "irreparable injury to the corporation is being suffered or is threatened by reason thereof;" or

(2) The acts of the directors or those in control of the corporation are "illegal, oppressive, or fraudulent;" or

(3) The shareholders are deadlocked in voting power, and have failed to elect successors to directors whose terms have expired during a period which includes at least two consecutive annual meeting dates; or

(4) The corporate assets are being "misapplied or wasted."

The quoted language in these provisions requires strong showings of potential or actual abuse or harm. In most cases shareholders will only be able to take advantage of clause (3) which is based solely on the lapse of time and not a finding of serious harm or serious abuse.

Some statutes contemplate the appointment of a receiver as an interim measure before dissolution is decreed. If a corporation is placed in receivership, control passes from the hands of the deadlocked shareholders; even if the business and assets are preserved during the receivership, it is probably unlikely that the cause of deadlock can be corrected and the business ever returned to its owners. Dissolution is usually the ultimate solution.

§ 12.6   Resolution of Deadlocks by Arbitration

Mandatory arbitration is sometimes used as a device by which a deadlock may be broken. In considering the desirability of arbitration, two questions should be considered: first, what kinds of controversies is the arbitrator likely to face, and second, what kinds of solutions will he be permitted to adopt.

Certainly many disputes leading to deadlock in a closely held corporation involve personality conflicts or broad differences in policy. An arbitrator may have no criteria for resolving such disputes, and even if he does resolve a specific dispute, it is unlikely that he will have cured the basic disagreement which led to the original deadlock. In Application of Burkin, 136 N.E.2d 862 (N.Y.1956), a well-known New York case, a minority shareholder in a corporation deadlocked because of an unanimity requirement and a disagreement with the majority shareholder sought arbitration of a claim that the majority shareholder should be removed as director. The court refused to order arbitration on the theory that the dispute was not justiciable, a result which was later overruled by statute. In this situation, the order of an arbitrator to remove the majority shareholder from the board of directors would in effect turn control of the corporation over to the minority shareholder, and as there was a unanimity requirement for the election of directors, the turnover of control would be permanent, at least until dissolution could be compelled pursuant to statute. Even if the majority shareholder had committed acts which might constitute cause for removal, it is doubtful whether an arbitrator should have power to favor permanently one faction over another in a pure struggle for control. There are other remedies of the minority shareholder to correct the acts which constitute cause for removal—e. g., a derivative suit—without turning the corporation over to the minority shareholder. Ultimately, if deep personal or policy conflicts continue, dissolution is the only suitable remedy because arbitration cannot cure the root cause of the disagreement.

The advantages of arbitration are speed, cheapness, informality (as contrasted with a court proceeding), and the prospect of a decision by a person with knowledge and experience in business affairs. Where the reason for deadlock is a question not involving a basic personal or policy matter, arbitration may satisfactorily resolve a dispute and permit the corporation to continue. For example, in Vogel v. Lewis, 268 N.Y.S.2d 237 (N.Y.App.1966), aff'd 224 N.E.2d 738 (1967) the issue was whether a corporation should exercise an option to purchase in a lease of real property. The court held that this issue should be submitted to arbitration, a result which seems reasonable under the circumstances.

§ 12.7 Special Close Corporation Statutes

State statutes assume that corporations will be conducted with a degree of formality: shareholders will meet to elect directors who will in turn meet to elect or appoint officers and to direct the affairs of the corporation. Even a moment's reflection will indicate that these assumptions are unjustified for the small closely held corporation. With only a few shareholders, all or most of whom are active in the conduct of the business, corporate matters are likely to be resolved by unanimous consent with a minimum of formality and no regard for the statutory niceties. This entirely understandable practice creates several possible legal issues:

(1) Will the ignoring of corporate formalities give rise to an argument that the corporate veil should be "pierced" and the participants held personally liable on corporate obligations? (See Chapter Six, particularly § 6.4.)

(2) Will the participants agree upon a control arrangement that is reasonable under the circumstances but violates the "statutory norms" so that the arrangement is legally unenforceable? (See § 8.9.)

(3) Will decisions made informally and without following the statutory norms be binding on the corporation and third parties? (See §§ 10.6–10.8.)

Special statutes relating to closely held corporations have been adopted in California, Delaware, and a number of other states. These statutes are designed to permit such corporations to conduct their affairs with essentially the same formalities as if they were partnerships. While there is considerable variation in the state statutes relating to close corporations they generally provide the following—

(1) Agreements that restrict the discretion of directors (and are therefore probably invalid under conventional principles (see § 8.9)) are specifically validatĕd.

(2) The corporation may elect to dispense with the board of directors entirely and have the business and affairs of the corporation conducted by the shareholders as though they were partners. If this option is elected, the liabilities otherwise imposed on directors are imposed on the shareholders acting as directors.

(3) The corporation may adopt special dissolution provisions that permit a minority shareholder, in specified circumstances, to compel the dissolution of the corporation. This provision, designed to eliminate the "locked in" feature of the close corporation (see § 12.1.) is the principal substantive provision of these statutes that addresses the basic problem of the minority shareholder in a closely held corporation. However, it has only limited usefulness since it is applicable only when specifically agreed to.

(4) In the event of a deadlock at the directoral level, courts are specifically empowered to break the deadlock by the appointment of impartial "provisional directors." This provision is designed to provide a simpler, more flexible and less drastic solution to deadlocked corporations than either the appointment of a receiver or dissolution. It is applicable to all close corporations and not limited to those that elect it; it is likely that the mere threat of the appointment of one or more provisional directors will be a strong stimulus to quarreling shareholders to make some kind of a mutual accommodation.

Close corporation statutes tend to be complex and prolix; much of the complicated language is addressed to problems such as determining which corporations are eligible to take advantage of these special provisions and what happens when an electing corporation loses its eligibility. Since corporations form a continuum in terms of size and number of shareholders, lines must to some extent be arbitrary, and the possibility that an electing corporation might become ineligible because of events over which it has little control has to be faced. A few states originally made the special statutes applicable to all corporations that fell within a broad statutory definition, but the trend is clearly toward making the special provisions completely elective by including appropriate provisions in the articles of incorporation of qualified corporations.

The definition of an eligible corporation involves a limitation on the number of shareholders (ranging from as low as 10 in some states to 35 or more in others), a requirement that there have been no registered public offering of shares, and a requirement that share transfer restrictions be imposed on all outstanding shares limiting their free transferability. Statutes also usually require appropriate notations on all certificates describing which special provisions the corporation has elected to make applicable.

Even though a number of states have adopted close corporation statutes, a rather limited sampling of the actual experience in several states indicates that they are not widely used. Florida even repealed its close corporation statute in 1975. While the reasons for the lack of use are speculative, it is probable that most attorneys are able to work out basic control relationships under the general corporation statutes and therefore do not feel it is necessary to use or experiment with these new and largely untried statutes. It is also possible that the sheer complexity of some of these statutes may have discouraged their widespread use.

[For unfamiliar terms see the Glossary]

CHAPTER THIRTEEN
THE PUBLICLY HELD CORPORATION

§ 13.1 Control and the Small Shareholder

The theoretical structure of a corporation assumes that shareholders select directors who in turn select corporate officers to carry out their directives. In some ways the large public corporation bears little resemblance to this theoretical structure. Consider, for example, the role of the small shareholder in selecting directors. He is presented with a list of candidates selected by the current managers of the corporation, and he may vote for or against them. However, since the overwhelming majority of the shareholders are going to vote in favor of the persons selected by management, it really does not make very much difference whether or not the small shareholder exercises his franchise.

For purposes of locating the real source of selection of directors, one must look not to the election process, but to some earlier point where an internal decision within the corporation was quietly made as to which names should be presented to the shareholders for approval as the management's candidates. It is at this point that the actual selection of directors occurs. The role of shareholders is to ratify this selection.

The managers and directors are usually shareholders of the corporation. Their holdings may vary from an infinitesimally small percentage to very substantial blocks. Except where the block approaches working control, however, their position in the corporation (not their voting power) is the source of their power. In many corporations, the directors and managers are virtually a self perpetuating body. The actual locus of power within the management structure of a corporation is more complex; it varies from corporation to corporation, depending on personalities, shareholdings, friendships, loyalties and the like.

Most shareholders routinely vote in favor of management. For one thing, they often have little choice. The managers control the "proxy solicitation" machinery. They have the list of shareholders, and their point of view is brought routinely before the shareholders as the experienced voice of those actually managing a complex business. Persons seeking to challenge them face formidable if not impossible obstacles. For another thing, there is natural self-selection by shareholders. Their financial interest in their own investment is paramount, and if they are dissatisfied with the management of their corporation, their natural inclination is to sell rather than to fight city hall. Thus, by a process of self-elimination, shareholders unhappy with management tend to disappear, and the remaining shareholders tend to be pro-management. Finally, the increased importance of institutional investors (described in the following section) has helped to solidify incumbent management. Institutional investors usually vote large numbers of shares and are natural supporters of management.

Management control, however, is not limitless. There are several sources of external pressure which may limit the power of management to do what it pleases. For one thing, a poor operating performance in terms of profits will result in depressed share prices and may lead indirectly to the ouster of management. This may possibly occur by forced dispossession by proxy fight, cash tender offer or exchange offer. More likely it will be the result of the power of large shareholders or other members of the financial community—commercial bankers, investment bankers, or institutional investors—to limit the sources of the corporation's long and short term financing. In addition, a palace coup may be a possibility. Even where total ouster is unlikely, however, other sources of pressure exist. The threat of filing of a shareholders' derivative suit produces pressure. The disclosure requirements of federal law create a kind of gold fish bowl atmosphere which also exercises a cautionary effect on management. Despite these factors, however, the threat that management will be turned out by an irate band of shareholders—as often occurs in political elections—is largely illusory in the large publicly held corporation.

§ 13.2 Institutional Investors

For many years the small shareholder described in the previous section was thought to epitomize the public shareholder. However, largely since World War II another type of public investor has grown tremendously in importance—the institutional investor. Institutional investors mainly collect and invest other people's money. They include life insurance companies, pension funds, investment companies (the "mutual funds"), bank trust departments, and similar organizations. Their assets have grown spectacularly, often by factors of 100 or more in the last thirty years. These institutional investors invest significant amounts of capital in a large variety of common shares traded on the major securities exchanges. As a group they are now the largest single owner of publicly held corporations; their holdings in the aggregate are in excess of forty per cent of the outstanding shares of listed publicly held corporations, and in specific corporations the percentage may run over fifty per cent. Accurate data on the full extent of institutional ownership is difficult to come by for several reasons, but it is clear that such investors are the predominant owners of American industry today.

Since institutional investors handle funds that ultimately belong to members of the general public in the form of pensions, life insurance proceeds, savings, or financial investments, their growth has been described as increasing the broad base of ownership of the means of production in modern society. However, in terms of potential control, the growth of institutional investors represent a narrowing of the base, since a relatively few persons may determine how large blocks of shares are voted.

Institutional investors often have the power, if they band together, to effectively dominate and control many large publicly held corporations. Most institutional investors, however, view their role as purely investors and disavow any interest in exercising control over the business and affairs of corporations. In part as a result of this attitude, institutional investors usually vote their shares in favor of management; if they are dissatisfied with management, they prefer to sell their shares rather than engage in a struggle for control. In some instances, however, institutional investors may be compelled to take affirmative roles in management rather than acting as a passive investor. In a struggle for control, for example, the blocks controlled by institutional investors may be absolutely critical, and by deciding who to support the investors effectively determine who should control the corporation.

Even though institutional investors view themselves as passive investors, their sheer size often raises unique market problems. For example, if an institutional investor decides to exercise its "market option" and sell its shares, the block may be so large that only other institutional investors have the capacity to absorb the shares. Large institutional holdings may therefore increase the volatility of share prices since an independent decision by several large institutional investors to dispose of their shares may markedly depress short-run prices.

§ 13.3   Registration of Securities in Street Name or in the Name of Nominees

One of the major problems of determining the role of institutional investors and others in the ownership of large publicly held corporations is created by the widespread use of nominees or street names in the registration of publicly held securities.

"Street names" refer to the names of several well-known brokers on Wall Street. Where a speculator purchases shares with a view toward reselling them promptly, he will probably not bother to have the shares registered in his own name. Indeed, he probably will not even take delivery of the certificates but will leave them with his broker. In order to facilitate such transactions, the practice has developed of registering often-traded shares in street names, and delivering them already endorsed by the registered owner. As a practical matter, such shares are bearer securities, but the problem is not a serious one since most transfers of street name securities are between brokers. Where shares are registered in street name, the corporation does not know who the beneficial owner is; indeed, it may not even know in which brokerage firm the shares are presently held. A person who buys securities for investment may take delivery of certificates registered in street name; more commonly, however, his broker will arrange for new certificates to be issued in the name of the investor, and those certificates will be delivered directly. The volume of securities held in street name at any one time is quite substantial.

Large institutional investors have developed a somewhat related practice of holding securities in the names of nominees, usually a partnership of employees using names such as "Abel and Company." This practice developed for completely innocuous reasons: to avoid onerous transfer requirements placed on corporations or fiduciaries selling shares. Since some institutional investors use several different nominees, it is difficult to ascertain the actual ownership of securities by such investors simply by looking at the corporation's records. In 1976, the Securities and Exchange Commission made an examination into this practice and concluded that it was consistent with the basic purposes of the securities acts administered by the Commission.

During the 1970s a new practice developed of using central clearing corporations to handle trading in securities. Within a central clearing corporation many off-setting trades between brokers can be netted, thereby greatly simplifying the transfer of certificates and reducing paperwork. As a result, large volumes of shares are now registered in the name of central clearing corporations, particularly the Stock Clearing Corporation, a subsidiary of the New York Stock Exchange. The nominee of Stock Clearing Corporation is Cede and Company. Shares registered in the name of Cede and Company may be beneficially owned by any one of hundreds of brokers participating in the Stock Clearing Corporation's clearing house functions.

§ 13.4   Directors of Publicly Held Corporations

In the large publicly held corporation, the business affairs of the corporation are usually run by the full-time management, not the board of directors. Management consists of a group of highly paid executives headed by a chief executive officer who may hold the title of president, chairman of the board, or some other title. For simplicity, such person is usually referred to as the CEO in the legal literature. The board of directors usually consists partly of management representatives ("inside directors") and partly of outsiders who have full-time jobs in other occupations and whose detailed knowledge of corporate affairs must of necessity be limited ("outside directors"). In these circumstances, it is not surprising that business management in fact rests with the corporate management not the directors.

The Model Business Corporation Act recognizes the theoretical role of the board of directors in the publicly held corporation in the following italicized language: "All corporate powers shall be exercised by or *under authority of*, and the business and affairs of a corporation shall be managed *under the direction of*, a board of directors . . ." (MBCA § 35).

The actual role of boards of directors in publicly held corporations is probably less than even the Model Act contemplates.

One empirical study concludes that boards in fact perform the following roles:

(1) They provide advice and counsel.

(2) They provide intellectual discipline for management which must appear before the board and present views and defend recommendations.

(3) They act in crisis situations, such as where the CEO unexpectedly dies or is incapacitated, or where the affairs of the corporation are in such bad financial shape that a change of CEOs seems desirable.

The same study concludes that by and large boards do *not* perform the following functions:

(1) They do not establish objectives, strategies and policies of the corporation.

(2) They do not ask discerning or "tough" questions at meetings of the board.

(3) They do not select the CEO except indirectly as a form of "corporate conscience."

(4) They do not decide what the corporation or the board of directors does.

Until relatively recently, the boards of many public corporations consisted primarily or exclusively of "inside" directors. The present trend appears to be in the direction of increasing the number and influence of "outside" directors. This group, however, may include former members of management, attorneys, investment bankers, and other suppliers of goods or services to the corporation. The trend toward more outside directors is in part the result of widespread disclosures of corporate misconduct during the 1970s, and in part a result of pressure on corporations by the Securities and Exchange Commission and the securities exchanges to "broaden" their boards. Whether or not this development has changed the locus of power within publicly held corporations is open to question.

Along with the broadening of boards by including more "outside" directors a trend has developed toward wider use of committees of boards consisting primarily of outside directors. Audit committees are now widely used; many corporations have also formed nominating and compensation committees in an effort to provide greater review of issues in these areas by the non-management members of the board. (See § 10.10.)

§ 13.5 Proxy Regulation In Publicly Held Corporations

Most modern law of proxy regulation is of federal rather than state origin. Section 14(a) of the Securities Exchange Act of 1934 makes it unlawful for any person to use the mails or any means or instrumentality of interstate commerce or the facilities of a national securities exchange "in contravention of such rules and regulations as the [Securities and Exchange] Commission may prescribe as necessary or appropriate in the public interest or for the protection of investors" to solicit any proxy in respect of any security registered pursuant to section 12 of the Act. Pursuant to this rather boundless grant of authority to regulate proxies, the SEC has issued comprehensive and detailed regulations.

Corporations subject to federal proxy regulation are those required to register under section 12 of the Securities Exchange Act: all corporations a) registered on a national securities exchange or b) having assets in excess of $1,000,000 and a class of equity security held of record by 500 persons or more. It should be noted that it is not the total number of security holders that is significant, but the number of holders of a *class* of security. A corporation with 400 shareholders of record holding common stock, and another 400 shareholders of record holding preferred stock is not required to register under section 12, and therefore is not subject to proxy regulation (unless, of course, its shares are registered on a national securities exchange). However, once a corporation is required to register under section 12, it remains subject to that section even though the number of shareholders drops below 500; registration under section 12 may be terminated only if the corporation has no class held of record by more than 300 persons.

The constitutional basis for federal proxy regulation is the use of the mails or an instrumentality of interstate commerce. As a practical matter, it is probably impossible to solicit proxies in connection with a security registered under section 12 on a broad scale without using the mails or facilities of interstate commerce.

The SEC proxy rules may be broken down into four broad categories:

(1) Requirements of disclosure of full information to shareholders relating to (a) proposals for action by shareholders presented by management through the proxy solicitation machinery, and (b) to a lesser extent, general information about the operations of the corporation.

(2) Prohibitions against the use of fraud or deceptive non-disclosure in the solicitation of proxies.

(3) Requirements that appropriate proposals submitted by shareholders be included in the proxy solicitation materials prepared by management, so that shareholders have an opportunity to consider them.

(4) Special requirements where there is a proxy fight.

In addition, the SEC has adopted regulations relating to cash tender offers and public exchange offers. These new devices are subject to regulation by the SEC under the Williams Act; they are related to proxy fights in the sense that they are alternative methods of ousting incumbent management and for purposes of convenience are discussed in that context.

§ 13.6 Disclosure Requirements in Connection With Proxy Solicitations

The SEC proxy regulations (rule 14a–3) provide that with certain exceptions no solicitation of a proxy may be made unless each person is furnished at the same time a proxy statement setting forth detailed information about the persons making the solicitation, about the background of all directors and nominees, about remuneration and other transactions with management and with others, and about any matter on which the vote of shareholders is sought. Excepted solicitations include those involving less than ten persons, solicitations by brokers to beneficial owners to determine how to vote shares held in the name of the broker, and newspaper advertisements which merely describe how holders may obtain copies of the proxy statement. Proxy statements under rule 14a–3 are one of the major sources of shareholder information about corporate affairs.

The SEC conducts a presolicitation review process for proxy documents. Such documents and other soliciting materials (such as letters, press releases, and the like), must be filed with the SEC at least ten days prior to the date it is proposed to mail definitive copies to all securities holders. Because the period for evaluation is short, as a practical matter the SEC review is based on an analysis of the filing and whatever else is in the Commission's files relating to the filing company. The SEC does not pass upon the accuracy of adequacy of the disclosures; however, it does indicate that revisions should be made if it concludes that some materials are inaccurate on the basis of information in its files. Most courts have recognized that this preliminary SEC review of proxy solicitation material should not be given great weight in subsequently evaluating the sufficiency of the disclosures.

The SEC disclosure requirements also indirectly require the distribution of annual reports. Rule 14a–3(b) provides that if a solicitation is made on behalf of management relating to an annual meeting of shareholders at which directors are to be elected, the proxy statement must be accompanied or preceded by an annual report of the corporation. This is the only basis in most states to require the distribution of an annual report,

perhaps the most helpful informational document for shareholders generally.

All of these disclosure requirements are posited on the assumption that the corporate management will find it necessary to solicit proxies. In most cases this will be necessary if there is to be a quorum at the meeting. (As a practical matter, the number of shares voted by shareholders who appear personally is likely to be numerically insignificant.) In some corporations subject to registration under section 12, however, management may own enough shares to constitute a quorum without any solicitation of public shareholders. However, a special section of the Securities Exchange Act of 1934 requires even such corporations to supply shareholders with the same information that would have been required if a proxy solicitation to its shareholders had been made. This section thus graphically illustrates that a major purpose of SEC proxy regulation is to ensure that significant information is made available to shareholders, whether or not they are requested to approve or disapprove some matter.

Section 13.3 discussed the practice of holding shares in street names or the names of nominees. This practice creates a problem for the SEC proxy disclosure process since the beneficial owners of such shares do not directly receive the proxy statements or annual reports (they are not the record owners). SEC regulations assume that brokers and dealers transmit proxy material to the beneficial owners of shares, and execute proxy forms in blank, and deliver them to the beneficial owners so that the shares may be voted by them, or directly vote the shares as the beneficial owners direct. Stock exchange rules require brokers and dealers to transmit such information if the solicitor of proxies reimburses the expenses of the broker or dealer; in addition, regulations under the Securities Exchange Act require issuers to provide nominee registered owners with sufficient copies of the proxy material so that they can be

transmitted to the beneficial owners. A 1976 study by the SEC concluded that this indirect method of distribution of proxy information worked surprisingly effectively.

SEC regulations also prescribe the form of proxy document itself and prohibit certain devices such as undated or post-dated proxies or broad grants of discretionary power to proxy holders. Shareholders must be given the option to vote for or against candidates for directors, and proxy holders must actually vote the shares as shareholders direct for the election of directors and on other issues presented for decision to the shareholders.

§ 13.7 Shareholder Proposals

Rule 14a–8 establishes a procedure by which a shareholder may submit proposals for inclusion in the management's proxy solicitation material. If the proposal is an appropriate one for shareholder action, and is timely, management must include the proposal even if opposed to it. If management does oppose a proposal (and management usually does), the shareholder may include a statement of not more than 200 words in support of his proposal. A shareholder may submit a maximum of two proposals in any proxy solicitation not exceeding an aggregate of 300 words. Management may explain the basis of its opposition without limitation.

Because shareholders may seek action on proposals of dubious relevance or propriety, or simply for personal publicity, the SEC has imposed specific requirements and limitations on shareholder's proposals. The application of these requirements and limitations has resulted in some litigation, and a substantial body of administrative rulings by the SEC. The SEC has also issued policy statements from time to time with respect to issues raised by shareholder proposals; for example, in 1978 the SEC announced that in the future it would recommend that important business-related proposals with policy implications such as whether a utility should develop nuclear power plants, should be included in proxy solicitations.

Under present SEC regulations, a shareholder's proposal may be omitted if:

(1) it is not a proper subject for action by security holders under the law of the issuer's domicile;

(2) it would require the issuer to violate any state, federal or foreign law, if implemented;

(3) it is contrary to any of the SEC's proxy regulations;

(4) it relates to the enforcement of a personal claim or the redress of a personal grievance, against the issuer, its management, or any person;

(5) it deals with a matter that is not significantly related to the issuer's business;

(6) it deals with a matter that is beyond the issuer's power to effectuate;

(7) it deals with a matter relating to the ordinary business operations of the issuer;

(8) it relates to an election to office;

(9) it relates to specific amounts of dividends;

(10) it is moot;

(11) it is either counter to a proposal by management or substantially the same as a proposal by another shareholder which will be included in the proxy materials; or

(12) substantially the same proposal has previously been submitted to the shareholders within the previous five years and failed to receive specified percentages of the vote, depending on the number of times it was submitted previously.

In considering the foregoing list of exclusions, it is important to recognize that over the years the SEC has issued numerous rulings applying many of these exclusions; as a result, phrases such as "proper subject" or "ordinary business operations" have been given considerable practical content, and the tests are not as open-ended as the language might indicate. For example, the SEC has ruled that important business related proposals are "proper subjects" for shareholder action under state law if they are phrased as recommendations to the board rather than specific directions. See the discussion of state law on this subject in § 8.6.

Most proposals of shareholders which appear in the proxy solicitation material are rejected by substantial votes if they are opposed by management. However, it is widely believed that even defeated proposals have an indirect educational effect. Certainly some shareholder proposals decisively rejected at the polls have been subsequently accepted and implemented by management.

§ 13.8   Private Actions for Violations of Federal Proxy Rules

Rule 14a–9 makes it unlawful to solicit proxies by communications which contain "any statement which, at the time and in the light of the circumstances under which it is made, is false or misleading with respect to any material fact, or which omits to state any material fact necessary in order to make the statements therein not false or misleading." For many years it was uncertain whether this broad prohibition created a private cause of action by shareholders, or whether it was enforceable only by the Securities and Exchange Commission. This question was definitively answered in J. I. Case Co. v. Borak, 377 U.S. 426 (1964). The Court held that rule 14a–9 created a private cause of action since, "private enforcement of the proxy rules provides a necessary supplement to Commission action. As in antitrust treble damage litigation, the possibility of civil damages or injunctive relief serves as a most effective weapon in the enforcement of the proxy requirements."

Since *Borak* there has been a substantial volume of private litigation under rule 14a–9. Such litigation is within the exclusive jurisdiction of the Federal courts so that state "security for expenses" statutes are inapplicable (see § 17.4). Rule 14a–9 litigation has largely been shaped by two subsequent decisions by the United States Supreme Court. In TSC Industries, Inc. v. Northway, Inc., 426 U.S. 438 (1976), in an opinion widely read as heralding a narrowing of the scope of the private cause of action under rule 14a–9, the Court defined a "material fact" as follows:

> "An omitted fact is material if there is a substantial likelihood that a reasonable shareholder *would* consider it important *in deciding how to vote*."

The competing test that was rejected would have defined material facts to include all facts "which a reasonable shareholder *might* consider appropriate." While the difference between the rejected and adopted tests may seem primarily semantic, the Court's distinction appears to constitute a warning to lower courts to limit rule 14a–9 to substantial misstatements; prior to this decision some courts had tended to find relatively minor misstatements or omissions to be "material" and therefore violations of rule 14a–9.

The other important case, Mills v. Electric Auto-Lite Co., 396 U.S. 375 (1970), involves the question of the required nexus between a material misstatement or omission and the approval of the proposal. It also discusses at some length the remedies available for a violation of rule 14a–9 after the transaction in question has been consummated, and the right of the plaintiff's attorney to recover attorneys' fees in rule 14a–9 cases.

In an appropriate 14a–9 case, the Court may, of course, issue a temporary restraining order (TRO), enjoining the distribution of proxy material, the voting of the proxies themselves, and the holding of the meeting, until after all misstatements or deficiencies in the proxy solicitation material under rule 14a–9 have been corrected. However, in many cases the plaintiff does not seek a TRO presumably because he is unable or unwilling to post the bond that may be required. In such a case, the meeting may be held, the proxies voted, and the transaction consummated, all before there is a judicial determination of whether the proxy solicitation material violates rule 14a–9. That is essentially what happened in *Mills*. Merganthaler Linotype Corporation owned about 54 per cent of the outstanding Auto-Lite shares, and therefore named all the directors of Auto-Lite. Merganthaler decided to merge with Auto-Lite, but in order to do so it needed the favorable vote of a substantial number of minority shareholders of Auto-Lite. The Auto-Lite management solicited proxies on the basis of a proxy statement that stated the Auto-Lite directors favored the proposed merger but did not disclose that these directors were all nominees of Mergenthaler. The merger proposed was approved and the merger consummated. Minority shareholders thereafter brought suit, claiming that the failure to disclose the relationship of the Auto-Lite directors to Mergenthaler constituted a material omission in violation of rule 14a–9. The lower courts agreed, but concluded that there was no showing that this violation of rule 14a–9 actually affected the outcome of the vote, and that since the terms of the merger were fair, no relief should be granted. The Supreme Court reversed without passing on the materiality of the omission. (This, it should be noted in passing, is the issue addressed in TSC Industries). It held that it was unnecessary to show a direct causal relationship between the violation and the vote; it was only necessary to show that the proxy solicitation was itself an essential step in the transaction under attack. The reason for this "rule of thumb" is that it is obviously impossible to inquire into the motivations of thousands of shareholders who voted to approve the merger. However, it does not necessarily follow that the merger should automatically be set aside. The remedy for a violation is in the discretion of the court, and unwinding the merger should be required only if "it would be in the best interests of the shareholders as a whole." If the merger is not to be set aside, a second possible type of relief may be money damages. The Court, however, made it clear that damages should be permitted only to the extent they can be proved, and as a practical matter, that may be impossible. If such proof is unavailable, and the merger should not be set aside, apparently the plaintiff/shareholder is left without remedy. However, in order to ensure that there will continue to be vigorous private enforcement of rule 14a–9 the Court then concluded that a court may award attorneys' fees when a proxy violation is found even though no monetary recovery is allowed. The possibility of champertous litigation, in the Court's eyes, was more than offset by the "therapeutic" effect vigorous enforcement of the proxy regulations has on fair and informed corporate suffrage. However, later decisions by the U.S. Supreme Court on the right to attorneys' fees have limited this aspect of the *Mills* holding. It is ironic that the Supreme Court remanded the *Mills* litigation for further proceedings and that the lower courts ultimately concluded that the omission was not "material" (an issue not passed upon by the Supreme Court in 1970) so that not only was no relief granted but also the attorneys were not eligible for fees for services after their initial victory in 1970 before the Supreme Court.

§ 13.9 Proxy Contests

A proxy contest is a struggle for control of a public corporation in which most of the high cards are held by management. In a proxy contest, a non-management group (usually referred to as "insurgents") compete with management in an effort to obtain sufficient proxies to elect a majority of the board of directors and thereby obtain control. Management has several advantages in a proxy fight: (1) it has the current list of shareholders, while the insurgents may have to go to court to get it; (2) within a broad range, management may finance its solicitation from the assets of the corporation, while the insurgents must finance their campaign from outside sources; and (3) for the reasons discussed earlier, shareholders tend to have a pro-management bias. (See §§ 13.1, 13.2.) However, despite these disadvantages, proxy fights do occur with some regularity, and insurgents are sometimes successful in ousting entrenched management.

An insurgent group, desiring to contest management control, usually first purchases a substantial block of shares in the open market before openly announcing its intentions. It must then obtain a list of the shareholders in order to conduct what is essentially a political campaign to persuade shareholders to cast proxies in their favor. A court proceeding may be necessary to obtain the list. Specialized proxy contest firms are available to assist both management and insurgents in the campaign. Large shareholders may be courted individually; with the modern growth of institutional investors, the support of this segment of the financial community may be essential if a bid for control is to have a chance of succeeding. The process can be expensive, running into the hundreds of thousands or millions of dollars.

In addition to seeking a list of shareholders by court proceeding under state law, an insurgent faction contemplating a proxy fight has limited rights under rule 14a–9, which requires management to provide minimal assistance to insurgent factions. Each issuer must supply the following information on demand to any shareholder:

(1) A statement of the approximate number of holders of record of the corporation's shares, or of the holders to be solicited by management;

(2) If management proposes to solicit beneficial holders of shares held in the name of bankers, brokers, or other persons, a statement of the approximate number of such beneficial owners; and

(3) An estimate of the cost of mailing a specified proxy statement, form, or other communication to shareholders and beneficial owners.

If the shareholder supplies copies of a proxy statement, form of proxy or other communication, plus the cost of postage and other expenses, the corporation must mail out the statement no later than it mails the management's proxy solicitation. Alternatively, the corporation may provide the shareholder with a reasonably current list of names and addresses by which the shareholder can substantially duplicate the mailing by management. This provision may be relied upon in connection with a proxy fight, though as a practical matter, the rule is not self-enforcing, and in any event management may elect to mail out the insurgents' literature rather than providing the all-important list of shareholders.

Proxy fights are not feasible in the very large corporation with hundreds of thousands or millions of shareholders, since the cost of solicitation is prohibitive. Further, if the corporation's business is profitable, a proxy fight is unlikely to be successful. The most likely candidate for a proxy fight is a small or medium-sized company with a poor earnings record and elderly management that has not paid attention to shareholders relations.

Proxy fights for public corporations subject to section 12 of the Securities Exchange Act of 1934 are subject to regulation by the Securities and Exchange Commission. Since this covers most proxy fights, state law on the subject tends to be rudimentary and there are very few reported state cases dealing with proxy fights.

One significant legal issue relating to proxy fights is the extent to which the corporation may be called upon to pay for its costs. From management's standpoint there appears to be no doubt that the corporation should pay for printing and mailing the notice of meeting, the proxy statement required by Federal law, and the proxies themselves. These are legitimate expenses because without the solicitation of proxies it is unlikely that a quorum of shareholders may be obtained. Most courts have gone further and allowed the corporation to be charged for the reasonable expenses of management of educating shareholders if the controversy involves a "policy" question rather than a mere "personal" struggle for control. Since virtually every proxy fight may be dressed up as a "policy" rather than "personal" dispute, and since what is involved is "education" of the management's side of the controversy, the net effect is to permit the deduction of all reasonable management expenses. While some judges have suggested that a narrower test should be applicable to management expenses, these suggestions have not prevailed.

A somewhat different question is presented if the insurgents are successful and seek to have the corporation also reimburse them for their expenses. If permitted, the net effect is usually to have the corporation pay the expenses of both sides, since management will usually reimburse itself for its expenses from the corporation before leaving office. The additional reimbursement of successful insurgents has been permitted if (a) approved by the shareholders and (b) the dispute involved "policy" rather than "personalities," and as a result the corporation ends up paying for the expenses of both sides. Again, there is a strong undercurrent of judicial opinion which would sharply limit or totally preclude insurgents' reimbursement, but this view has not prevailed.

Law review writers have sometimes suggested that reimbursement should be permitted for *un*successful insurgents since they may perform a socially useful function. Most economists and legal writers view proxy fights as basically desirable phenomena that help to rid corporations of inefficient or ineffective management. Not surprisingly, however, there appears to be no instance where management has voluntarily paid unsuccessful insurgents, and any such proposal would have to be carefully structured to avoid possible abuse such as encouraging groundless proxy fights.

§ 13.10 Federal Regulations Relating to Proxy Contests

The Securities and Exchange Commission has promulgated special regulations applicable to proxy contests. These regulations require "participants" other than management in a proxy contest to file specified information with the SEC and the securities exchanges at least five days before a solicitation begins. "Participant" is defined to include anyone who contributes more than $500 for the purpose of financing the contest. The information that must be disclosed relates to the identity and background of the participants, their interests in securities of the corporation, when they were acquired, financing arrangements, participation in other proxy contests, and understandings with respect to future employment with the corporation.

The general philosophy of the proxy contest regulations is well expressed by Judge Clark, of the Second Circuit: "Appellants' fundamental complaint appears to be that stockholder disputes should be viewed in the eyes of the law just as are political contests, with each side free to hurl charges with comparative unrestraint, the assumption being that the opposing side is then at liberty to refute and thus effectively deflate the 'campaign oratory' of its adversary. Such, however, was not the policy of Congress as enacted in the Securities Exchange Act." SEC v. May, 229 F.2d 123, 124 (2d Cir. 1956).

§ 13.11   Tender Offers as a Substitute for a Proxy Contest

A *cash tender offer* is a public invitation to the shareholders of the "target" corporation to tender their shares to the "aggressor" corporation for purchase at a specified price, usually 15–20 per cent in excess of the then current market price. A *public exchange offer* involves the offering of a "package" of the aggressor's securities (which may include some cash) for the outstanding securities of the target corporation. In the late 1960s, there were numerous cash tender and public exchange offers that were largely based on the element of surprise, virtually blitzkrieg tactics. Since then developments in various areas have greatly modified the manner in which takeover bids are now pursued. These developments include—

(1) Adoption of the Williams Act, an amendment to the Securities Exchange Act of 1934, which is briefly described below.

(2) Adoption by many states of takeover statutes designed to regulate (and, some may argue, make more difficult) unwanted takeover attempts of businesses active in the state in question.

(3) The increasing sophistication of defensive tactics by potential targets.

During the 1970s the trend has been away from the surprise onslaught on an unexpecting target. Rather takeover attempts may involve the taking of an "investment position" in the target's securities, followed by a direct invitation to the target's management for a merger or amalgamation. This process is described as a "bearhug" in the slang of Wall Street. Only in rare cases today is a cash tender or exchange offer vigorously pursued in the face of implacable or strong opposition by the target.

The principal advantage of a tender offer as compared to a proxy fight is that the probability of success in a tender offer appears to be greater. In a cash tender offer, the individual shareholder's decision tends to be an investment-type of decision rather than a choice between competing factions for control. He may think in terms of "I paid X for this stock I am now offered Y. Should I sell?" On the other hand in a proxy contest, the shareholder's choice is pretty clearly a choice between competing factions for the right to run the corporation in which the shareholder will have a continuing interest.

When a cash tender offer is made, the open market price for the shares increases dramatically close to the tender price. (Whether it equals or exceeds the tender offer price depends on a complex variety of factors, including the probability that a competing offer at a higher price might be made, whether the offer is likely to be over-subscribed, and so forth.) Persons owning shares thus have the choice of selling their shares in the open market at a discount or tendering their shares. Most shares sold on the open market are ultimately tendered. A group of speculators, known as *arbitragers*, purchase shares in the open market at prices below the tender offer price in order to tender them and profit by the difference between the two prices. In some tender offers, the volume of transactions effected by arbitragers have been very substantial. Arbitragers may also be active in connection with public exchange offers, buying the target corporation's shares and at the same time selling "short" or on a "when issued" basis the "package" to be received on the tender.

Both cash tender offers and public exchange offers are subject to regulation by the Securities and Exchange Commission. A public exchange offer involves a public offering of securities by the aggressor corporation and is subject to registration under the Securities Act of 1933 in the same way as any other public offer. In 1968, the Williams Act amended the Securities Exchange Act of 1934 to provide for mandatory disclosure of information in connection with cash tender offers. The details of this legislation are complex and the following is only a brief summary. Any person who makes a cash tender offer for a corporation registered under section 12 must disclose information as to the source of funds used in the offer, the purpose for which the offer is made, plans the aggressor may have if successful, and contracts or understandings with respect to the target corporation. Filing and public disclosure is also required of anyone who acquires more than 5 per cent of the outstanding shares of any class of a section 12 corporation. Similar requirements are also imposed upon (1) issuers making an offer for their own shares, or (2) issuers in which a change of control is proposed to be made by seriatim resignations of directors. The cash tender offer legislation also imposes miscellaneous substantive restrictions on the mechanics of a cash tender offer, and imposes a broad prohibition against the use of false, misleading or incomplete statements in connection with such an offer.   In Piper v. Chris-Craft Industries, Inc., 430 U.S. 1 (1977), the Court held that a defeated tender offeror did not have standing to sue for damages under this provision of the Williams Act.

One of the outstanding issues awaiting resolution as this is written is whether the numerous state takeover statutes have been preempted by the Williams Act and the regulations issued thereunder.   The Fifth Circuit held that such statutes were preempted in Great Western United Corp. v. Kidwell, 577 F.2d 1256 (5th Cir. 1978) but the Supreme Court reversed without reaching this issue.   Leroy v. Great Western United Corp., 443 U.S. 173 (1979).   The SEC has adopted regulations apparently designed to create direct conflicts between federal and state law on takeover attempts; a definitive judicial determination of the validity of these regulations is also expected in the future.

[For unfamiliar terms see the Glossary]

CHAPTER FOURTEEN

FIDUCIARY DUTIES OF DIRECTORS AND OFFICERS

§ 14.1 Fiduciary Duties In General

Because of their broad powers of management, directors occupy a unique position within the corporate structure, and they are usually said to owe a high degree of fidelity and loyalty to the corporation. Directors are sometimes referred to as "fiduciaries," and their duties are analogized to those of a trustee of a trust. However, directors of corporations are not strictly trustees, and their duties and liabilities are not necessarily identical with those of other fiduciaries. Acts which might be considered breaches of trust by other fiduciaries have not always been so regarded in cases of corporate directors. The relationship between director and corporation, in short, is a unique one.

The relationship between other corporate officers and agents and the corporation depends to some extent on the position occupied by the officer or agent and the type of liabilities that are being imposed. A managing officer may owe substantially the same duties to the corporation as a director. Officers or agents in subordinate or limited positions may owe a correspondingly lesser degree of duty, though even the lowest agent owes the principal certain minimum duties of care, skill, propriety in conduct, and loyalty in all matters connected with his agency (see § 11.6).

In most instances, directors owe duties to the corporation as a whole rather than to individual shareholders or to individual classes of shareholders. However, if a director deals with a shareholder directly, or if he acts in a way which injures a shareholder, he may become directly liable to that shareholder.

Since shareholders as such have no power to manage the business and affairs of the corporation, it is not surprising that the relationship of a shareholder to the corporation differs from the relationship of a director or officer to the corporation. It is often said that a shareholder as such owes no fiduciary duty to his corporation. Such statements, however, are too broad. Shareholders may owe a duty to their corporation or their fellow shareholders in some circumstances. Controlling shareholders, for example, owe duties to creditors, holders of senior securities and minority shareholders when they transfer control of the corporation to a third party. And, even minority shareholders do not have an open license to abuse or sell their voting power, or exercise it fraudulently.

§ 14.2 Sources of Law—Common Law, State and Federal Statutes, "Federal Common Law"

The basic relationship between a corporation and its directors, officers and agents traditionally has been established by common law decision rather than statute. Many of the duties hereafter discussed are common law in origin: (1) a duty of exercising due care in administering the corporation's business; (2) a duty of loyalty to the corporation; and (3) as a subdivision of the general duty of loyalty, a prohibition against usurping business opportunities belonging to the corporation. These common law duties have given rise to a great deal of litigation; they define fundamental obligations in a complex relationship. State corporation acts supplement the common law duties by imposing liability on directors for certain specific acts. Directoral liability to the corporation is the principal method by which certain statutory prohibitions are enforced.

Federal law is also an important source of legal principles relating to duties and obligations within a corporation. The Federal securities acts are the genesis of this development with much of it based on rule 10b–5 promulgated by the Securities and Exchange Commission under the Securities Exchange Act of 1934. The phrase "Federal Corporation Law" was often used to describe this development, particularly during its meteoric rise during the 1960s and early 1970s. Indeed, at one time it appeared that much of the law of fiduciary duties would become federalized. However, as a result of a series of limiting United States Supreme Court decisions during the 1970s, this trend has been abruptly halted. The ultimate scope of the federal law of corporations cannot now be determined; however, it seems probable that both federal and state law will continue to have their place in the area of fiduciary duties.

§ 14.3   Duty of Care

A director may be liable to the corporation for losses incurred as a result of his failure to exercise proper care in managing the corporation's affairs. The test that is usually quoted is that duties must be discharged "in good faith in a manner he reasonably believes to be in the best interests of the corporation, and with such care as an ordinarily prudent person would use under similar circumstances. (MBCA § 35, 2d ¶.) Another test that is often quoted is that degree of diligence, care and skill "which ordinarily prudent men would exercise under similar circumstances in their personal business affairs." [This language is taken from a leading Pennsylvania case, Selheimer v. Manganese Corp. of America, 224 A.2d 634 (Pa.1966).] There probably is little practical difference in these two formulations; general language of this sort rarely helps to resolve concrete cases.

Courts feel that they should not second-guess corporate managers with the benefit of hindsight, and, whatever the language employed, liability is apt to be found in only the most extreme situations. Most cases in which liability has been found involve some element of self-dealing as well as negligence or misjudgment. The test must depend to some extent on the circumstances: the character of the corporation, the condition of the corporation's business, the usual methods by which such corporation's affairs are managed, and any other relevant facts that throw light upon what is the proper discharge of the duty of directors under the circumstances. There is language in a number of early cases, for example, that directors of banks owe a particularly strong duty of care and prudence to the public.

The strongest kind of case is where the director knowingly participates in a wrongful act. Thus, personal liability has been imposed on directors where they authorize the improper use of corporate funds, knowing that the use is not in furtherance of corporate affairs, or where they assent to the corporation's use of a financial statement to obtain credit when they know that it is false or fraudulent. Directors have also been held liable for a tortious act of the corporation if they personally participated in the act. On the other hand, in recent years all attempts to hold directors or officers personally liable for antitrust fines imposed on the corporation or for bribes or improper payments made by the corporation have been unsuccessful, despite evidence in some cases of the directors' or officers' personal involvement in the conduct or payments in question. Of course, the amounts in such situations are usually extemely large when compared to the wealth of even well-to-do individuals. Directors also are not automatically liable if they approve an act that turns out to be ultra vires. In some cases actual knowledge of the wrongful act is lacking but the claim is that the directors should have known of it. It is difficult to find any cases outside of the bank director area where such liability has actually been imposed.

Honest business decisions made in good faith are usually not actionable, even though experience shows that the decision was mistaken or unfortunate. This is usually referred to as "the business judgment rule." However, due care also involves some minimal notion of prudence, particularly where the corporation is a bank or other financial institution. In one leading New York case, Litwin v. Allen, 25 N.Y.S.2d

667 (Sup.Ct.1940), liability was imposed on directors as a result of a complex option arrangement "because the entire arrangement was so improvident, so risky, so unusual and so unnecessary as to be contrary to fundamental conceptions of prudent banking practice." Again, there may be some element of self dealing in many of the cases in which liability is found.

Sometimes the claim is made that a director should be liable for mismanagement because he totally failed to direct. The director may be aged, ill, resident of a distant state, or merely lazy or unduly trusting. He may feel that he was elected only as a figurehead and was not intended to have any significant function—certainly an erroneous notion. As an abstract matter, when a person agrees to be a director he accepts certain responsibilities and obligations, and if these are too burdensome, the proper course is to resign rather than fail to meet them. Again, however, only a few cases impose liability on a director for total failure to direct. Barnes v. Andrews, 298 F. 614 (S.D.N.Y.1924) is a leading case which holds that a director who was negligent in failing to direct can be held liable only if the plaintiff shows a causal relationship between this failure and some specific loss. If this is correct, the burden of proof is certainly difficult if not insuperable. Also often helpful to defendants in "failure to manage" cases is the principle that directors, in the absence of other information, may assume that managers and officers are honest. The Model Act (§ 35), and the statutes of several states, including Delaware, further qualify the duty of due care by exempting directors who rely in good faith on information, opinions, reports or statements prepared by responsible corporate officials, counsel, or committees of the board. However, a director is not considered to be acting in good faith "if he has knowledge concerning the matter in question that would cause such reliance to be unwarranted."

Finally, courts have sometimes buttressed their conclusion that directoral liability does not exist in due care cases by arguing that too stringent a test would discourage able and competent persons from assuming the position of director.

§ 14.4 Duty of Loyalty: Self Dealing

The duty of loyalty, unlike the duty of care, has produced a steady stream of litigation in which directors and officers have often been held liable. These cases may be divided into three general types: (1) cases involving transactions between a director and his corporation; (2) cases involving transactions between corporations with common directors; and (3) cases involving a director taking advantage of an opportunity which arguably may belong to the corporation.

The danger of self-dealing transactions between a corporation and a director is the risk that the corporation may be treated unfairly in such a transaction. When such a transaction is questioned, the burden is on the director to prove the propriety of the transaction rather than on the person questioning the transaction. The form the transaction takes is not significant. The courts apply essentially the same test to transactions involving the sale of corporate property to a director, the sale of property to a director's spouse, the sale of property by a director to a corporation, a contract between the corporation and a director for the director to perform services such as selling stock or managing the business, or a loan by a director to his corporation.

The early common law took the position that all self-dealing transactions were automatically voidable at the election of the corporation. It was eventually recognized, however, that a black-and-white rule of this type did not fit business needs. Even though self-dealing transactions may be suspect, many of them in fact are entirely fair and reasonable; indeed, in many situations directors may give their corporations terms that are more favorable than the corporation might obtain elsewhere. For example, loans by directors to the corporation are often made when the corporation could not borrow elsewhere; such transactions should obviously be encouraged.

While many transactions between directors and their corporation have been held to be valid, considerable confusion exists in the case law as to the circumstances which validate such transactions. If one examines the results of the cases (as contrasted with statements in the opinions), the following comments accurately reflect most decisions:

(1) If the court feels the transaction to be fair to the corporation, it will be upheld;

(2) If the court feels that the transaction involves fraud, undue overreaching or waste of corporate assets (*e. g.*, a director using corporate assets for personal purposes without paying for them), the transaction will be set aside; and

(3) If the court feels that the transaction does not involve fraud, overreaching or waste of corporate assets, but is not convinced that the transaction is fair, the transaction will be upheld only where the interested director can convincingly show that the transaction was approved (or ratified) by a disinterested majority of the board of directors without participation by the interested director, or by a majority of the shareholders after full disclosure of all relevant facts.

The opinions themselves do not establish a single, neat set of principles from which the foregoing results may be obtained. For example, courts have struggled with the question whether a fair transaction may be avoided if it is not ratified either by disinterested directors or by the shareholders. For example, all the directors may be interested in a fair transaction, and shareholder ratification is not sought. Many cases either state or intimate such a transaction is voidable since it has not been properly approved; other opinions, however, emphasize the fairness of the transaction and have not insisted on formal approval or ratification. The same essential conflict is also represented in section 41 of the Model Business Corporation Act, which purports to validate all fair transactions and other transactions which have received formal approval of disinterested directors or shareholders. Such a provision seems obviously overbroad to the extent it allows ratification of fraudulent or overreaching transactions.

Two recurring issues relating to ratification are who may be considered disinterested for purposes of ratification, and what degree of specific knowledge or notice is required to constitute an effective ratification. There is a tendency in the cases to relax these requirements in situations where the transaction appears to be fair and to stiffen them when the transaction seems questionable. Most courts have permitted interested directors to vote their shares, as shareholders, in favor of upholding the transaction in which they are interested. This does not leave the minority at the complete mercy of a self-dealing majority because transactions involving fraud, undue overreaching or waste of corporate assets cannot be ratified by a simple majority vote.

Suit for rescission is the proper remedy to avoid a voidable transaction. In such a suit, the corporation must be prepared to return any consideration received by it in the transaction. It may not simultaneously retain the consideration and attack the validity of the transaction.

§ 14.5   Interlocking Directors

Transactions between corporations with common directors may lend themselves to the same evil as self-dealing transactions between a director and his corporation, since the interest of a common director may be small in one corporation and large in the other. The standard for setting aside transactions between corporations with common directors is simply one of manifest unfairness to one corporation. The role of the common director in approving the transaction also is inquired into. If the corporation on the losing side of the transaction relied on the views of the common director without a full evaluation of the risks, or without disclosure that the director was interested in the other corporation, the chances that the transaction will be set aside are greatly improved. The stated test, however, is an objective one of fairness, not a procedural test based on the degree of the common director's participation.

§ 14.6 Executive Compensation

Directors of a corporation often serve as corporate officers or agents, and may be compensated for their services. The establishment of the amount of compensation payable to a director involves a specific application of the principles relating to self-dealing. Obviously, if all the directors are also officers, the problem is compounded because of the mutual back-scratching element.

Much modern law relating to executive compensation is directly or indirectly related to the Federal income tax. The issues differ in publicly owned corporations and in closely held corporations.

(1) In a closely held corporation, all the shareholders may be employees of the corporation; if so, the salaries paid to them are likely to be set so as to minimize the aggregate tax liabilities imposed on the corporation and the shareholders. A salary payment may be deductible by the corporation while payment of the same sum in the form of a dividend may not. If some shareholders are not employees, however, they will be adversely affected by the payment of substantial salaries to other shareholders and obviously would much prefer that the same sum be distributed pro rata in the form of a dividend, even though the tax obligations of the corporation are higher. In a closely held corporation, the Internal Revenue Service often reviews the reasonableness of corporate salaries and may disallow deductions for unreasonably large salaries. The total amount paid is still taxable to the shareholder-recipient either as

a dividend or as compensation; the issue is the deductability at the corporate level. If a payment is treated as a dividend for tax purposes, there is no requirement that it be distributed pro rata to all shareholders, though the disallowance of a salary deduction may suggest to a minority shareholder that the payment may also have been improper under general corporate fiduciary principles as well.

(2) In publicly held corporations, executive compensation is not considered to be a manner of distributing earnings. The executive is receiving "other people's money", and the effect of his compensation on the earnings per share of the stock he owns is minimal. However, compensation in public corporations may be very substantial and the major question is under what circumstances may a court set aside compensation on the ground that it is excessive and therefore improper.

Courts generally are reluctant to conclude that executive compensation is excessive, particularly if procedures are adopted which minimize the appearance of self-dealing. The rationale of this view is set forth in an often-quoted statement from the leading New York case of Heller v. Boylan, 29 N.Y.S.2d 653 (Sup.Ct.1941):

> "Yes, the Court possesses the power to prune these payments, but openness forces the confession that the pruning would be synthetic and artificial rather than analytic or scientific. . . .

> "If comparisons are to be made, with whose compensation are they to be made—executives? Those connected with the motion picture industry? Radio artists? Justices of the Supreme Court of the United States? The President of the United States? Manifestly, the material at hand is not of adequate plasticity for fashioning into a pattern or standard . . . ..

> "Courts are ill-equipped to solve or even to grapple with these entangled economic problems. Indeed, their solution

is not within the juridical province. Courts are concerned that corporations be honestly and fairly operated by its directors, with the observance of the formal requirements of the law; but what is reasonable compensation for its officers is primarily for the stockholders. This does not mean that fiduciaries are to commit waste or misuse or abuse trust property, with impunity. A just cause will find the Courts at guard and implemented to grant redress . . .."

As suggested by the last paragraph of this quotation, the tests applied by the courts to determine whether compensation is excessive is spoilation or waste. Total compensation must bear some minimal relation to the services rendered. If it does not, the payment constitutes waste of corporate assets. The leading case of Rogers v. Hill, 289 U.S. 582 (1933), involved a compensation plan for executives of the American Tobacco Company based on profits which yielded the President of the Corporation more than $680,000 of extra compensation in 1929 and more than $1,300,000 in 1930. The United States Supreme Court held that these payments were so excessive as to be subject to examination and revision by the courts. In this case, the court expressly recognized that the compensation plan was reasonable and valid in 1912 when it was approved by the shareholders; subsequent developments, however, resulted in payments so large as to raise the question that they constituted waste.

Relief has also been granted in a few instances in which large, specific payments have raised questions of fairness. Thus, a complaint attacking a very generous pension granted to a CEO shortly before his retirement, and funded by a single cash payment of several million dollars, was held to state a cause of action. However, examples of the exercise of this power are rare.

The contrast between the very cautious approach taken on compensation questions in publicly held corporations, and the tax cases dealing with deductibility of compensation in close corporations, is striking. Of course, in the latter there is a legislative command to limit deductions only to "reasonable" amounts; in addition, protection of the national fisc may require a more active review and consideration of the reasonableness of compensation.

§ 14.7 Corporate Opportunity

The corporate opportunity doctrine requires a corporate director to render to Caesar at the best possible price that which is Caesar's. As a fiduciary, a director owes a duty to further the interest of the corporation and to give it the benefit of his uncorrupted business judgment. He may not take a secret profit in connection with corporate transactions, compete unfairly with the corporation, or take personally profitable business opportunities which belong to the corporation.

Very often the application of the doctrine of corporate opportunity to a specific situation ultimately comes down to a judicial evaluation of business ethics. Serious problems of definition and evaluation lie close to the surface: When is an opportunity a corporate opportunity? When may a director take advantage of a corporate opportunity on the ground that the corporation is unwilling or unable to take advantage of it? Under what circumstances may a director enter into a business which competes with the corporation? These questions are considered below.

The basic test established by modern cases as to when an opportunity is a corporate opportunity combines a "line of business" test with the pervasive issue whether it is unfair for the director under the circumstances to take advantage personally of the opportunity. The "line of business" test simply compares the closeness of the opportunity to the types of business in which the corporation is engaged. The closer it is, the more likely it is to be a corporate opportunity. Other courts have adopted narrower tests as to the relation between the opportunity and the corporate business. An earlier test was that the opportunity must involve "property wherein the corporation has interest already existing or in which it has an expectancy growing out of an existing right." Another test that has been adopted by some courts is that the opportunity must in some sense arise out of the corporation's business as it is then conducted. Both tests are somewhat narrower than the "line of business" test, but in the last analysis, the verbal formulation of the test is less important than the court's sensitivity to reasonable business ethics.

In evaluating the fairness of a director's decision to take advantage of an opportunity, weight is given to the following factors among others: (1) whether there were prior negotiations with the corporation about the opportunity, (2) whether the opportunity was offered to the corporation or to the director as an agent of the corporation, (3) whether the director disclosed the opportunity to the corporation or took advantage of it secretly, (4) whether the director learned of the opportunity by reason of his position with the corporation, (5) whether the director used corporate facilities or property to take advantage of the opportunity, (6) whether the director competed with the corporation in selling shares of stock or in the business the corporation is engaged in, (7) whether the director acquired at a discount claims against the corporation when the corporation could have done so, and (8) how substantial was the need of the corporation for the opportunity.

Even if an opportunity is a corporate opportunity, directors are not necessarily precluded from taking advantage of it. The corporation may voluntarily relinquish it, though such a relinquishment will be scrutinized by the courts for fairness and good faith, including full disclosure and free acquiescence in the relinquishment by the disinterested directors. A persuasive policy reason for the relinquishment, *e. g.*, a decision that under the circumstances it would be unwise to expand the corporation's business, helps to make it clear that the corporation voluntarily decided not to pursue the opportunity. Directors may also take advantage of a corporate opportunity if the corporation is incapable of taking advantage of the opportunity, *e. g.*, on the ground the opportunity would be ultra vires, in violation of law, or because the third person refuses to deal with the corporation. Directors have also sought to justify their utilization of a corporate opportunity on the ground that the corporation is financially unable to capitalize on the opportunity. This defense is often a troublesome one, since directors may be tempted to refrain from exercising their strongest efforts on behalf of the corporation if they can thereafter take advantage personally of a profitable opportunity. There is some support for a "rigid rule" prohibiting directors from taking advantage of a corporate opportunity on this ground; in this view, if the directors do not wish to lend the necessary funds to the corporation, they must forego the opportunity. Such a rule seems unnecessarily strict, however, and most courts have permitted directors to utilize corporate opportunities under such circumstances upon a convincing showing that the corporation indeed lacked the independent assets to take advantage of its opportunity.

Directors generally may engage in a similar line of business in competition with the corporation's business where it is done in good faith and without injury to the corporation. A number of cases, however, have found a competing director guilty of a breach of fiduciary duty on several possible theories: conflict of interest, corporate opportunity, misappropriation of trade secrets or customer lists, or wrongful interference with contractual relationships. In this area, tort concepts of unfair competition are close to fiduciary duties. Again, judicial notions of fairness or fair play seem dominant, and a close appraisal of the fiduciary's conduct in light of ethical business practice is necessary.

§ 14.8 Fairness to Minority Shareholders

The preceding sections dealing with various aspects of the director's fiduciary duties to his corporation demonstrate that the law is moving in the direction of applying a test of fairness as the principal criterion for evaluating the propriety of specific transactions. This test is explicitly a criterion in evaluating transactions between corporations with common directors and in determining which opportunities constitute corporate opportunities; it appears to be on the way to becoming the preponderant test in evaluating all self-dealing transactions. The test of fairness adequately serves all interests in the corporation, since well meaning officers and directors should not be discouraged from dealing with the corporation. Reasonable transactions should not be set aside merely because of some formal or technical defect in corporate procedure. On the other hand, the fairness test protects shareholders and creditors alike from overreaching or unwise transactions.

The test of fairness is also applicable to a variety of transactions which defy precise categorization, but which may be lumped loosely under the title "fairness to minority shareholders." For example, in the absence of preemptive rights, a controlling shareholder may not cause the corporation to issue to himself new or treasury shares to cement his control, even at a fair price, since to do so would unfairly dilute the voting power of minority shareholders. Another example is Zahn v. Transamerica Corp., 162 F.2d 36 (3d Cir. 1947). In this case the directors of the Axton-Fisher Tobacco Company knew that the inventory of the corporation had appreciated greatly in value over the value reflected on the books of the corporation. To obtain the greatest portion of this appreciation for itself, the majority shareholder, Transamerica

Corporation, caused the corporation to call a senior security (a convertible participating preferred). The corporation did not disclose the inventory appreciation and, as a result, most of the holders of the senior securities permitted their holdings to be redeemed at $80.00 per share rather than converting them into common worth considerably more. The court held that the transaction violated a duty owed to the minority shareholders: in effect, the directors are required to treat fairly each class of stock and may not take actions which are designed to enhance the value of one class at the expense of another. It is important, however, that this principle be put into context. Directors elected by the common shareholders may declare extra dividends on the common so long as the required provision is made for the senior securities; the directors may call a senior security for redemption in order ultimately to improve the position of the common shareholders. These powers are specifically granted to the directors by the articles and are part of each shareholder's contract with the corporation. The holders of senior securities have no complaint if these powers are exercised ultimately to benefit the common shareholders who have the power to elect the directors. The holders of senior securities, however, may legitimately expect to be given accurate information so that they will not be misled and may make an intelligent selection of the various options available to them. The original opinion in the *Zahn* case contains language which intimates that the mere call for redemption constituted the breach of fiduciary duty, but on a subsequent appeal on the issue of damages, the Third Circuit adopted the theory that the failure to disclose relevant information constituted the breach, Speed v. Transamerica Corp., 235 F.2d 369 (3d Cir. 1956).

§ 14.9 The Business Judgment Rule

The phrase "the business judgment rule" is a helpful shorthand description of the basic principle that courts are reluctant to interfere with the discretion of the directors in operating the company, and are unwilling to stigmatize every transaction that with hindsight turns out badly as being improper. Generally, the business judgment rule should not be applied to self-dealing transactions but to claims based on alleged mismanagement. The rule protects decisions made by an honest, unbiased judgment.

Examples of acts which are not actionable under the business judgment rule even though they may turn out badly include:

(1) A reorganization of a subsidiary company, including a distribution of surplus, reduction of stated capital, and distribution of a share dividend.

(2) Election of a manager and president.

(3) A sale of part of the assets of a telephone company.

(4) Acceptance of a note for a judgment rather than enforcing it by execution.

(5) The closing down of an unproductive mine.

The most important recent type of case in which the "business judgment" rule has been applied is in the discontinuance of derivative litigation. (See § 17.1.) Suit is brought by a minority shareholder seeking a recovery in favor of the corporation against one or more officers or directors, *e. g.*, for causing the corporation to make improper foreign bribes or other payments. The members of the board of directors who are not defendants or involved in the acts complained of are formed into a "Litigation Committee" to review the wisdom of the corporation's pursuing the suit. Several cases, including decisions by the United States Supreme Court and the New York Court of Appeals have recently held that the "business judgment rule" is applicable to the question of the continuance or the discontinuance of such litigation so that a decision to discontinue is binding on the plaintiff shareholder. The result is that the plaintiff is totally foreclosed from litigating the merits of his case because of the impartial directors' business judgment that pursuing such litigation is not in the best interest of the corporation; the minority shareholder may only litigate issues such as the independence and uninvolvement of the members of the committee recommending discontinuance of the litigation.

There is some potential overlap between the cases in which the "fairness" test described in the previous sections is applied and the cases described in this section dealing with the business judgment rule. This is illustrated by Sinclair Oil Co. v. Levien, 280 A.2d 717 (Del.1971), a case involving transactions between a parent corporation and its largely (but not solely) owned subsidiary. The minority shareholders of the subsidiary attacked several transactions including decisions (1) to pay large dividends by the subsidiary to ease the cash needs of the parent, (2) to channel oil development into other subsidiaries of the parent, and (3) to cause the subsidiary not to pursue claims for breach of contract against the parent. The alternative rules potentially applicable, the Court stated, are the standards of "intrinsic fairness," on the one hand, or of "business judgment" on the other. Under the latter, actions will be upheld unless there is a showing of "gross or palpable overreaching." The Court held that the questions of the excessive dividends and channeling of business opportunities should be evaluated by the "business judgment" rule while the refusal to enforce the contract claim should be judged on the basis of "intrinsic fairness." The basic test is whether the transaction involves self-dealing, that is, whether the parent received something from the subsidiary "to the exclusion and detriment of the minority shareholders." Since the dividends were paid proportionally to all shareholders, there was no self-dealing and the business judgment rule should be applied. So far as the business opportunities were concerned, there was no showing that they were ever corporate opportunities of the subsidiary and thus were not taken improperly by the parent. Giving up a contract claim by the subsidiary against the parent, however, constituted self-dealing, and should be judged by "intrinsic fairness."

§ 14.10 Shareholder Ratification

Ratification by shareholders of a transaction between a director and his corporation will sometimes validate a transaction that otherwise might be voidable. However, not all self-dealing transactions may be ratified by majority vote. Transactions which involve fraud, undue overreaching, or waste of corporate assets (*e. g.*, a director using corporate assets for personal purposes without paying for them) can only be ratified by a unanimous vote, and even then may be attacked by representatives of creditors if the corporation becomes insolvent. The theory is that all the shareholders may dissipate the corporate assets as they wish, so long as creditors are not injured, but that any individual shareholder may object to a clearly improper use of corporate assets.

§ 14.11 Exoneratory Provisions in Articles of Incorporation

Provisions are sometimes placed in the articles of incorporation of a corporation which purport to permit transactions between directors and the corporation which otherwise might be voidable under the principles described elsewhere in this chapter. These clauses are not construed literally to validate fraudulent or manifestly unfair acts. Such clauses may (1) permit an interested director to be counted in determining whether a quorum is present, or (2) exonerate transactions between corporation and director "from adverse inferences which might be drawn against them." Despite such clauses, courts examine with care transactions which may involve conflicting loyalties, and thus the usefulness and effectiveness of such clauses are limited.

§ 14.12 Statutory Duties and Statutory Defenses

State business corporation acts impose liabilities on directors for certain transactions which violate specific statutory provisions. This liability is in addition to all other liabilities, and usually is not dependent on bad faith. While provisions vary from state to state, liability for the following actions are typical:

(1) Paying dividends or making distributions in violation of the act or of restrictions in the articles of incorporation. Liability is usually limited to the excess of the amount actually distributed over the amount whch could have been distributed without violating the act or restriction.

(2) Purchasing its own shares by a corporation in violation of the act. The liability again is usually limited to the consideration paid for such shares which is in excess of the maximum amount which could have been paid without violating the statute.

(3) Distributing assets to shareholders during the liquidation of the corporation without paying and discharging, or making adequate provision for the payment and discharge of, all known debts, obligations, and liabilities of the corporation.

(4) Permitting the corporation to commence business before it has received the minimum required consideration for its shares. In most states, the liability is limited to the unpaid part of the minimum, and the liability terminates when the required consideration has actually been received. However, in some states liability extends to all debts or liabilities incurred before the required capital has been paid in.

(5) Permitting the corporation to make a loan to an officer or director, or to make a loan secured by shares of the corporation. The liability is limited to the amount of the loan until it is repaid.

Business corporation acts also usually provide for joint and several liability imposed on all directors present at the meeting at which the action is taken, unless a director's negative vote is duly entered in writing in the corporate words or the secretary is notified in writing by registered mail of his negative vote.

Prior to 1974, the Model Business Corporation Act contained statutory defenses that were limited to the statutory liabilities described above, and the statutes of a large number of states still follow this pattern. The most common provision relieves directors of liability for unlawful dividends or similar violations if in the exercise of ordinary care, the director relied in good faith upon "written financial statements of the corporation represented to him to be correct" by appropriate corporate officials, or if he uses book values in determining the amounts available for distribution. A few states also added a defense based on good faith reliance upon the written opinion of an attorney for the corporation.

In 1974, the Model Act was amended to make these statutory defenses generally applicable to all suits based on the obligation of due care. (See § 14.3.) Some states have amended their statutes to broaden the statutory defenses, and it is probable that more states will do so in the future.

There has been virtually no litigation over the scope of these defenses. Indeed, there has also been very little litigation over the statutory liabilities for unlawful distributions.

§ 14.13   Purchase or Sale of Shares or Claims at Common Law

The common law relating to transactions in corporate shares by directors and officers, or by the corporation itself, has been largely overshadowed by the development of federal law, particularly rule 10b–5, discussed in the following Section. As a result, there is relatively little case law on some of the problems discussed in this Section. However, with the apparent decline of federal corporations law resulting from Supreme Court decisions, greater attention may be paid in the future to the state law in this area.

(1) *Purchase or Sale of Shares by an Officer or Director on the Basis of Undisclosed Information.* An officer or director of the corporation may have knowledge about corporate affairs which is unknown to the general public or to the shareholders. He may be tempted to either purchase or sell shares, depending on the nature of the information, without disclosing the in-

formation in order to make a personal profit. Failure to disclose "material" information constitutes a clear violation of rule 10b-5 and most cases of this type are now brought in federal court under that rule. The common law did not develop a simple test for handling such situations. If an affirmative misrepresentation was made, of course, normal fraud principles dictate that the defrauded person might rescind the transaction. In addition, where the facts were of critical importance and peculiarly within the knowledge of the insider, some courts found a duty to disclose "special facts" without attempting to define which facts are "special." The leading case is Strong v. Repide, 213 U.S. 419 (1909). Chances of recovery in these early cases appear somewhat greater if the outsider could prove that he relied on the insider. Rescission has also been ordered where the insider concealed his identity from the purchaser, though the identity of the purchaser itself may be a "special fact." Kansas early adopted a stricter rule to protect outsiders, though the difference between these cases and the cases applying the "special facts" rule appears to be one of degree. The broadest rule was articulated in Diamond v. Oreamuno, 248 N.E.2d 910 (N.Y.1969) where the court permitted the corporation to recover profits made by insiders in securities trading on the basis of inside information. Relying on analogies with the federal securities laws, the court in effect concluded that inside information was corporate property and the insider should not be permitted to profit from the use of that corporate property even though the corporation was not injured thereby. In this case the information was unfavorable, and the insiders sold shares before the news was publicly disclosed and the market reacted negatively. This view has not yet been accepted by any other state court, and has been flatly rejected by some.

(2) *Purchase at a Discount of Claims Against the Corporation.* A corporate officer or director may purchase claims against a *solvent* corporation at a discount, and enforce them at face value, though in some circumstances the opportunity to acquire

a claim at a discount may itself be a corporate opportunity. It follows that claims validly bought at a discount when a corporation is solvent may share at face value in a subsequent distribution in insolvency or bankruptcy. A different rule, however, is applicable to claims purchased at a discount when the corporation is *insolvent*, and on the verge of, or in, bankruptcy or liquidation. The theory is that when insolvency, liquidation, or reorganization has occurred or is imminent, corporate directors should attempt to settle or discharge claims against the corporation on the best possible terms from the corporation's standpoint in order to benefit other creditors and the shareholders rather than seeking to share personally in the distribution.

(3) *Purchase or Sale of Shares in Competition with the Corporation.* In some circumstances an officer or director may attempt to sell his personal stock in competition with the corporation's attempt to raise capital by selling stock. Such conduct is actionable if the opportunity to sell shares to a third person is itself a corporate opportunity. The same principle should be applicable to corporate opportunities to repurchase its own shares as well.

(4) *Purchase or Sale of Shares by a Corporation in a Struggle for Control.* If outsiders are seeking to wrest control of a public corporation away from incumbent management, the incumbents may attempt to use the corporation in order to preserve their position. They may cause the corporation to make open market purchases of its own shares in order to drive up the price. Or they may cause the corporation to buy out the insurgents at a premium price in order to eliminate them. Or they may issue additional shares to themselves or to friendly persons in order to cement their position. Similarly, in a closely held corporation, the majority may decide to have the corporation purchase at a generous price the shares owned by a particularly obstreperous minority shareholder in order to be rid of him.

The general test of propriety adopted by the courts to evaluate all such transactions is one of underlying purpose: "[I]f the actions of the board were motivated by a sincere belief that the buying out of the dissident stockholder was necessary to maintain what the board believed to be proper business practices, the board will not be held liable for such decision, even though hindsight indicates the decision was not the wisest course . . . . On the other hand, if the board has acted solely or primarily because of the desire to perpetuate themselves in office, the use of corporate funds for such purposes is improper." Cheff v. Mathes, 199 A.2d 548 (Del.Ch.1964). This test may be criticized on the ground that it is possible to dress up virtually every transaction as a "proper business practice." However, a number of cases have invalidated transactions of the type described, so that the test obviously has some teeth.

§ 14.14 Rule 10b–5

Rule 10b–5, promulgated by the Securities and Exchange Commission under section 10(b) of the Securities Exchange Act of 1934, is the source of most current principles relating to transactions in securities by officers, directors, and others. Rule 10b–5 has some of the attributes of a roller coaster: a dizzying growth followed by a sudden decline as the Supreme Court attempts to limit the growth of the jungle of case law. The end of the downhill slide may not yet be in sight and it may well be that future developments will limit even more sharply the scope of this rule. The deceptively simple language of rule 10b–5 should be quoted:

"It shall be unlawful for any person, directly or indirectly, by the use of any means or instrumentality of interstate commerce, or of the mails or of any facility of any national securities exchange,

(1) to employ any device, scheme, or artifice to defraud;

(2) to make any untrue statement of a material fact or to omit to state a material fact necessary in order to make the

statements made, in light of the circumstances under which they were made, not misleading, or

(3) to engage in any act, practice, or course of business which operates or would operate as a fraud or deceit upon any person,

in connection with the purchase or sale of any security."

It should be emphasized at the outset that rule 10b–5 is a federal regulation and claims arising under it are federal claims. There is no need for diversity of citizenship, suit may be brought only in federal court, and state security for expenses statutes (see § 17.4) are not applicable. While many 10b–5 cases probably could have been brought in state court on state fiduciary or fraud principles, the federal forum is preferred by plaintiffs for several reasons. The procedures may be simpler and discovery procedures broader. There is nationwide service of process and broad venue provisions. The doctrine of pendent jurisdiction permits the joinder of both state and federal claims in a rule 10b–5 suit, but a rule 10b–5 claim cannot be joined with state causes of action in a state court. Further, in the past at least, the principles applicable under rule 10b–5, have been more favorable to plaintiffs than the correlative principles of state law. Also, there are more rule 10b–5 precedents than state court precedents and hence "more law" on which to build one's case. There is also the feeling, perhaps unjustified, that federal judges may be more sympathetic to minority shareholder complaints than state court judges. For all these practical reasons, rule 10b–5 has been traditionally preferred over state-based claims, and as a result rule 10b–5 prospered while state law languished. Two Supreme Court opinions, however, may have served to restore the balance.

In Ernst & Ernst v. Hochfelder, 425 U.S. 185 (1976), the United States Supreme Court held that a private plaintiff under rule 10b–5 must allege and prove "scienter," that is, "intentional wrongdoing" or a "mental state embracing intent to deceive, manipulate or defraud." The Court rejected several lower court holdings that mere negligence was sufficient. The Court, however, reserved the issues whether in some circumstances recklessness might satisfy the scienter requirement and whether a lesser standard of conduct might satisfy rule 10b–5 when injunctive relief is being sought by the Securities and Exchange Commission rather than a private plaintiff. (The latter issue was resolved against the SEC in a later case, Aaron v. SEC, 100 S.Ct. 1945 (1980).

In a second case, Santa Fe Industries, Inc. v. Green, 430 U.S. 462 (1977), the United States Supreme Court further limited rule 10b–5 to situations involving deception; in other words, a transaction (*e. g.,* a merger) that is adequately disclosed cannot be attacked under rule 10b–5 no matter how unfair its terms. Roughly contemporaneous with this decision are decisions by the Delaware Supreme Court holding that unfair merger transactions could not be validated by literal compliance with the requirements of the state business corporation acts, but that a valid business purpose must be demonstrated and the transaction must meet a test of "entire fairness." *E. g.,* Singer v. Magnavox Co., 380 A.2d 969 (Del.1977). Other state courts have adopted a similar view. These developments obviously have the potential of returning some of the prior rule 10b–5 litigation to the state courts.

(1) *Rule 10b–5 as an antifraud provision.* It is now firmly established that a private cause of action exists under rule 10b–5, on behalf of a person who bought or sold securities in a transaction violating the rule. Further, the rule is applicable to closely held shares as well as publicly held shares; it is triggered by the use of facilities of interstate commerce—*e. g.,* the telephone—or the mails. To use a classroom example: if the president of a small Denver corporation offers over the telephone to purchase the shares owned by a shareholder living in Denver without disclosing "material" facts about the corporation, he has probably violated rule 10b–5 without even leaving

his Denver office. Rule 10b–5 is obviously a far-reaching anti-fraud provision.

Rule 10b–5 proscribes not only affirmative misrepresentations and half-truths but also a failure to disclose "material facts;" mere silence may constitute a violation. The question of what is "material" is necessarily a relative one. The basic test is whether a reasonable man would attach importance to the information in determining his course of action—in other words, if the information would, in reasonable and objective contemplation, affect the value of the securities, it should be considered "material." The leading case is still Securities and Exchange Comm. v. Texas Gulf Sulphur Co., 401 F.2d 833 (2d Cir. 1968). Certain things are clearly material: *e. g.,* a significant ore strike, a resale contract for the shares or corporate assets, or a merger opportunity. (See also the discussion of a related issue in § 13.8.)

A person having knowledge of "material facts" can avoid liability only by disclosing them to the other party to the proposed transaction. If he does not, the transaction may be rescinded by the innocent party, or damages may be computed on the assumption that the contract had not been entered into. If disclosure is improper or impractical, the insider must forego the transaction to avoid liability.

(2) *Rule 10b–5 as a prohibition against insider trading.* The above principles have also been applied in the publicly held corporation. Here, however, transactions are usually not with a single known individual, but are effected anonymously over securities exchanges or through brokers. It is usually impractical for the insider to disclose the material facts since that is a corporate function. The result is that persons with material information about corporate matters simply must forego the transaction until after the facts are made public and have been reasonably disseminated by wire services and the like. In Securities and Exchange Comm. v. Texas Gulf Sulphur Corp., the

court held unlawful, under rule 10b–5, transactions entered into very shortly after the news of the ore strike had been released. After this decision, the New York Stock Exchange published guidelines as to when it was appropriate for an insider to purchase shares of his own corporation. These guidelines suggest periodic investment purchases (*e. g.,* buying a few shares every month) or limiting transactions to brief periods after public information is released. However, where a development of major importance has occurred, uncertainty may exist as to when an insider may trade even after the information has been released.

A problem may also arise as to which persons or employees of a corporation are subject to this ban on trading. Rule 10b–5 in terms is applicable to "any person." While this should perhaps not be construed literally, it has been held to be applicable to corporate employees in a responsible position, *e. g.,* a geologist employed by a mining company. It also may be applicable to some non-employees, *e. g.,* brokers or dealers who obtain information about a corporation before the information is generally available. In Chiarella v. United States, 100 S.Ct. 1108 (1980) the Supreme Court set aside a criminal conviction under rule 10b–5 of an employee of a printing plant who traded on information obtained at the place of his employment. A majority held that such an employee owed no duty to the general public to disclose the information he obtained. The possibility that a criminal conviction under rule 10b–5 might be based on the employee's duties to his employer was suggested by a dissent but not squarely addressed by the majority.

Rule 10b–5 has been applied to "tippees," *i. e.,* persons who are given inside information by corporate officers or employees. Such a person differs from the printer in *Chiarella* in that the tippee is acting on information obtained directly from the corporation in breach of a duty owed to the corporation. A tippee has been held liable to the corporation for profits made by him on the basis of the inside information. The person giving a tip (the "tipper") is also liable to the corporation for the same profits. If the tipper is liable for his tippee's profits, it is doubtful whether he has an "action over" because of the *in pari delicto* principle. The case law has also considered the liability of a tipper who gives his tippee knowingly false information; an argument may be made that *in pari delicto* should apply in this type of case also to bar recovery, but some courts have rejected this argument and simply held the tipper liable for the consequences of the false information he released.

If a person subject to rule 10b–5 has improperly traded on the basis of undisclosed material facts, the person who by chance engaged in the transaction with the insider may have a claim for rescission. Such a claim makes little sense since the plaintiff in no way relied on the fact that he was trading with an insider. Courts have also directed insider profits to be held by the corporation for the benefit of possible injured members of the public, presumably persons who actually entered into transactions with the insider; if no such persons appear, the corporation may keep the profits. The theory is to remove the incentive for insider trading (even though the corporation may receive a windfall) and yet preserve the remote possibility that an injured private plaintiff may appear.

(3) *Rule 10b–5 as a Protection Against Corporate Deception.* Rule 10b–5 is potentially applicable when a corporation issues or acquires its own shares. In other words, the phrase "purchase or sale" is literally construed to cover such transactions. If shares are issued or acquired by a corporation as a result of deception or a failure of some persons to disclose material facts to the corporation, the corporation may have a claim under rule 10b–5, and this claim may be asserted derivatively by a minority shareholder. For example, stock options granted to officers of Texas Gulf Sulphur Corporation

who knew of a major ore strike were cancelled since the recipients did not advise the members of the option committee of the ore strike. Similarly, a rule 10b–5 violation occurs if the corporation is fraudulently induced to issue shares for inadequate compensation even though such conduct also constitutes a violation of state-created fiduciary duties.

(4) *Rule 10b–5 as a general prohibition against wrongful conduct.* Several courts have permitted rule 10b–5 to be cast adrift from its mooring as an antifraud provision, and have applied the rule to situations in which bad conduct has occurred and there is some relationship either to the securities market or to trading in securities. The leading case involving this free wheeling approach is Superintendent of Ins. of New York v. Bankers Life & Cas. Co., 404 U.S. 6 (1971), where the United States Supreme Court found a rule 10b–5 violation when a corporation sold treasury bonds and the proceeds were fraudulently diverted to third parties. Thus, for a relatively brief period rule 10b–5 appeared to have an apparently limitless growth potential. The major limiting principle (that had been wholly or partially rejected by some courts of appeals) was the "Birnbaum doctrine," that the last clause of rule 10b–5, "in connection with the purchase or sale of any security" required the plaintiff to be a purchaser or seller of securities. This doctrine, based on Birnbaum v. Newport Steel Corp., 193 F.2d 461 (2d Cir. 1952) was firmly embraced by the United States Supreme Court in Blue Chip Stamps v. Manor Drug Stores, 421 U.S. 723 (1975). Indeed, some of the language and argument of Mr. Justice Rehnquist's opinion appears to show blatant and open hostility to an expansive construction of rule 10b–5 adopted by lower federal courts; indeed this opinion signalled the end of the era of uncontrolled growth of that rule.

(5) *Rule 10b–5 as a regulator of corporate publicity.* The *Birnbaum* rule requires that the plaintiff be a purchaser or seller of shares. There is no similar limitation on defendants; a

person may violate rule 10b–5 even though he neither purchases nor sells a security. If a person issues a false or misleading statement which might cause reasonable investors to rely and thereby purchase or sell the corporation's securities, he has violated rule 10b–5. *Texas Gulf Sulphur* is the leading case applying this principle to a corporate press release. Pre-*Hochfelder* cases (see the beginning of this section) held that an evil intent or wrongful purpose was unnecessary; a misleading statement containing inaccuracies caused by negligence may be as injurious to a "free and open public market" for securities as a statement published intentionally to further a wrongful purpose. Scienter is now clearly required under *Hochfelder* and *Aaron*.

In the course of the *Texas Gulf* litigation, individual shareholders who relied on the misleading press release were permitted to recover damages from *Texas Gulf Sulphur.* Obviously, the potential liability to the corporation as a result of a misleading press release may be very substantial, though the amounts actually recovered in *Texas Gulf Sulphur* were not large.

§ 14.15　Section 16(b) of the Securities Exchange Act of 1934

Section 16(b) of the Securities Exchange Act of 1934 is an *in terrorem* provision designed to prevent specified persons from trading in a corporation's securities on an in-and-out basis on the strength of inside information. The following comments outline the scope of this statutory liability:

(1) Unlike rule 10b–5, section 16(b) is only applicable to corporations registered under section 12 of the Securities Exchange Act—that is to corporations (1) with securities traded on a national securities exchange or (2) with assets of more than $1,000,000 and more than 500 shareholders of record of any class of equity security.

(2) Section 16(b) is only applicable to specified persons, namely officers, directors and ten per cent shareholders of the issuer.

(3) Section 16(b) is applicable only if there is an offsetting purchase-and-sale or sale-and-purchase of an equity security of the issuer within any six-month period. For example, if there is a sale on January 1, section 16(b) is applicable if there is an offsetting purchase made at any time from six months before to six months after the sale. The sequence of the transactions or the fact that different certificates are involved, is irrelevant. However, a transaction on June 2, six months and one day after the offsetting transaction cannot be matched.

(4) The words "purchase" and "sale" are construed broadly. A gift may be a sale, as may be a redemption, conversion or a simple exchange of shares pursuant to a merger or consolidation. The grant of a warrant may be a purchase; a conversion may also be a purchase of the conversion securities, and so forth. The test is not a dictionary one; rather a transaction will be considered a "purchase" or a "sale" for purposes of section 16(b) if it is of a kind which can possibly lend itself to the speculation encompassed by section 16(b). Under this test, commentators and lower courts have struggled with whether all sorts of transactions, such as recapitalizations, exchanges, conversions, mergers, puts and calls should be considered "purchases" or "sales."

(5) Actual use of inside information is not a prerequisite for section 16(b) liability. Even a sale for entirely justifiable reasons—*e. g.,* unexpected medical expenses—will trigger section 16 (b) if there has been an offsetting transaction within the six-month period.

(6) Profits are payable to the corporation. However, if the corporation fails to take steps to recover the profit, any shareholder may bring suit. It is not necessary that the shareholder have owned shares when either of the transactions took place.

(7) Profits are computed by comparing the highest sale price with the lowest purchase price, the next highest sale price with

the next lowest purchase price, and so forth. The purpose is to squeeze out all possible profits; in this computation, all loss transactions are ignored. It is possible to have a substantial loss in a trading account and yet have a section 16(b) profit under this method of computation. The United States Supreme Court has never passed on this rather draconian measure of recovery.

(8) All transactions by covered persons must be reported to the SEC and this information is published. Certain attorneys regularly review all these filings in order to find section 16(b) violations. They are motivated by the attorneys fees that may be awarded in a successful section 16(b) suit. Suits brought by these attorneys in the name of nominal shareholder plaintiffs may be champertous, but are the principal enforcement device of section 16(b). As a result, it is unlikely that a violation of section 16(b) will escape litigation.

(9) The Securities and Exchange Commission has authority to exempt classes of transactions from section 16(b). While it has exercised this power in a number of instances, the exemptions tend to be narrowly drawn to cover specific situations.

(10) Like rule 10b-5, the jurisdiction of section 16(b) suits is exclusively federal.

The foregoing statement of principles gives little picture of the substantial volume of section 16(b) litigation despite its apparent automatic liability. The United States Supreme Court has struggled with the application of section 16(b) to takeover situations where an unsuccessful aggressor acquires over ten per cent of the target's shares and then sells that interest or has it "merged out" within six months thereafter. In Reliance Electric Co. v. Emerson Electric Co., 404 U.S. 418 (1972), the Court held that a 13.2 per cent shareholder could dispose of its holding by first selling 3.2 per cent subject to section 16(b) and thereafter dispose of the balance free of section 16(b) since it was then less than a ten per cent shareholder. In Kern County Land Co. v. Occidental Petroleum Corp., 411 U.S. 582 (1973), in a complex series of transactions, the Court refused to treat either an "involuntary" merger or an option to sell as "sales" triggering section 16(b). And in Foremost-McKesson, Inc. v. Provident Securities Co., 423 U.S. 232 (1976), the Court finally "solved" the application of section 16(b) to the unsuccessful tender offeror by holding that the initial purchase that puts the aggressor over ten per cent was not a section 16(b) purchase. In Blau v. Lehman, 368 U.S. 403 (1962) the Supreme Court considered the circumstances in which transactions by a partnership not itself a ten per cent holder may violate section 16(b) because one of the partners is a director of the issuer. The test in such a case is whether the partnership "deputized" the partner to represent the partnership on the board.

The purchase and sale matched under section 16(b) must both generally be of the same class of equity security. There is no meaningful basis, for example, for matching a sale of common with a purchase of preferred. However, if the preferred is convertible into common and is trading at or close to the conversion price, matching may be permitted since the two securities are trading as economic equivalents.

People do not knowingly violate section 16(b); most of the violations appear to be a result of ignorance rather than the actual misuse of inside information. Most inadvertent violations probably are a result of the failure to appreciate how broadly the words "purchase" and "sale" may be construed. However, despite its shortcomings and erratic imposition of liability, section 16(b) has been effective in eliminating the in-and-out trading evil that was thought to exist prior to 1934.

§ 14.16 Transfer of Control

For purposes of this section, a "controlling shareholder" is a person who owns either an outright majority of the shares or a minority of the shares but the balance is so fragmented that he has working control and can deliver such control to a purchaser of his shares. The simplest method of "delivering" control is by the seriatim resignation of directors and their successive replacement by nominees of the purchaser.

When a controlling shareholder sells his interest to third persons, he is selling more than the property represented by the shares. He is also selling control of a going business in which other persons—minority shareholders, senior security holders, and unsecured creditors—may have a substantial interest. Shares owned by a controlling shareholder command a premium over other shares simply because they represent the power to control the business, to designate the corporate officers, and so forth. This premium is usually referred to as the "control premium."

Generally a controlling shareholder may sell his shares for whatever price he can obtain in the same way as any other property. However, the courts recognize that the seller and buyer are not the only persons interested in this transaction and have imposed duties on the selling shareholder with respect to whom he sells. The "looting" cases are a good illustration. Several cases have imposed liability on a controlling shareholder when he has sold his shares to unscrupulous third persons who thereafter "loot" the corporation by stealing corporate assets. The controlling shareholder has a duty to make a reasonable investigation of potential purchasers and not to transfer control to outsiders under circumstances that might awaken suspicion that the outsiders plan to wrongfully convert the assets of the corporation, or to use them to pay the purchase price. Danger signs include, (1) an excessive price for the shares willingly paid, (2) interest in the liquid and readily salable assets owned by the corporation, (3) insistence by the buyers on an immediate transfer of control, (4) insistence by the buyers that the liquid assets be made available immediately, (5) a failure to investigate carefully the background of the potential purchasers, (6) little interest being indicated in the operation of the corporation's business, and (7) the insistence that the purchase be handled with dispatch. Since the liability is based on negligence, the recovery may be based on the damage suffered, *i. e.,* the amount looted, rather than on the purchase price paid on the amount of the control premium.

Outside of the looting cases, courts have not evolved consistent theories about the propriety of a controlling shareholder receiving a "control premium." Some cases in which the controlling shareholder has been compelled to share the control premium with minority shareholders contain broad statements to the effect that a director owes a fiduciary duty to the corporation and to the minority shareholders. *E. g.,* Perlman v. Feldmann, 219 F.2d 173 (2d Cir. 1955). Such statements are little more than make-weight since they do not explain when the premium may be recovered and when it may not. Law review commentators have suggested that all control premiums in good conscience should be shared with all shareholders. These commentators essentially argue that since shares of stock are fungible, the control premium represents the pure power to control which should, if anything, be a corporate asset available to all shareholders. The cases, however, have not taken such a firm position. Many cases, including some rather recent ones, have permitted the selling shareholder to keep the premium. A form of control premium is also involved in cases such as Honigman v. Green Giant Co., 309 F.2d 667 (8th Cir. 1962), where a class of voting shares agreed to share the voting power with a larger class of nonvoting common in exchange for a larger slice of the "equity." Such transactions have been approved where the premium is not excessive, or to put it a different way, where the transaction seems fair. On the other hand, the decision in Jones v. H. F. Ahmanson & Co., 460 P.2d 464 (Cal.1969), though involving unique facts, goes furthest toward acceptance of the theory that control premiums are inherently improper. In this case, the majority shareholders of a savings and loan association created a holding company and exchanged their shares for holding company shares. Minority shareholders in the association were not permitted also to exchange their shares for holding company shares. The holding company then made a public offering and a public market was created for the holding company's shares from which the minority shareholders of the association were precluded. The court held that this conduct violated the majority's fiduciary responsibility to the minority, and that recovery might be based either on the appraised value of the shares when the holding company was created or the value of a "derived block" of the holding company shares on the date litigation was commenced.

Some cases have permitted the recovery of a control premium on a theory of "corporate action" or usurpation of corporate opportunity. If the purchaser first offers to buy the assets of the corporation at an attractive price, but the controlling shareholder suggests that the transaction be recast in the form of a purchase of the controlling shares, a reasonable argument may be made that the favorable sale opportunity was a corporate opportunity belonging to all the shareholders, rather than to the majority shareholder. The facts of Perlman v. Feldmann arguably present this pattern, though the opinion itself only partially articulates this theory. Other cases adopt the theory that the control premium is for the sale of a corporate office rather than a sale of stock, and since a sale of office is against public policy, the excess payment may be recovered by the corporation for the benefit of the minority shareholders. The problem with this argument is that it proves too much—all sales of control stock at a premium may be analyzed in this fashion. This argument is most likely to be accepted either where an additional payment is conditioned on the immediate transfer of offices or where the selling shareholders own a miniscule proportion of the outstanding shares and the sales agreement carefully provides for a seriatim resignation of directors. Petition of Caplan, 246 N.Y.S.2d 913 (Sup.Ct.1964), is the leading case accepting this argument. In that case the selling shareholders owned only 3 per cent of the outstanding shares.

Liability for a control premium has also been based on a theory of nondisclosure or misrepresentation. In these cases a controlling shareholder contracts to sell more shares than he owns, planning to purchase the additional shares; if he purchases the additional shares without disclosing the resale contract, he is liable under state or federal law. (See §§ 14.13, 14.14.) However, frontal attacks on the sale of control premiums under rule 10b–5 have been largely unsuccessful because of the *Birnbaum* principle that the plaintiff must be a purchaser or seller of securities. See § 14.14.

Where a control premium is recoverable, courts have permitted either the corporation or the minority shareholders to recover, depending on the theory adopted. If the theory of recovery is corporate opportunity, corporate action, or sale of corporate office, logically the corporation should recover. If the theory is misrepresentation or violation of rule 10b–5, the minority shareholders should recover. Since a corporate recovery enriches the purchaser paying the premium, however, the leading case of Perlman v. Feldmann permitted recovery directly by the minority shareholders, even though the theory adopted apparently was corporate opportunity. The court argued that the purchaser who paid the control premium should not be permitted to share in its recovery. This holding creates some anomalous consequences and appears to be inconsistent with the substantive theory adopted by the court.

§ 14.17 Indemnification by the Corporation

"Indemnification" by the corporation simply means the corporation reimburses a defendant who is a corporate officer or director for (a) expenses incurred in defending against a claim or prosecution, particularly legal fees but including other expenses as well, and (b) amounts paid in settlement of suits or to satisfy a judgment entered against or a conviction of the defendant officer or director.

There are basic policy questions posed by indemnification. Policy justifications for indemnification of officers and directors include: (1) it encourages innocent directors to resist unjust charges, (2) it encourages responsible persons to accept the position of director, and (3) it discourages groundless shareholder litigation. There can be little objection to indemnification of expenses if a director is absolved of liability. However, indemnification against many kinds of wrongful acts clearly violates public policy. Perhaps the clearest example is attempted indemnification against liabilities under section 16(b) of the Securities Exchange Act of 1934. Such indemnification would create complete circularity, and would obviously vitiate the policy underlying that section. Indemnification should not be permitted whenever the defendant is found guilty of some sort of wrongful misconduct and is held liable to a third person in damages for such misconduct. In such situations indemnification of expenses is as objectionable as indemnification against the judgments themselves. Further, serious doubts arise as to the propriety of indemnification of amounts paid in settlements (since such settlements may or may not reflect wrongdoing), or in suits in which only negligence has been alleged.

State statutes attempt to work out a compromise of these various competing considerations. Modern indemnification provisions developed in the Delaware statute and in section 5 of the Model Business Corporation Act have been particularly influential. However, a number of states have only very general statutes authorizing indemnification which give little indication of the outer limits.

Under the modern statutes a defendant is entitled to indemnification as a matter of statutory right if "he is successful on the merits or otherwise." Under these statutes a defendant who prevails because of the statute of limitations or because of pleading defects is as entitled to indemnification as the defendant who prevails on the merits. In other situations, indemnification is permitted (but as a matter of discretion, not as a matter of right) if the defendant director has "acted in good faith and in a manner he reasonably believes to be in or not opposed to the best interests of the corporation;" indemnification may even be permitted against criminal fines if he "had no reasonable cause to believe his conduct [was] unlawful." Judgments as to entitlement to indemnification under these standards may be made (a) by the disinterested directors, (b) the shareholders, or (c) independent legal counsel in a written opinion. No presumption that a person acted in bad faith is made merely because he settles litigation or pleads *nolo contendere* or even if he is convicted criminally or found liable civilly. Of course, a criminal conviction or civil judgment will usually involve a determination of bad faith and prevent indemnification.

The Model Act and Delaware statutory provisions do not purport to be exclusive and many corporations have indemnification provisions in their articles of incorporation or bylaws. The same public policy considerations discussed above of course limit indemnification under special corporate provisions as well as under the general statute. The major purpose of these special provisions is to create a right of indemnification wherever it is permitted, so that defendants who may be indemnified consistently with public policy under the statute become automatically entitled to indemnification whether or not the directors then in office choose to grant indemnification.

§ 14.18 Liability Insurance

Insurance against directors' and officers' liabilities (usually called "D & O" insurance) is a relatively new phenomenon. It provides useful but limited protection against costs and liabilities for negligence, for misconduct not involving dishonesty or knowing bad faith, and for false or misleading statements in disclosure documents. Companies writing D & O liability insurance are not eleemosynary institutions; they write policies that cover only insurable risks. Thus wrongful misconduct, dishonest acts, acts in bad faith with knowledge thereof, or violations of statutes such as section 16(b) are specifically excluded, and in any event are not insurable events. Also excluded are actions entered into for personal profit or gain or suits based on claims of libel or slander. There is also an exclusion for failing to disclose contingent liabilities on the application for insurance. D & O insurance is purchased by the corporation to cover all its officers and directors. The cost of the premium is shared: a typical pattern is for the corporation to pay 90 per cent and the covered persons 10 per cent. This division in cost reflects the fact that D & O insurance protects the corporation's obligation to indemnify officers and directors under statute or bylaw provisions, as well as the officers and directors themselves.

Many state statutes specifically permit corporations to purchase D & O insurance. Where there is no statutory authorization, the power to purchase such insurance is usually thought to be implicit in the corporate power to provide executive compensation. Corporate bylaws often specifically authorize the purchase of such insurance.

§ 14.19 Liability to Creditors

Generally, the liabilities of officers and directors discussed in this chapter run to the corporation rather than to creditors. Certainly, in the absence of insolvency, a corporate creditor has an adequate remedy against the corporation itself, and there is no reason to permit a creditor to proceed also against an officer or director who has acted wrongfully. Where the corporation is insolvent, the usual recourse of a corporate creditor is through a receiver or bankruptcy trustee; to permit a direct suit by a creditor against a director or officer in effect whould permit the creditor to obtain a priority or other advantage over other creditors. Of course, bankruptcy trustees, receivers, and assignees for the benefit of creditors are charged with collecting the assets of the corporation and distributing them equitably among the creditors; among the assets may be claims against directors or officers for wrongful action. Basically, however, the representative of creditors is suing on behalf of the corporation, and the corporation or specific shareholders are the persons in whose favor the duties set forth in this chapter run.

[For unfamiliar terms see the Glossary]

CHAPTER FIFTEEN

INSPECTION OF BOOKS AND RECORDS

§ 15.1 Inspection by Directors and Shareholders Compared

Both shareholders and directors have the right to inspect corporate books and records in certain circumstances. However, the right of a director is considerably broader than the right of a shareholder and rests on an entirely different theoretical base. A director is a manager of the corporation and owes certain duties to it and to all the shareholders. Indeed, he may be liable for negligent mismanagement if he does not adequately acquaint himself with the business and affairs of the corporation. Hence, the directors' right to inspect books and records is virtually absolute and unqualified. However, as with many supposedly absolute principles, there are exceptions. Courts have sometimes denied inspection rights to directors where it was clear that the director was acting with manifestly improper motives and adequate information prepared by unbiased persons was available to the director. Such cases, however, are exceptional and unusual.

The right of a shareholder to inspect books and records, on the other hand, is considerably narrower. A shareholder of course has a financial interest in the corporation, and the common law recognizes a right to inspect books and records to protect this interest. However, because the shareholder is not charged with management responsibility and is not subject to a broad fiduciary duty, his right to inspect is available only for "proper purposes," and is otherwise hedged with restrictions. The balance of this chapter deals exclusively with the more limited inspection rights of shareholders.

§ 15.2 Common Law and Statutory Rights of Inspection

From the standpoint of the corporation, a shareholder's demand to inspect books and records almost certainly will be viewed as a hostile and threatening act. The practice therefore developed of denying the request out-of-hand and compelling the shareholder to litigate, relying on whatever pretext may be available for the denial. In an effort to combat this attitude, the statutes of most states supplement the common law right of inspection with a statutory right of inspection which includes a "penalty" on corporate officers who arbitrarily refuse to permit proper examination of books and records.

The statutory right of inspection is typically available to persons (1) who have been shareholders of record for at least six months prior to the demand or (2) who own at least five per cent of the outstanding shares of the corporation. (MBCA § 52). Some states use different numbers but the principle is the same. The statutory right to inspect, like the common law right, also requires a showing of "proper purpose" for the inspection which must be stated in the shareholder's written demand. However, in the event a shareholder qualifies for the statutory right of inspection the corporation has the burden of showing the plaintiff does not have a proper purpose; shareholders who do not qualify under the statute continue to have the common law burden of establishing that their purpose is a proper one.

Under the Model Act, a corporate officer or agent who refuses to grant a statutory right of inspection is liable for a "penalty" equal to ten per cent of the value of the shares owned by the shareholder (§ 52). State statutes vary widely: several states have made the penalty one or two per cent of the value of the plaintiff's shares; others have imposed a maximum penalty of $500; still others have imposed a per diem penalty of $25 or some other amount. Several states require five days written demand in advance. As a practical matter, these provisions are pretty much a dead letter because the basic test of eligibility—a proper purpose—is a vague and uncertain one. While the potential of a substantial penalty may have a healthful, *in terrorem* effect, there appears to be no recent reported case in which a penalty was successfully imposed.

§ 15.3   What Records may be Examined?

Business corporation acts require each corporation to keep minutes of meetings, books and records or accounts, and information about shareholders.   The Model Act, and the statutes of many states, permit these records to be kept on tape or machine-readable form capable of being converted into written form in a reasonable time.

The right to inspect extends not only to all such records but to corporate records in general.   Case law, for example, has authorized the examination of "records, books of account, receipts, vouchers, bills and all other documents evidencing the financial condition of the corporation."   Another case authorized the examination of the books of a subsidiary controlled by the corporation.   Corporate contracts and even the correspondence of the chief executive officer have been held to be subject to inspection in appropriate cases.   The right generally extends to all relevant records necessary to inform the shareholder about corporate matters in which he has a legitimate interest.   The corporation cannot defeat this right by offering summaries, substitute papers, or financial statements prepared by the corporation's auditors.

§ 15.4   What is a "Proper Purpose"?

The basic test of inspection by shareholders is a "proper purpose."   A purpose is proper if it is directed toward obtaining information bearing upon or seeking to protect the shareholder's interest and that of other shareholders of the corporation.   The inspection may be to determine the worth of the shareholder's holdings. It may be to seek reasons for a decline in profits. It may be to communicate with other shareholders. It may be to ascertain whether there has been mismanagement or alarming transactions. All of these are "proper purposes."

A corporation cannot deny the right to inspect by arguing that the shareholder has an improper purpose simply because he is unfriendly to management. An improper purpose is one with ulterior or vindictive motives. Obvious examples are general harassment of management or a desire to obtain trade secrets for a competitor. Probably mere idle curiousity is not a proper purpose, though it is a rare shareholder who cannot allege a more specific purpose. Some courts appear to be more willing than others to countenance "fishing expeditions."

Obviously, substantial and difficult factual issues arise as to the shareholder's true purpose. The issue may come down to predominant motive and intent. The burden of proof, discussed earlier, may be significant. It is probably fair to conclude that careful coaching of testimony may lead to the conclusion that the purpose for inspection is proper, while the outspoken or unusually forthright witness may run into difficulty.

§ 15.5 Who Is Entitled to Inspect?

A person who is a beneficial owner of shares but is not the record owner has a common law right of inspection, and depending on the wording of the statute, may have a statutory right as well. In some states, pledgees or judgment creditors have a statutory right to inspect. Holders of voting trust certificates also have a statutory right to inspect under the Model Act and the statutes of many states.

§ 15.6 Inspection of Shareholders Lists

Every corporation must maintain "a record of its shareholders, giving the names and addresses of all shareholders and the number and class of the shares held by each." (MBCA § 52). This record is subject to the statutory or common law right of inspection possessed by every shareholder [unlike the voting list compiled immediately before the meeting (see § 9.3) which is automatically open to inspection]. There has been a substantial volume of litigation over shareholders lists in publicly held corporations since such lists are, to quote a colorful phrase, "the line of scrimmage for contests involving incumbent management, dissident shareholders, acquisition-minded corporations, and those who have been described in current fiction as 'corporate raiders'." Also, a list of names and addresses of numerous well-to-do persons (as shareholders are likely to be) is itself valuable, and may be sought in order to sell it to mail-solicitation firms. Indeed, some state statutes, including New York's, specifically provide that a shareholders list need not be produced if the applicant has offered to sell or assisted another person in the sale or offering for sale of a shareholders list within the preceding five years.

Much of the litigation dealing with shareholders lists also involves the "proper purpose" test. Generally it has been held that it is a proper purpose to desire to communicate with other shareholders about matters of corporate concern: to solicit proxies, to initiate a proxy contest, to publicize mismanagement, to discuss a derivative suit, to discuss proposals of management, to form a protective committee and the like. It has also been held to be a proper purpose to offer to purchase the shares of the corporation. Courts probably tend to be more lenient in granting access to shareholders lists than to other books and records. However, it is not a proper purpose to seek to sell to the shareholders securities of unrelated corporations. Similarly it is not a proper purpose to seek the list in order to communicate one's own social or political views to shareholders. The mere fact that the shareholder making the request is a competitor of the corporation does not necessarily make his purpose proper though such a demand may raise suspicions.

§ 15.7 Inspection of Shareholders Lists of Publicly Held Corporations

Where a corporation is large enough to be registered under section 12 of the Securities Exchange Act of 1934 (500 shareholders of record of any class and $1,000,000 of assets), the federal proxy regulations give additional rights of inspection. Rule 14a–7 requires a corporation either to supply a shareholders list or to mail solicitations to shareholders on behalf of a shareholder upon payment of the postage by that shareholder. The corporation will usually elect the latter alternative so that the insurgent faction may have to seek to obtain the production of the shareholders list under state law. The insurgent faction needs the list (rather than merely communicating with shareholders) in order to make personal solicitation and personal contact with large shareholders. However, a solicitation of shareholders asking them to join in a request for a shareholders list (in order to meet the 5 per cent requirement of state law) is itself a solicitation under the proxy rules, and requires filing with the Securities and Exchange Commission if more than ten such solicitations are made. Studebaker Corp. v. Gittlin, 360 F.2d 692 (2d Cir. 1966).

In a large public corporation, the right to copy by hand a list of tens of thousands of shareholders is of dubious value. What is obviously needed is a copy of the list itself or permission to reproduce it in its entirety by xerography or similar process. State statutes only refer to a right to "make extracts" from the records, but that language has been used to support an order that a list be made available for reproduction purposes.

[For unfamiliar terms see the Glossary]

CHAPTER SIXTEEN

CORPORATE DISTRIBUTIONS AND REDEMPTIONS

§ 16.1 Dividends in General

The profits of a business corporation—the purpose or goal of such a corporation—may be accumulated by the corporation or paid out, in whole or in part, in the form of dividends. The decision whether or not to pay dividends rests in the hands of the board of directors of the corporation.

The dividend policy of a corporation depends in part on whether the corporation is publicly held or a close corporation. In the large public corporation, dividends are often paid on a periodic basis, in amounts that remain stable from period to period. Public shareholders, without effective voice in the management of the business, may look in part to the history of dividends by the corporation to determine whether to purchase shares of the corporation. Probably greater attention, however, is paid to the prospects of dividends in the future and to the hope that the market price of the shares will rise.

In the closely held corporation, on the other hand, the principal owners of the business prefer, for tax reasons, to distribute earnings in the form of salaries, interest or rent to the principal shareholders, or to let the earnings accumulate, planning ultimately to sell the business. See § 2.3.

The term "dividend" refers to distributions of *earnings*; where a distribution of capital in partial liquidation is made from sources other than current or retained earnings, the term "distribution" rather than "dividend" should generally be used, though this usage is not uniform—*e. g.*, it is not uncommon to refer to a "liquidating dividend" rather than a "liquidating distribution."

It is useful to classify true dividends into three categories: cash dividends, dividends-in-kind or property dividends, and share dividends.

A cash dividend—the most common—as the name implies, divides cash (from legally available funds) among the shareholders. The amount may be expressed either as so many cents or dollars per share or as a percentage of the par or stated value of the shares. An informal or irregular payment may be a "dividend" for some purposes. For example, excessive payments in the form of salary, rent or interest may be treated as a dividend for tax purposes. Such payments, of course, usually will not be proportionate to share holdings.

A property dividend is a division of assets other than cash or shares of the declaring corporation among the shareholders. The property so divided is usually fungible; it may consist, for example, of shares of a subsidiary corporation or of a corporation in which the declaring corporation has an investment. A share dividend or stock dividend distributes additional shares of the declaring corporation among the shareholders. Share dividends are usually of the same class as the original shares. However, this is not necessarily so; a holder of common shares may receive a dividend in the form of preferred shares, or vice versa. The source of shares may be either treasury shares (*i. e.*, shares previously issued and later reacquired by the corporation) or authorized but unissued shares.

A share dividend is not a true dividend in the sense of cash or property dividends, since a distribution of additional shares does not reduce the real worth of the corporation or increase the real worth of the shareholder. A share dividend increases the number of ownership units outstanding but is not itself a distribution of assets. This is true even though treasury shares are used as the basis for the distribution. The *acquisition* by a corporation of its own shares decreases the real worth of the corporation by the amount of the consideration paid, but the *reissuance* of the shares as a dividend without consideration does not affect the assets of the corporation. If a shareholder sells the additional shares he receives as a share dividend, he thereafter owns a smaller percentage of the enterprise than he owned before the dividend. It is surprising that many people apparently are unaware that a share dividend is unlike property or cash dividends. Where shares are publicly traded, a share dividend, other things being equal, will reduce the market price for each share proportionately; however, other things usually are not equal, and other factors may cause a price change which masks the decline attributable to the dividend. If no decline occurs, a small shareholder may sell his dividend shares for cash and yet have a diluted investment with undiminished market value. The dilution in such situations may be so slight as to be unimportant.

A share dividend is often expressed as a ratio. Thus, a 20 percent distribution means that a shareholder receives a 20 percent increase—one additional share for each five shares held; if he owns less than five shares or a number of shares not divisible by five, he will receive either a fractional share or "scrip," or at the election of the directors the fair value in cash. "Scrip" differs from fractional shares in that it grants no voting or dividend rights; it represents merely the right to a fraction of a full share and may be bought or sold so that a full share may be assembled from the rights to fractional shares.

A share "dividend" and a share "split" are closely related. A share dividend increases the capital accounts of the corporation by the par value of the new shares, while a "split" simply divides the shares into a greater number without any change in the aggregate stated capital. A share split, like a share dividend, does not decrease the real worth of the corporation. Since cash dividend rates are usually not adjusted for a share dividend, such a dividend may increase slightly the effective rate of dividend pay-outs. The dividend rate is usually partially adjusted in a stock split; for example, if a share of a corporation which regularly pays dividends of $1.00 per share is split two-for-one, the dividend on the split shares may be set at $0.55 cents per share, or an effective rate on the old shares of $1.10.

"Rights" or "warrants" are simply options to purchase additional shares at a price usually below the current market price of the shares. Most rights are short lived (usually a period of weeks at the most); where they remain in effect for longer periods they are usually called "warrants". Rights or warrants when distributed to shareholders are also not a true dividend, though they may be so regarded by recipients. The effect of a distribution of rights or warrants is that a shareholder must add new capital to the enterprise in order to retain his relative ownership interest in the corporation. In order to be attractive, the rights or warrants must permit new shares to be purchased below current market values. Rights or warrants issued by publicly held corporations are themselves traded, the price fluctuating with the price of the underlying shares. If a shareholder sells his rights or warrants, he has diluted his proportionate interest in the corporation.

§ 16.2 Shareholder's Rights to a Dividend

A dividend is distributable to shareholders of record on a specific date. This date may be determined in several different ways similar to the determination of eligibility to vote at meetings (See § 9.2). (1) The directors may specify that the share transfer books be closed for a period of up to 50 days prior to the date the dividend is to be paid, and the shareholders shown in the share transfer books are entitled to the dividend. (2) The bylaws, or in the absence of a bylaw the board of directors, may specify the record date for determining entitlement to the dividend: the record date may be set any time not more than 50 days prior to the payment of the dividend. (3) If no record date is fixed, the shareholders of record as of the date on which the resolution of the board of directors declaring the dividend is adopted are entitled to the dividend. Most corporations do not close the share transfer books but set a record date under either alternative (2) or (3).

Generally, when a dividend has been declared it becomes a debt of the corporation and cannot be rescinded or repealed by the directors.

Where shares are transferred after the record date, it is customary to agree upon who is entitled to the dividend. Such agreement, of course, is binding between the purchaser and seller but not binding on the corporation who will simply pay the dividend to the record owner as of the record date. Securities exchanges have promulgated conventions or rules dealing with who is entitled to dividends on publicly held shares. A share goes "ex dividend" on the date the seller becomes entitled to keep the dividend. Under the New York Stock Exchange rules, shares normally are traded on an ex dividend basis on and after the fourth business day before the record date for the dividend. For example, a dividend may be made payable on March 28 to shareholders of record on March 14. The stock goes ex dividend on March 10. A purchaser of the stock on March 9 is entitled to the dividend; a purchaser on March 10 is not. In either event the dividend will be paid on March 28 to whoever is the record owner on March 14. In contracts for the purchase and sale of shares after the ex dividend date the seller retains the right to the dividend, and the amount of the dividend is not included in the contract price. This does not necessarily mean that when ex dividend dealings commence the market price will decline from the previous closing price by exactly the amount of the dividend, as other factors may also affect the market price simultaneously, bringing about a greater or lesser change than the adjustment due to the shares going ex dividend. Where the corporation issues "rights," shares go "ex rights" on the same basis as they go ex dividend.

§ 16.3 Restrictions on the Declaration of Dividends

Restrictions on the distribution of dividends are basically designed to assure that such payments are made out of current or past earnings and not out of capital. Restrictions are phrased in accounting terms applicable to the right hand side of the traditional balance sheet. (If this reference is unclear read § 7.4.) Unfortunately the language of state statutes vary widely, and an examination of the specific statute is necessary to ascertain whether specific payments are prohibited. The principal requirements are as follows:

(1) *Solvency.* All states prohibit the payment of a dividend if the corporation is "insolvent" or the payment of the dividend will render the corporation insolvent. "Insolvency" is usually defined in the equity sense of being unable to meet corporate obligations as they mature; a few states define insolvency in the bankruptcy sense of the corporate liabilities exceeding the corporate assets. A payment in violation of the insolvency test may also constitute an act of bankruptcy under the Federal Bankruptcy Act.

(2) *Surplus Test.* A number of states permit dividends to be paid from "surplus" as contrasted with "capital." Under statutes of this type, dividends usually may be paid from earned surplus or capital surplus, or both. The statutes of this type may be phrased in terms of prohibitions against impairment of "capital" or "capital stock."

(3) *Net Profits Test.* A number of states permit distributions from current profits even if there is an earnings deficit from operations for prior periods. These dividends are sometimes called "nimble dividends." The leading case holding that current earnings may be distributed without being used to eliminate prior deficits is Goodnow v. American Writing Paper Co., 69 A. 1014 (N.J.1908). Some states do not permit nimble dividends.

(4) *Earned Surplus Test.* An increasing number of states follow the provisions of the Model Business Corporation

Act, and permit dividends to be paid only from "earned surplus." (As described in the following section statutes also usually permit distributions from capital accounts such as capital surplus but they are not "dividends" in the strict sense.) In these statutes earned surplus is a composite income item determined by adding together all net profits, income, gain and losses during each accounting period going back to the original creation of the corporation with reductions for prior dividends or transfers to other accounts.

Randall v. Bailey, 23 N.Y.S.2d 173 (Sup.Ct.1940), raised the question whether it was permissible for directors to write up the value of appreciated assets on the books of the corporation in order to increase the amount available for distribution as dividends. In holding that it was permissible to use such writeups, the court relied in part on the language of the New York statute that only prohibited dividends that "impaired capital stock." It is questionable whether similar writeups are permissible to increase earned surplus available for dividends in Model Act states, and if written up, it is also questionable whether they may thereafter have to be written down.

§ 16.4 Distributions from Capital

Modern statutes based on the Model Business Corporation Act often permit distributions to be made from capital accounts when there is no earned surplus. The Model Act, for example, permits distributions of capital surplus to common shareholders simply with the approval of the holders of a majority of the shares. (MBCA § 46.) Distributions of capital surplus to holders of cumulative preferred shares in discharge of cumulative dividend rights are also permitted. The justification for permitting preferential dividends to be paid from capital surplus is that it permits a corporation to avoid building up preferred arrearages during the early years of operation when there may be no earned surplus. It also permits dividends to be paid to common shareholders at an earlier time and in a greater amount. While not all states are this liberal, some distributions from capital surplus are permitted in most states.

Distributions from capital surplus may not be made if the corporation is insolvent or the distribution will render the corporation insolvent. Further, a distribution to common shareholders may not be made unless all preferential cumulative dividends have been paid, and the capital remaining in the corporation is sufficient to cover all preferential rights on liquidation.

All payments made from capital surplus must be identified as such when made to shareholders.

Amendments to the Model Business Corporation Act are being considered that would greatly simplify the financial and accounting provisions of the Act. Distinctions between capital and earned surplus distributions would be eliminated and general insolvency tests would become the sole criteria for the validity of a distribution.

§ 16.5   Restrictions on Surplus

The Model Business Corporation Act generally permits dividends to be paid from "unrestricted" earned surplus and distributions from "unrestricted" capital surplus. Restrictions on surplus arise from the acquisition of treasury shares by the corporation. When treasury shares are acquired, the earned or capital surplus used for their acquisition must be restricted so that the same surplus may not be used again for distributions or dividends. Restrictions on surplus rather than reductions of surplus are used in this situation because the treasury shares may later be reissued, in which event the restrictions may be removed *pro tanto* to the extent of the consideration received for the treasury shares. If the treasury shares are instead cancelled, the restrictions are changed to permanent reductions in the appropriate surplus accounts.

Amendments to the Model Business Corporation Act propose the elimination of the concept of treasury shares, and with it, the need for imposing restrictions on surplus. Under the proposed amendments, reacquired shares would automatically revert to the status of authorized but unissued shares. (See § 7.8).

§ 16.6   Reduction of Stated Capital

The Model Business Corporation Act permits the reduction of stated capital by the simple expedient of amending the articles of incorporation to reduce the par value of outstanding shares. (MBCA § 60(b)). Stated capital represented by no par shares or by amounts previously transferred from other accounts to stated capital may be reduced by a simple procedure involving approval by the shareholders and directors. (MBCA § 69). In some states the surplus created by the reduction of stated capital is called "reduction surplus." Under the Model Act, however, it is considered simply capital surplus. As a result of these provisions it is not safe to assume that even stated capital is irrevocably "locked in" the corporations.

§ 16.7   Contractual Provisions Relating to Declarations of Dividends

Because of the great liberality of many modern business corporation statutes in permitting distributions to shareholders and reductions of stated capital, much of the modern law of dividends is contractual in nature. Creditors of a corporation are naturally anxious that the assets of the corporation not be dissipated through unwise distributions. Therefore provisions are often inserted in loan agreements to prohibit or restrict the power of the corporation to make distributions to stockholders. The nature of such restrictions vary widely. If the debtor is a publicly held corporation with an established history of regular dividend payments, the loan agreement may permit dividends of specified amounts provided that certain ratios are maintained between assets and liabilities, or between current assets and current liabilities. Other restrictions may permit any distribution so long as a minimum net worth and minimum cash balance is maintained. Loan agreements with closely held corporations may prohibit all dividends, and may even impose restrictions on salary payments, bonuses, and other distributions which have the effect of a dividend.

Contractual provisions relating to dividends also often appear in articles of incorporation. Where preferred as well as common shares are authorized, provisions relating to dividends are apt to be complex. Not only must the preference rights of the senior security be defined (*e. g.,* cumulative, noncumulative, or cumulative to the extent earned), but provisions may be inserted restricting a portion of earned surplus from being distributed to the junior securities, prohibiting the reduction of stated capital or the distribution of capital surplus, limiting senior indebtedness, and so forth. The preferred shareholder otherwise receives scant protection under most business corporation acts since his claim to preferential dividends, even if cumulative, are not corporate debts but a mere priority to possible future distributions.

§ 16.8 Liability of Directors and Shareholders for Illegal Dividends

Directors who vote for or assent to a declaration of dividends or the distribution of assets to shareholders which is wholly or partially in violation of statutory limitations or a provision in the corporation's articles of incorporation, are jointly and severally liable to the corporation for the illegal portion of the dividend or distribution. This statutory liability is ameliorated in many states by possible defenses discussed earlier. See § 14.12. Shareholders "who accepted or received such dividend or assets knowing such dividend or distribution to have been made in violation" of the statute or the articles also may be required to restore the unlawful payment received. This provision thus protects the innocent shareholder who relies on the declaration of a dividend not knowing that the dividend is in violation of statute.

§ 16.9 Shareholders' Right to Compel a Dividend

Minority shareholders in closely held corporations are likely to be unhappy about the dividend policy established by the corporation. For tax reasons, the shareholders in control of the corporation usually prefer to pay high salaries to themselves or make other tax-deductible payments than to pay the same funds in the form of dividends. They may also prefer to allow earnings to accumulate in the corporation rather than pay dividends. What, if anything, can the minority shareholder do to secure a more favorable dividend policy? The two most likely approaches involve suits either (1) to compel the controlling shareholder to return part of the amounts distributed to him as being irregular dividends or amounts paid in violation of fiduciary duties, or (2) to compel the declaration of a dividend to all shareholders.

Historically, suits to compel the declaration of a dividend faced serious obstacles. The discretion of the board of directors with respect to business decisions was so broad that a strong showing of fraud, bad faith or abuse of discretion was necessary. In short, there must be shown an abuse of power or a clear failure to exercise it honestly for the corporation and all its shareholders. Dodge v. Ford Motor Co., 170 N.W. 668 (Mich.1919) was one of the first cases in which minority shareholders were successful in compelling the declaration of a dividend, though the Court there appeared to rely heavily on the unusual frankness of the majority shareholder and the Court's own view of social policy. Other cases have also compelled the declaration of a dividend, though in a "head count" of such cases, plaintiffs come off as clear losers. A major concern of courts in ordering a dividend to be paid is that there appears to be no standard to guide the court as to how much may safely be paid out and how much should be retained by the corporation for contingencies and future growth. Judges are usually not businessmen and in any event have little knowledge or familiarity with the specific business before them. Hence even where a finding of bad faith may be made in connection with refusing to declare a dividend, a court is likely to be extremely cautious in establishing the amount of any judicially-declared dividend.

§ 16.10   Tax Consequences of Failure to Pay Dividends in Closely Held Corporations

Section 531 of the Internal Revenue Code imposes a special penalty tax on corporations "formed or availed of for the purpose of avoiding the income tax with respect to its shareholders" by the expedient of permitting earnings and profits to accumulate rather than distributing them in the form of taxable dividends. A tax is imposed on that portion of current earnings which is retained in excess of the "reasonably anticipated" needs of the business. The tax is at a rate of 27½ per cent on the first $100,000 and 38½ per cent on the balance, and is in addition to the regular Federal income taxes applicable to corporations. However, a deduction may be taken for dividends paid shortly after the close of the taxable year, and an aggregate of $150,000 may be accumulated without any justification. A test based on the "reasonably anticipated" needs of a business is obviously very imprecise, and in fact has given rise to a substantial amount of litigation. Guidelines for the proper application of this test appear in IRS regulations.

Section 531 is often administered informally. An internal revenue agent auditing a closely held corporation may raise an issue about paying a dividend without actually seeking the imposition of a section 531 penalty tax. The corporation may take the hint and declare a dividend in the immediate future.

§ 16.11   Corporate Repurchase of Its Own Shares

A purchase by a corporation of its own shares is somewhat analogous to a corporation declaring a dividend; in both cases the corporation distributes cash or property to the shareholders but receives nothing of value in exchange. Shares of itself repurchased by a corporation and held as treasury shares have no more inherent value than authorized but unissued shares. The true effect of a corporate purchase of its own shares is to increase the proportionate interest of the remaining outstanding shares in a group of assets reduced by the amount of the payment used to acquire the shares. Therefore, essentially the same safeguards for creditors and preferred shareholders are applicable to repurchases of shares as are applicable to dividends.

Repurchases or "redemption" of shares, however, create several problems that are not present in the dividend area. Since redemption usually is not proportionate, the shareholders' relative positions among themselves are affected by the corporate repurchase, and delicate ethical questions may arise. For example, a Massachusetts case has held that it is a breach of fiduciary duty for the majority shareholder to cause the corporation to purchase a portion of a family member's shares at inflated prices. Donahue v. Rodd Electrotype Co. of New England, Inc., 328 N.E.2d 505 (Mass.1975). In effect this case recognizes a reverse preemptive right on the purchase of shares.

All in all, the problems involved in repurchases of shares are considerably more lively than the problems relating to dividends, though again the volume of litigation—at least non-tax litigation—is not particularly great.

§ 16.12   Purposes for Which Reacquisition may be Prohibited or Permitted

A corporation may desire to purchase its own shares for a variety of reasons, depending in part on whether the corporation is closely held or whether it is a public corporation with an active market for the shares in question. At common law some states considered the purchase by a corporation of its own shares as ultra vires, but that view has now been universally rejected. In a close corporation, the usual reason to reacquire shares is to eliminate the interest of one of the shareholders in the enterprise. The remaining shareholders may not wish to increase their investment in the business by purchasing the shares personally, or they may lack the liquid assets to do so. An installment purchase may be worked out so that most or all of the purchase price may be paid from (hoped for) future earnings. It is in these types of transactions that the legal restrictions on repurchase of shares discussed in the following section are most apt to have application. In a public corporation, on the other hand, a corporation may reacquire its own shares in order to have them available for stock options or other compensation plans, or for acquisitions of other corporations. Many corporations purchase large amounts of their own shares for these purposes. Publicly held corporations may purchase their own shares for financial reasons, planning to retire them. In these situations the corporation has made the judgment that the market has underpriced the corporation's securities. Retirement of shares may have the effect of increasing the earnings per share of the remaining outstanding shares; this, assumes of course, that the corporation has idle cash which is surplus to its reasonably anticipated business needs and its use to retire shares will not significantly reduce earnings.

Corporate management which is faced with the threat of a takeover by an outside corporation may cause the corporation to purchase its own shares as a defensive measure. Purchases on the open market may drive up the price of the shares, thereby tending to defeat a cash tender offer or public exchange offer. A filing under the Williams Act may be required before such transactions are undertaken. Or the insurgent group may be willing to sell its block of shares (at a premium over what it paid for them) and management may not wish to use their personal funds to purchase the shares. The appropriate test in such a case, according to the Delaware Supreme Court, is whether the directors were "motivated by a sincere belief that the buying out of the dissident stockholder was necessary to maintain what the board believed to be proper business practices" or whether the board "sanctioned the use of corporate funds to advance the selfish desires of directors to perpetuate themselves in office." Cheff v. Mathes, 199 A.2d 548 (Del.1964). Since most transactions involve elements of both factors, the usefulness of this test is debatable.

§ 16.13   Statutory Restrictions on Reacquisition of Shares

Statutory restrictions on the power of a corporation to repurchase its own shares are analogous to statutory restrictions on the payment of dividends, and are phrased in accounting terms applicable to the right hand side of the traditional balance sheet. (If this reference is unclear read § 7.4.) In addition there are general prohibitions: in most states, no matter what the capital accounts of the corporation show a corporation may not repurchase its shares when (1) the purchase is prohibited by the articles of incorporation, (2) there is a reasonable ground for believing that the corporation is insolvent, or will be rendered insolvent by such purchase, or (3) in some states, after such purchase, the fair value of its total assets will be less than the total amount of its debts.

In states whose statutes are based on section 6 of the Model Business Corporation Act, shares may be purchased from earned surplus by simple resolution of the board of directors or from capital surplus by resolution of the board of directors and approval by the holders of a majority of all shares entitled to vote. Also, shares may be purchased for the following purposes without limitation as to source of funds:

(1) To eliminate fractional shares.

(2) To collect or compromise indebtedness owed by or to the corporation.

(3) To pay dissenting shareholders entitled to payment for their shares under the act.

(4) To effect the purchase or redemption of its redeemable shares in accordance with the provisions of the act.

While all state acts are not as liberal as the Model Act, most states allow not only earned surplus but also capital surplus to be used for the repurchase or redemption or corporate shares. States that do not follow the Model Act may have quite different provisions. California, for example, requires assets to be maintained at least equal to one and one fourth times specified liabilities. Delaware simply prohibits reacquisitions that would cause "any impairment of capital." Other statutes may be even more liberal then Delaware.

Corporations often repurchase their own shares in installments over a period of time. Often the corporation will deliver promissory notes to the selling shareholder representing the future payments of principal. Usually, an installment sale occurs because the corporation lacks the assets to buy the shares outright and it is contemplated that future payments will be made in whole or in part out of future earnings. Where an installment sale is made the question arises whether the insolvency and availability of surplus requirements should be applied only when the shares are reacquired and the notes issued, or whether those requirements should be repetitively applied to determine the validity of each payment when it is made. The limited case law tends to apply the tests to each payment but a pending revision of the Model Act proposes that whatever test is appropriate it should be applied only when the shares are acquired and the notes issued. The argument for this position is that the transaction should be treated no differently than if the corporation borrowed the purchase price from a bank in order to acquire the shares for cash. The alternative view would require at least the insolvency test to be applied at the time of each payment.

§ 16.14 Redeemable Securities

Corporations may, when permitted by their articles of incorporation, issue shares of "preferred or special classes which are subject to the right of the corporation to redeem any of such shares at the price fixed by the articles of incorporation for the redemption thereof." (MBCA § 15(a)). In some states, however, common shares may not be made redeemable unless they also have a liquidation preference. Most states do not permit redeemable common shares, which are thought to raise serious public policy issues in terms of corporate democracy. One commentator has stated that even the suggestion of redeemable common shares is "corporate heresy."

In modern financing practice within publicly held corporations, preferred shares are usually cumulative, redeemable, and often convertible into common shares (the "conversion shares") on a predetermined ratio. If the market price of the underlying common rises to the point that the conversion shares are worth more than the preferred security priced without the conversion feature, the preferred will fluctuate in price with the common. If such securities are thereafter called for redemption, preferred shareholders should rationally elect to convert rather than permit the shares to be redeemed. Such conversions are described as "forced."

Most redeemable shares are redeemable at the option of the corporation, though shares redeemable at the option of the holder are sometimes encountered.

§ 16.15   Tax Consequences of a Corporate Acquisition of Shares

The most important tax question in connection with the purchase by a corporation of its own shares is whether the shareholder should be treated as having received a dividend or as having sold his stock. The former gives rise to ordinary income, the latter to capital gain or loss. The basic test set forth in Section 302 of the Internal Revenue Code is that a redemption transaction will be treated as a sale or exchange of the stock if it meets one of the following requirements: (1) it is "not essentially equivalent to a dividend," (2) it results in substantially disproportionate treatment, or (3) it results in the complete termination of the shareholder's interest. The substantially disproportionate and complete termination exceptions provide fairly objective standards by which capital gains treatment may be obtained though in a sense they are subsumed in the "not essentially equivalent to a dividend" standard. It is clear under these tests that a proportional redemption of shares is "essentially equivalent to a dividend" and taxable as such.

[For unfamiliar terms see the Glossary]

CHAPTER SEVENTEEN

SHAREHOLDER'S SUITS

§ 17.1 Direct and Derivative Suits in General

Actions by shareholders as such may be divided into two basic categories: direct and derivative. A direct suit involves the enforcement by a shareholder of a claim belonging to him on the basis of his being an owner of shares. Examples are suits to recover dividends, to examine corporate books and records, and to compel the registration of a securities transfer. These are suits involving the shareholder, the shares themselves, or rights relating to the ownership of shares. A derivative suit is an action brought by one or more shareholders to remedy or prevent a wrong to the corporation as such. In a derivative suit, the plaintiff shareholders do not sue on a cause of action belonging to themselves as individuals. They sue in a representative capacity on a cause of action that belongs to the corporation; the real party in interest is the corporation though it may be formally aligned as a defendant for procedural purposes. In effect, the shareholder is suing as a champion of his corporation. The derivative suit raises a number of procedural and substantive questions and is the principal topic of this chapter.

A class suit is a direct suit in which one or more shareholder plaintiffs purport to act as a representative of a class or classes of shareholders, for injuries to the interests of the class as such. It differs from a derivative suit in that the claim being sued upon is direct: all shareholders of a particular class (or all shareholders) are claiming they were injured as shareholders by an act which was not an injury to the corporation as such. A derivative action, it should be added, often has some aspects of a class action: usually, a shareholder is suing to protect the interest of all other shareholders when righting a wrong done to the corporation.

§ 17.2   The Distinction Between Derivative and Direct Claims

Since different procedural and substantive rules are applicable to direct and derivative claims, it is important to distinguish between them.   Unfortunately, however, the line between the two classes is sometimes hazy.   Anything that harms the corporation also harms the shareholder by reducing the value of his shares.   However, it is clear that a shareholder may not transmute a derivative claim into a direct one merely by alleging a direct reduction in value of his shares because of injury to the property of a corporation, or the impairment or destruction of its business.   Generally, the individual shareholders have no separate and independent right of action for injuries suffered by the corporation which merely result in the depreciation of the value of their stock.   Where such an injury occurs each shareholder suffers relatively in proportion to the total number of shares he owns, and each is made whole if the corporation recovers damages from the wrongdoer.   Such an action brought by the corporation obviously avoids a multiplicity of suits by the various shareholders;   also, the damages so recovered by the corporation are then available for the payment of the corporation's creditors, and ultimately for proportional distribution to the shareholders as dividends.

Many cases have considered whether a claim is derivative or direct.   A suit charging officers and directors with misapplication of corporate assets or other breaches of duty is derivative in character.   Suits to recover improper dividends or to require a controlling shareholder to account for a premium on the sale of his shares have also been held to be derivative since the benefit inures to the corporation.   However, a suit charging that it was improper for a majority shareholder to vote on a resolution authorizing the corporation to repurchase the shares owned by the majority shareholder is direct—to prevent the dilution of the voting power of the complaining shareholder's shares. Cases also have held that a conspiracy of the directors to use their powers to depress the market price of the shares so that they can be bought at less than fair value states a direct rather than a derivative claim. A suit claiming a denial of preemptive rights seems direct; however, it may also be considered derivative if it is alleged that the corporation was induced to issue the shares for inadequate consideration through fraud or a violation of federal securities law.

As these examples indicate, not only is the line sometimes hazy, but careful pleading may affect the categorization. In some situations a single claim may give rise to both a direct and a derivative claim.

§ 17.3   Jurisdiction of Federal Courts

In recent years, the bulk of shareholder class and derivative litigation has been brought in the federal courts, usually under the federal securities laws, but sometimes on the basis of diversity of citizenship. For purposes of diversity in derivative suits, if it appears on the face of the pleadings and by the nature of the controversy that the corporation is antagonistic to the enforcement of the claim, the corporation should be aligned as a defendant for purposes of determining diversity.

As federal corporation law developed, plaintiffs increasingly became able to state a cause of action under both federal and state law. Suits involving such situations are usually brought in the federal courts since the concept of "pendent jurisdiction" permits the federal courts to determine both the federal and state claim in a single proceeding even in the absence of diversity of citizenship. In contrast, state courts do not have jurisdiction over claims arising under the federal securities acts, and thus cannot adjudicate all claims for relief in a single proceeding. The preference for the federal forum also may be based on generous discovery rights, nationwide service of process under the federal securities acts, and the avoidance of state security-for-expense statutes. Substantive advantages that are sometimes cited—a belief that federal courts are more sympathetic to minority plaintiffs than state courts and the greater liberality of federal securities law—are doubtful, particularly in light of recent restrictive decisions of the United States Supreme Court. (See Chapter 14, particularly § 14.14.)

The Federal Rules of Civil Procedure contain carefully drawn and elaborate procedural requirements for maintaining class (rule 23) and derivative (rule 23.1) suits in the federal courts. Many states have adopted similar rules in whole or in part. These requirements are discussed briefly in the following sections.

§ 17.4   Prerequisites for Derivative Suit

(a) *Demand on the corporation and the directors.* Generally, in a derivative suit, the burden rests upon the plaintiff to allege and prove that he made a good faith effort to first obtain action by the corporation on the claim. Thus a good faith demand on the directors is usually a prerequisite to such a suit, and since usually nothing is lost by making such a demand, it probably is a necessary prerequisite to suit. A similar requirement is also applicable under rule 23.1 of the Federal Rules of Civil Procedure which states: "the complaint shall also allege with particularity the efforts, if any, made by the plaintiff to obtain the action he desires from the directors or comparable authority . . . and the reasons for his failure to obtain the action or for not making the effort." In the alternative, the plaintiff may allege and prove such a state of facts as makes it clear that an appeal to the directors would have been useless. One such example, might be where "the wrongdoers are in complete control and management of the corporation."

To phrase the applicable legal principle somewhat differently, the plaintiff must allege and prove that he exhausted his remedies within the corporate structure unless it is clear that such attempts would be futile.

(b) *Demand upon shareholders.* The Federal Rules of Civil Procedure (as well as the rules of several states) also require either a demand on shareholders, or the showing of some adequate reason for not making the effort. Adequate reasons for omitting a demand on shareholders include the following: (1) the wrongdoers own a majority of the shares and hence favorable shareholder action is impossible; (2) the number of shareholders is so large that it is unreasonable to require the plaintiff to incur the expense of what is essentially a proxy solicitation when there is little chance of success, or (3) the acts complained of cannot be ratified by the shareholders, so that action by the shareholders is useless. While some cases have required a demand on shareholders even when the cost would be substantial, many cases have held that such an act may be omitted on one ground or another. Massachusetts appears to have adopted the most stringent rule, requiring a demand in every case where a majority of shareholders are not wrongdoers. Other state courts have proceeded on a case-by-case basis, not requiring a demand when there are thousands of shareholders, and considering the motives of the plaintiff, the number of shareholders joining in the action, and the proximity to the next shareholders meeting.

(c) *Contemporary ownership.* The Federal Rules of Civil Procedure require a plaintiff in a derivative suit to allege that he "was a shareholder or member at the time of the transaction of which he complains or that his share or membership thereafter devolved on him by operation of law." This is the "contemporary ownership" requirement, which was included in federal law primarily to prevent the collusive establishment of diversity citizenship but which has been accepted by several states to prevent "the buying of a lawsuit." Of course, if "buying a lawsuit" is the only concern, the contemporaneous ownership requirement might be safely liberalized to allow suit by plaintiffs who discover the facts giving rise to the lawsuit only after becoming a shareholder.

(d) *Security for expenses.* Security-for-expenses statutes require certain plaintiff shareholders in derivative suits to give to the corporation "security for the reasonable expenses, including attorneys fees" which the corporation or other defendants may incur in connection with a derivative suit. The security is usually in the form of a bond with sureties, though it also may be in the form of cash or marketable securities. The expenses for which security may be required include not only the direct expenses of the corporation, but also the expenses of other defendants for which the corporation may become liable by indemnification or otherwise. Such expenses may be substantial, running into the tens or hundreds of thousands of dollars. The requirement of posting security of this magnitude obviously creates a major obstacle to the successful prosecution of a derivative suit, and a decision that the securities-for-expenses statute is applicable may well be the substantive decision that ultimately results in the litigation being terminated.

Security-for-expenses statutes usually do not define when the corporation may actually look to the security for reimbursement; rather they usually state in effect that "[t]he corporation shall have recourse to such security in such amount as the court having jurisdiction shall determine upon the termination of such action." (MBCA § 49, last Par.) In the absence of such a provision, the corporation normally has no right at all to be reimbursed for any of its expenses; thus security-for-expenses statutes have the secondary effect of creating a right of reimbursement as well as providing that security may have to be posted in the first place. As a further consequence, an unsuccessful shareholder plaintiff posting security-for-expenses may well end up paying the expenses of both sides of the litigation.

Shareholder plaintiffs who are required to post security-for-expenses (and who therefore may become liable to pay the corporation's expenses) are defined in different ways in the state statutes. In the older statutes, where the purpose to discourage derivative litigation is most manifest, shareholders are classified by size of holding. A typical provision is that a plaintiff must post security-for-expenses unless he holds five per cent of the outstanding shares or his shares have a specified market value, *e. g.,* $25,000 or $50,000. The more modern statutes require security-for-expenses only upon a court finding that the suit was apparently brought without reasonable cause or seems patently without merit.

While statutes are silent on the question, it appears likely that in the older type of statutes, intervening shareholder plaintiffs may have their shares counted toward meeting the statutory minima, though a solicitation of shareholders for this purpose may be deemed a proxy solicitation subject to the proxy solicitation rules adopted by the Securities Exchange Commission.

Security-for-expenses statutes are applicable under the *Erie* principle to suits in federal court based on state-created causes of action. Federal jurisdiction over such causes may be based on diversity of citizenship or on the doctrine of pendent jurisdiction. However, such statutes are not applicable to suits in federal court based on claimed violations of the federal securities acts. Nor are they applicable to direct class actions brought either in the federal or state courts since such statutes are only applicable to derivative suits.

One purpose of security-for-expenses statutes is to deter "strike" suits, that is, suits brought not to redress an injury to the corporation but in the hope of securing a settlement profitable to the plaintiff shareholders and their attorneys. However, the older statutes do not distinguish between "strike" suits and bona fide shareholder suits. Rather, they are applicable to all shareholder suits, and thus have the effect of making all such suits more difficult. They were upheld against constitutional challenge, despite the arbitrary numerical limit in Cohen v. Beneficial Industrial Loan Corp., 337 U.S. 541 (1949). Such statutes also probably have the incidental effect of encouraging suits to be brought under the federal securities acts rather than under state law.

§ 17.5   Defenses in a Derivative Suit

Defenses in derivative suits may be grouped into three broad classes. One class involves alleged failure to comply with requirements which are peculiar to such suits. A failure to make a demand on the directors, or a failure to post security-for-expenses when required to do so, for example, will result in the dismissal of the suit. A second class of defenses are those which would be available to the third party defendants if the corporation had sued directly on the claim that is the underlying basis of the derivative suit. If the action is barred by the statute of limitations or statute of frauds, for example, the derivative suit based on the same claim is also barred. Presumably, such defenses may only be raised by the third party defendants, not the corporate defendant. Somewhat similarly, a defense based on ratification of the transaction by directors or shareholders may be available if the transaction is voidable rather than void, or if it arguably falls within the ordinary business judgment of the directors. Such defenses may arise from director or shareholder action after the claim is presented by the plaintiff shareholder, and presumably may be raised by the corporate defendant. A third class of defense may be available against the specific plaintiff shareholder but not against other shareholders. Derivative suits basically involve two separate claims: the substantive claim by the corporation against a third person and the claim by the shareholder that he should be permitted to represent or champion the corporation. Laches, for example, may bar some shareholders but not others from acting as plaintiff. If the plaintiff shareholder actually participated in the wrongful transaction, or assented to it, he may be estopped from questioning the transaction. Shares owned by such a person may be considered "tainted shares" or "dirty stock" and even innocent transferees of such shares may be estopped from questioning the transaction. Such a transferee may also be barred if there is a contemporaneous ownership requirement.

§ 17.6　Procedural Problems in Derivative Suits

In derivative suits, the shareholder is aligned as a nominal plaintiff and the corporation is aligned as a nominal defendant even though recovery usually runs exclusively in favor of the corporation. The corporation is a necessary party in a derivative suit; without it, the action cannot proceed. The unique roles of the plaintiff shareholder and defendant corporation have other procedural consequences as well. It has been held for example, that the plaintiff shareholder may not combine individual or direct actions with a derivative action in the same suit, though many cases are more liberal. Similarly, the traditional view is that the plaintiff shareholder may not be subject to personal counterclaims.

A derivative suit has class as well as derivative aspects since the plaintiff shareholder brings suit not only as a champion of the corporation but also as a representative of the class consisting of shareholders. Multiple derivative suits may therefore be filed by several different shareholders; in the absence of other considerations, the suit first filed is generally permitted to proceed while later actions may be stayed or dismissed, or consolidated with the initial suit. Intervention by other shareholders is permitted and indeed may be encouraged. Presumably, holdings of intervening shareholders may be counted toward meeting the security-for-expenses minima, but intervention may also be encouraged because for some reason the representation of the original plaintiff shareholder may be considered inadequate: perhaps the original plaintiff may be subject to a defense that is personal to him, or a collusive settlement is feared.

Counsel for the shareholder first bringing suit is usually permitted to control the litigation from the plaintiff's standpoint, though the court undoubtedly has discretion to designate an attorney for another shareholder as the principal counsel for plaintiffs. This decision may be of importance in determining fees at a later date. In all such matters, the trial court has "great discretion."

Even though the corporation is technically a defendant, its interest in the litigation is usually adverse to the interest of the other defendants. Therefore, generally, common counsel will not be permitted to represent the defendant corporation as well as other defendants; problems arising from common representation are often complicated because some defenses may be available to some defendants but not to others.

Derivative suits are equitable in nature, a categorization which may be significant in resolving procedural questions. In Ross v. Bernhard, 396 U.S. 531 (1970) the United States Supreme Court held that a right to jury trial may exist in derivative suits brought in federal courts where the issue is of a "legal" (as contrasted with an "equitable") nature.

§ 17.7   Private Settlement of Derivative Suits

Historically, the secret settlement of shareholders' suits was a serious evil. "Strike" suits were thereby encouraged, and the settling shareholder received substantial sums which in fact was a payment to ignore a corporate wrong. This evil has now been largely resolved by bringing the process of settlement of derivative or class suits under judicial control. The Federal Rules of Civil Procedure provide that derivative actions may "not be dismissed or compromised without the approval of the court, and notice of the proposed dismissal or compromise shall be given to shareholders or members in such manner as the court directs." A similar provision is applicable to class suits.

In exercising discretion to review proposed settlements, courts consider several factors, including:

(1) The size of the potential recovery and the size of the suggested settlement;

(2) The probability of ultimate success; and

(3) The financial position of the defendants. Shareholders may appear at the hearing on a proposed settlement and object to its terms.

Courts have held that where a secret settlement has led to a payment to the shareholder plaintiff, other shareholders may bring a derivative suit in the name of the corporation against the settling shareholder to recover the amount of the settlement received by him.

§ 17.8   To Whom Recovery is Paid in a Derivative Suit

A recovery in a derivative suit is usually payable to the corporation rather than to individual shareholders on a pro rata basis. This principle normally protects fully the interest of shareholders and creditors alike, and does not involve the court in making a business judgment as to whether corporate funds should be distributed to some or all of the shareholders.

If an individual wrongdoer is also a shareholder, a corporate recovery permits him to share indirectly in the recovery. In a few instances, courts have been persuaded to grant shareholders a pro rata recovery in order to limit the recovery to "innocent" shareholders. For example, in Perlman v. Feldmann, 219 F.2d 173 (2d Cir. 1955) a control premium paid to a former controlling shareholder was held to be recoverable and payable to the nonselling shareholders pro rata on the theory that it was improper for the persons presently in control (who had paid the control premium to the defendants) to share in the recovery.

Similarly, if the corporation is controlled by the wrongdoers, the court may order a pro rata recovery by the innocent shareholders on the theory that it is improper to permit the funds recovered to revert immediately to the control of the wrongdoers. Such situations, however, are unusual, and a pro rata recovery often gives rise to serious logical and practical problems. In the Perlman case, for example, the pro rata recovery by nonselling shareholders creates the possibility that the persons presently in control may themselves resell at a premium and then argue that the remaining shareholders have already been compensated for the loss of the central premium and should not be permitted to question the propriety of the second sale.

§ 17.9 Res Judicata Effect of Derivative Suits

A final judgment on the merits in a derivative suit is res judicata, binding on all other shareholders, including any who were original parties to the suit but thereafter withdrew. This assumes that the plaintiff shareholder was an adequate representative of the class of shareholders. A court-approved settlement ordinarily has the same effect as a final judgment on the merits, though problems may arise as to whether shareholders are bound if they were not notified of the proposed settlement.

The res judicata effect of a dismissal of a derivative suit depends on the reason for the dismissal. A voluntary dismissal, or a dismissal because the plaintiff shareholder is not a proper plaintiff, *e. g.,* for not being a contemporaneous owner or for not posting security-for expenses, is "without prejudice" and does not bind the class. On the other hand, a dismissal on the merits may be binding upon the class. In some situations, the court may order notice be given to all other shareholders before a derivative action is dismissed voluntarily. Such action may then be continued by intervening shareholders, or if none appear, the action may be dismissed "with prejudice."

§ 17.10   Reimbursement of Plaintiff's Expenses

If the plaintiff is successful, he may be awarded his expenses, including attorneys' fees. Such a recovery is justified in equity as encouraging meritorious shareholder suits. Usually the recovery will be paid out of the funds obtained by the corporation as a result of the suit; however, expenses may be awarded even where the corporation receives no money so long as the result of the suit "was of some benefit to the corporation." Thus, expenses may be awarded in a suit which results only in an injunction against the officers and directors of a corporation engaging in improper conduct. It should be noted that a payment of the plaintiffs' expenses by the corporation does not compel the "losing party" to pay the other's expenses since both the corporation and the plaintiff are winning parties.

The size of the attorneys' fee to be awarded depends on a variety of factors: the nature and character of the litigation, the skill required, the amount of work actually performed, the size of the recovery, the nature of the harm prevented, and other factors. The size of the fee is a question of fact. To choose one example more or less at random, a fee of $200,000 in a suit leading to a $1,025,000 settlement was upheld.

[For unfamiliar terms see the Glossary]

CHAPTER EIGHTEEN

ORGANIC CHANGES: AMENDMENTS, MERGERS AND DISSOLUTION

§ 18.1   Amendments to Articles of Incorporation

Under modern statutes, articles of incorporation may be freely amended subject only to two broad requirements:

(1) The amended articles may contain only such provisions as may be lawfully contained in original articles of incorporation at the time of the amendment; and

(2) If a change in shares or rights of shareholders, or an exchange, reclassification or cancellation of shares or rights is to be made, the provisions necessary to effect such change, exchange, reclassification, or cancellation must be specifically set forth.

Under modern statutes no shareholder has a vested right in any specific provision in articles of incorporation. Obviously, the exercise of the broad power of amendment contained in a business corporation act may adversely affect the holders of one or more classes of securities to the advantage of holders of another class of securities. The only protection against abuse of such power in most states lies in the right to vote by classes on specified kinds of amendments discussed below. Some states also grant shareholder a statutory right of dissent and appraisal similar to that granted in most states for mergers. (See § 18.6.) Outside of class voting or a statutory appraisal right, minority holders have no basis for objecting to amendments validly approved which they consider adverse to their interest.

Some early decisions evolved the theory that certain rights, such as accrued cumulative dividend rights of preferred shares, are "contractual" or "vested" rights and cannot be eliminated over the objection of the owner by an amendment to the articles of incorporation. In order to reverse such decisions, decisively and unambiguously, the statutes of most states contain a "laundry list" of permissible amendments which itself is not exclusive. This "laundry list" includes very broad powers of which the following are illustrative:

"(d) To increase or decrease the aggregate number of shares, or shares of any class, which the corporation has authority to issue . . . .

"(f) To exchange, classify, reclassify or cancel all or any part of its shares, whether issued or unissued.

"(g) To change the designation of all or any part of its shares, whether issued or unissued, and to change the preferences, limitations, and relative rights in respect of all of any part of its shares, whether issued or unissued . . . ..

"(i) To change the shares of any class, whether issued or unissued, and whether with or without par value, into a different number of shares of the same class or into the same or a different number of shares, either with or without par value, of other classes.

"(j) To create new classes of shares having rights and preferences either prior and superior or subordinate and inferior to the shares of any class then authorized, whether issued or unissued.

"(k) To cancel or otherwise affect the right of the holders of the shares of any class to receive dividends which have accrued but have not been declared." (MBCA § 58.)

It should be added parenthetically that not all statutes contain such broad provisions; in those states there may be some limited continued vitality to the notion of "vested rights."

In the absence of specially tailored voting provisions in the articles of incorporation, the major protection of shareholders against unacceptable amendments imposed by other classes of shares is the right of class voting. The scope of this right depends on the specific statute, but generally, the objective is to require class voting on all amendments that are burdensome to the class as such and beneficial to other classes. In most states such amendments must be approved by the required percentage (usually two-thirds) of each class voting as such, and in addition, two thirds of all shares voting not by classes. Shares that are otherwise nonvoting may be entitled to vote as a class on amendments burdensome to the class of nonvoting shares. The basic idea is that if the specified percentage of a class of shares is willing to accept a burdensome amendment, the balance must accept it as well.

There is also a broad equitable principle that majority shareholders and directors must act in a fair way toward the corporation and minority shareholders. This principle may provide entry into the courtroom for minority shareholders who claim that an amendment serves no purpose other than injuring minority shareholders. The test may be phrased as "good faith" or "reasonableness." Also, if there is a failure to provide accurate and complete information about the effect of a proposed amendment, the amendment may be attacked under federal or state law discussed earlier. (See § 14.8.)

§ 18.2   Mergers and Consolidations

Business corporation acts specifically authorize certain kinds of corporate amalgamations:

(1) The merger of one domestic corporation into another domestic corporation;

(2) The consolidation of two domestic corporations into a new domestic corporation;

(3) The merger of one domestic corporation into the subsidiary of another domestic corporation; and

(4) The merger or consolidation of a domestic corporation and a foreign corporation. The surviving or new corporation may be either a domestic or a foreign corporation.

Technically a "merger" of corporation A into corporation B means that corporation B survives and corporation A disappears while in a "consolidation" of corporation A and corporation B, both corporation A and corporation B disappear and a new corporation C is created.

These statutory methods of amalgamations are often simply described as "statutory mergers" to distinguish them from the asset-purchase and stock-purchase transactions described immediately below.

A statutory merger or consolidation is only one of several possible ways of effecting a corporate acquisition or creating an amalgamated corporation out of formerly independent operations. The Internal Revenue Code has its own set of definitions: it describes a statutory merger or consolidation as a class "A" reorganization.

A class "B" reorganization occurs when one corporation purchases all or most of the outstanding shares of the other corporation, and thereafter liquidates or merges the acquired corporation into the parent corporation, perhaps using the short form merger procedure discussed below. The purchase price may be paid in cash, debt, stock, other property, or in a combination of forms. The distinguishing feature of a class B reorganization is that it involves an acquisition of stock. Two possible disadvantages of a stock acquisition is that the acquiring corporation may have to deal with a fairly large number of sellers, and the acquired business remains liable for undisclosed or unknown liabilities, such as income tax deficiencies of prior years. This transaction often is referred to as a "stock purchase" or "stock acquisition" transaction.

A class "C" reorganization occurs when one corporation purchases the assets of another corporation. The purchase may include all or most of the assets of the acquired corporation, or may include only the assets used in one line of business. Again, the purchase price may consist of cash, debt, stock, or other property. After the transaction is completed, the acquired corporation remains in existence with assets consisting primarily of the proceeds of the sale. Usually such a corporation will thereafter liquidate after making provision for liabilities not assumed by the purchaser, distributing the remaining proceeds to its shareholders. However, such a corporation may continue in existence operating as a holding or investment corporation. This transaction is often referred to as an "asset purchase" or "asset acquisition" transaction.

Clearly, the same basic economic result can be reached by casting a transaction in the form of a statutory merger, a stock purchase, or an asset purchase. The question as to which form a particular transaction should take is a complex one, involving a variety of tax and nontax considerations. Often the parties to a specific transaction may have different views on this question, one preferring an asset purchase, the other a stock purchase or statutory merger.

Because of the similar economic effect no matter which form is followed, there is a possibility that the selection of a particular form to achieve some goal, such as not assuming certain types of liabilities, will not be successful. A court may reject form, "look at substance", and recast the transaction into a different form. This is the "de facto merger" notion, first adopted in Farris v. Glen Alden Corp., 143 A.2d 25 (Pa.1958). The court held in that case that dissenting shareholders had the appraisal rights of a statutory merger despite the fact that the transaction was cast as an asset transaction where the "selling" corporation sold assets and received shares of the acquiring corporation and was required to dissolve and distribute the shares to its shareholders after the completion of the transaction.   The court referred to this transaction as a "hybrid form of corporate amalgamation" and said:

> "[I]t is no longer helpful to consider an individual transaction in the abstract and solely by reference to the various elements therein determine whether it is a 'merger' or a 'sale.'   Instead, to determine properly the nature of a corporate transaction, we must refer not only to all the provisions of the agreement, but also to the consequences of the transaction and to the purposes of the provisions of the corporation law said to be applicable."

Several cases are contra to *Farris*, and most academic writing has been critical of that case.

§ 18.3   Triangular Mergers, Cash Mergers, Short Form Mergers and Related Developments

Until about 1960, statutory mergers and consolidations contemplated that all shareholders in disappearing corporations would receive shares in the surviving corporation or corporations in exchange for their shares in the disappearing corporation or corporations.   Apparently, the first broadening of this notion arose in connection with complex transactions, the so-called triangular or reverse-triangular merger.   In a triangular merger the acquiring corporation forms a wholly owned subsidiary into which the acquired corporation is merged, the shareholders of the acquired corporation receiving shares of the acquiring corporation (not, it should be noted, shares of the subsidiary into which the acquired corporation is merged).   A reverse-triangular merger is an even more complex transaction in which the wholly owned subsidiary is merged into the acquired corporation;   the shares of the subsidiary held by the acquiring corporation are exchanged for newly issued shares of the acquired corporation and the shareholders of the acquired corporation receive shares of the acquiring corporation in exchange for their shares of the acquired corporation. As a result, the acquired corporation is the surviving corporation though it is a wholly owned subsidiary of the acquiring corporation. The critical point here is not the detail of the transactions: indeed, one commentator has stated that the "procedure is a magical one" and those who claim to understand it fully "are under an illusion." Rather, the critical point is that in both instances the acquired corporation's shareholders receive shares of the parent corporation even though the merger is with a subsidiary of the parent corporation. (In these situations, the parent corporation is usually a publicly held corporation and a market exists for its shares; the subsidiary is created solely for the purpose of the particular transaction and obviously there is no market for its shares). Traditional merger statutes in most states contemplated that the shareholders in the disappearing corporation would receive shares in the surviving corporation, and therefore it was unclear whether the shares of another corporation—the parent—could be substituted validly for the shares of the party to the merger—the subsidiary. There was, therefore, some uncertainty about the validity of triangular mergers under many statutes.

In order to clearly validate all triangular mergers, the merger statutes of many states were amended to provide expressly that mergers were not limited to share-for-share exchanges, that some parties to the merger might have their shares converted into "shares, obligations or other securities of the surviving corporation *or any other corporation, or in whole or in part, into cash or other property.*" (MBCA § 71(c).) Such amendments led to another type of transaction, the "cash merger" in which certain shareholders were compelled to accept cash or property for their shares. In effect a corporation might merge into its own subsidiary with the majority shareholders receiving stock in the subsidiary and other shareholders being compelled to accept a specified amount of cash for their shares. In effect, such a merger was essentially a device to force out or chase out the interest of some shareholders. This procedure was used to attempt to force out an unwanted minority shareholder, *e. g.,* Bryan v. Brock & Blevins Co., Inc., 490 F.2d 563 (5th Cir. 1974) or to eliminate all public shareholders in a "going private" transaction. It also could be used in a two-step acquisition of all the outstanding shares of an unwilling target corporation. The first step is acquiring a majority of the outstanding shares of the target by open market purchases or a tender offer; the second step is the merger of the target into the aggressor or a subsidiary of the aggressor in which, or on terms by which, the remaining shareholders of the target were compelled to accept cash for their shares. Transactions of this nature raise two basic questions to be addressed in a later section: (1) may such transactions be attacked on the ground that they lack any business purpose other than freezing or squeezing out a minority and (2) are statutory appraisal rights an adequate protection for the frozen or squeezed-out shareholder?

A somewhat parallel development to cash mergers has occurred in a related area: mergers between parent corporations and largely but not solely owned subsidiaries. Such a merger is referred to as an "up stream" merger if the surviving corporation is the parent corporation and a "down stream" merger if the surviving corporation is the subsidiary. Many states have adopted statutes that provide a special summary merger procedure by which a parent corporation owning a large majority (*e. g.*, 90 or 95 per cent) of the outstanding shares of each class of a subsidiary corporation may merge the subsidiary into the parent without a shareholders' vote of either corporation. (MBCA § 75.) This procedure is usually called a "short form merger." The theoretical basis of omitting both votes is that (1) a vote of the subsidiary's shareholders is unnecessary because the minority shareholders are, in any event, unable to block the merger, and (2) a vote of the parent's shareholders is unnecessary because the merger will not materially affect their rights which already include a 90 or 95 per cent interest in the subsidiary. The latter conclusion is based on the relatively slight increase in the parent's interest in the subsidiary resulting from the merger. The major practical justification for the short form merger statute is to effectuate a saving of the cost of proxy solicitations and meetings where the parent corporation is publicly held. Moreover, the short form merger procedure creates no appraisal rights on the part of dissenting shareholders of the parent.

The most difficult theoretical problem with the short form merger statute lies in its treatment of the minority shareholders of the subsidiary. In a merger between independent corporations, it is unlikely that the shareholders of a corporation will approve a merger that is unfair to them. However, in the merger of a subsidiary into its parent, no such automatic protection exists against terms unfair to the subsidiary's minority shareholders; indeed, terms which are unfair to the minority shareholders may be advantageous from the standpoint of the majority shareholder who is the parent. The short form merger statute attempts to avoid this problem by a special appraisal procedure similar to that followed in ordinary (often called "long form") mergers. (See § 18.6.)

§ 18.4 "Business Purpose" Tests

The development of cash mergers, going private transactions, short form mergers, and related practices promptly raised the question whether courts should have any role in judging or evaluating such transactions so long as the formal statutory procedural requirements were complied with. Despite some academic argument that courts should not judge motive or subjective fairness, and should be satisfied if the minority protection devices granted by statute are made available, the case law appears to be developing in the opposite direction.

Several state cases have flatly recognized that cash mergers and related practices should be judged by a "business purpose" test and an evaluation of the "intrinsic" or "entire" fairness of the transaction. The leading cases are Singer v. Magnavox Co., 380 A.2d 969 (Del.1977) and Gabhart v. Gabhart, 370 N.E.2d 345 (Ind.1977), though other cases may also be cited for the same proposition. In Delaware, following *Singer,* the Court held that a business purpose was established in the merger of a 31% owned subsidiary into the parent by showing that the merger facilitated the parents' long term debt financing. Tanzer v. International General Industries, Inc., 379 A.2d 1121 (Del.1977). Some commentators have felt that this reading may constitute a watering down of *Singer.*

The "business purpose" and "intrinsic fairness" tests have been developed by state courts as a matter of state law. An attempt to find a "fairness" standard in rule 10b–5 to evaluate such transactions was rejected by the United States Supreme Court in Santa Fe Industries, Inc. v. Green, 430 U.S. 462 (1977), holding that the essence of a rule 10b–5 violation was nondisclosure or misrepresentation of material facts. As a result of this holding, judicial controls over the transactions described in the previous section appear to be solely within the province of state courts.

§ 18.5 Disposition of Substantially All The Assets of A Corporation

A sale, lease, exchange or other disposition of all, or substantially all, the property and assets of a corporation, not in the usual and regular course of business, must under the statutes of most states be approved by the shareholders as an organic change in the corporation. If the transaction is in the ordinary course of business, which is conceivable but not likely, shareholder approval is not usually required. Most states specifically consider a pledge, mortgage, or deed of trust covering all the assets of the corporation to be within the ordinary course of business and therefore shareholder approval is not required.

In most states, shareholders have a statutory right of dissent and appraisal in connection with transactions involving the disposition of substantially all the assets of the corporation not in the ordinary course of business.

§ 18.6   Appraisal Remedies

State statutes give shareholders the right to dissent from certain types of transactions and to obtain the appraised value of their shares through a judicial proceeding. Since the right is entirely the creature of statute, it is available only when the statute specifically so provides and may be lost if the elaborate statutory procedures are not precisely followed. If the right is lost, the dissenting shareholder must go along with the objectionable transaction.

The appraisal right is usually extended only to certain kinds of transactions: regular mergers, short form mergers (shareholders of the subsidiary only), sales of substantially all corporate assets not in the ordinary course of business, and (in some states) adverse amendments to articles of incorporation. The statutes of a number of states purport to make the statutory dissent and appraisal procedure the exclusive remedy for dissenting shareholders, though there appears to be a trend toward allowing direct attacks on unfair transactions (or transactions without business purpose) that may give rise to an appraisal right despite the language about appraisal being the exclusive language. (See § 18.4.)

The statutory procedure usually requires that a written notice of dissent be filed by the dissenting shareholder before the vote of shareholders on the proposed action. Because appraisal claims may constitute serious cash drains, it is not uncommon in merger and other agreements to provide an "out" for the parties if an excessive number of dissents are filed. Following the affirmative vote on the proposal, the dissenting shareholder automatically has the status of creditor rather than shareholder. Most statutes provide an elaborate procedure by which the shareholder must designate in writing a price at which he is willing to sell; the corporation must respond by setting a written price at which it is willing to buy; if negotiation fails, a court proceeding to establish the appraised price follows. This appraised price is usually to be fixed as of a time immediately before the transaction in question is to occur, but no account is to be taken of the potential impact of the transaction on the value of the shares. After the appraised price is finally determined, the corporation has a limited time to pay that price in cash.

The appraisal remedy has a superficial appeal and plausibility. However, from the dissenting shareholder's point of view it is not an attractive remedy, and there has been considerable litigation seeking to avoid remitting the shareholder to that remedy. Not only does the process involve potentially long delays while the price is established, but litigation over the value of shares is likely to be viewed as expensive and unrewarding. Since the corporation is an active participant in the judicial proceeding seeking to establish the lowest possible valuation, the cards are to some extent stacked against the dissenting shareholders. They must accept the judicially determined price which may be based primarily on the evidence and materials presented by the corporation with its extensive knowledge about its own affairs and virtually unlimited resources.

Most appraisal statutes provide that if a shareholder fails to comply with any procedural requirement relating to the appraisal remedy, that remedy is irrevocably lost and the shareholder has no choice but to accept the transaction to which he originally dissented.

§ 18.7 Voluntary Dissolution

Most state statutes contain a variety of dissolution provisions. These include streamlined provisions for dissolution before commencement of business by the incorporators or initial directors and dissolution at any time with the unanimous consent of the shareholders. The latter is widely used in closely held corporations. The regular dissolution process involves adoption of a resolution to dissolve by the board of directors and approval of it by a majority or some other specified percentage of the shareholders. In this regard, dissolution is similar to other organic changes by the corporation.

Some states require the filing of a notice of intent to dissolve, followed by a period in which the business and affairs of the corporation are wound up, followed by the filing of final articles of dissolution. In other states, only articles of dissolution are filed when the corporate affairs are wound up. Irrespective of the type of statute involved, notice to creditors must be given, and final dissolution is permitted only after all franchise and other tax obligations have been fully satisfied.

State statutes provide that the existence of a corporation continues after dissolution for a stated period so that the corporation may be sued on pre-dissolution claims.

For obvious reasons, there is no statutory right of appraisal in connection with a voluntary dissolution. There may be, however, some equitable limitations on the power to dissolve. These involve situations where a voluntary liquidation is arguably unfair to minority shareholders or which may constitute a "freeze out" of such shareholders. Standards, however, are elusive. Where the business prognosis is bad and the corporation is losing money, the majority should not be required to wait until the corporation is insolvent and their investment lost. On the other hand, a proposed dissolution may be suspect as, for instance, where the sales price of assets is grossly inadequate. Cases have arisen where the objective of dissolution is obviously to eliminate some shareholders from sharing in the profits of a good business, or where the proposal is not to discontinue the business, but to turn it over to a new corporation which is owned by some but not all of the original owners. Were such behavior sanctioned, a minority could be ejected from a successful venture through the process of dissolution as readily as through a cash merger. If so, the tests of "business purpose" or "entire fairness" developed in the merger cases would appear to have potential applicability in liquidations as well.

[For unfamiliar terms see the Glossary]

*

GLOSSARY

ADOPTION is a contract principle by which a person agrees to assume a contract previously made for his benefit. An adoption speaks only from the time such person agrees, in contrast to a "ratification" which relates back to the time the original contract was made. In corporation law, the concept is applied when a newly formed corporation accepts a preincorporation contract made for its benefit by a promoter. See § 5.5.

AGGRESSOR CORPORATION is a corporation that attempts to obtain control of a publicly held corporation, often by a direct cash tender or public exchange offer to shareholders, but also possibly by way of merger, which requires agreement or assent of the target's management.

AMOTION is the common law procedure by which a director may be removed for cause by the shareholders. See § 8.3.

ANTIDILUTION PROVISIONS appear in convertible securities to guarantee that the conversion privilege is not affected by share reclassifications, share splits, share dividends, or similar transactions that may increase the number of outstanding shares without increasing the corporate capital.

APPRAISAL is a limited statutory right granted to minority shareholders who object to certain transactions. In an appraisal proceeding a court determines the appraised value of their shares and the corporation pays such appraised value to the shareholder in cash. An appraisal right exists only to the extent specifically provided by statute. See § 18.6.

ARBITRAGERS are market investors who take offsetting positions in the same or similar securities in order to profit from small price variations. An arbitrager, for example, may buy shares on the Pacific Cost Exchange and simultaneously sell the same shares on the New York Stock Exchange if any price discrepancy occurs between the quotations in the two markets.

AUTHORIZED SHARES are the shares described in the articles of incorporation which a corporation may issue. Modern corporate practice recommends authorization of more shares than it is currently planned to issue. See § 7.2.

BASIS in tax law is roughly the equivalent of the amount invested in property by the taxpayer. To compute gain or loss on the sale or exchange of property, the basis of property is generally subtracted from the amount realized from the sale or exchange.

BENEFICIAL HOLDERS OF SECURITIES are persons who have the equitable or legal title to shares but who have not registered the shares in their names on the records of the corporation. See also **RECORD OWNER.**

BLOCKAGE is a price phenomenon: a large block of shares may be more difficult to market than a smaller block, particularly if the market is thin. The discount at which a large block sells below the price of a smaller block is blockage. Blockage is generally a phenomenon of shares which do not represent the controlling interest in a corporation. Compare **CONTROL PREMIUM.**

BLUE SKY LAWS are state statutes that regulate the sale of securities to the public. Most blue sky laws require the registration of new issues of securities with a state agency that reviews selling documents for accuracy and completeness. Blue sky laws also often regulate securities brokers and salesmen.

BONDS are long term debt instruments secured by a lien on some or all the corporate property. Typically a bond is payable to bearer and interest coupons representing annual or semi-annual payments of interest are attached. The word bonds is sometimes used more broadly to refer also to unsecured debt instruments, *i. e.*, debentures. **INCOME BONDS** are hybrid instruments that take the form of a bond, but the interest obligation is limited or tied to the corporate earnings for the year. **PARTICIPATING BONDS** are another type of hybrid instruments that take the form of a typical debt instrument but the interest obligation is not fixed so that holders are entitled to receive additional amounts from excess earnings or from excess distributions, depending on the terms of the participating bond.

BONUS SHARES are par value shares issued without consideration, usually in connection with the issuance of preferred or senior securities, or debt instruments. Bonus shares are considered a species of watered shares and may impose a liability on the recipient equal to the amount of par value. See § 7.7.

BYLAWS are the formal rules of internal governance adopted by a corporation. Bylaws define the rights and obligations of various officers, persons or groups within the corporate structure and provide rules for routine matters such as calling meetings and the like. Most state corporation statutes contemplate that every corporation will adopt bylaws. See generally § 3.13.

CALL FOR REDEMPTION. See **REDEMPTION.**

CAPITAL SURPLUS. In Model Business Corporation Act nomenclature, capital surplus is an equity or capital account which reflects the capital contributed for shares not allocated to stated capital: the excess of issuance price over the par value of issued shares or the consideration paid for no par shares allocated specifically to capital surplus. See §§ 7.4, 7.5. Capital surplus may be distributed to shareholders under certain circumstances or used for purchase or redemption of shares more readily than stated capital. See § 16.4.

CAPITALIZATION is an imprecise term that usually refers to the amounts received by a corporation for the issuance of its shares. However, it may also be used to refer to the proceeds of loans to a corporation made by its shareholders (which may be in lieu of capital contributions) or even to capital raised by the issuance of long term bonds or debentures to third persons. Depending on the context, it may also refer to accumulated earnings not withdrawn from the corporation.

CASH FLOW refers to an analysis of the movement of cash through a venture as contrasted with the earnings of the venture. For example, a mandatory debt repayment is taken into account in a cash flow analysis even though such a repayment does not reduce earnings. See **NEGATIVE CASH FLOW.**

CASH MERGER is a merger transaction in which certain shareholders or interests in a corporation are required to accept cash for their shares while other shareholders receive shares in the continuing enterprise. Modern statutes generally authorize cash mergers, though some courts have tested such mergers on the basis of fairness and business purpose. See § 18.3.

CASH TENDER OFFER is a technique by which an aggressor corporation seeks to obtain control of a target corporation by making a public purchase offer for a specified fraction (usually a majority) of the target corporation's shares.

CEO stands for "chief executive officer" of a publicly held corporation. **CEO** is a preferred and useful designation because official titles of such persons vary widely from corporation to corporation.

CLASS VOTING permits classes of shares to vote on a proposal by class, and approval by each class is necessary for the proposal to be adopted. Class voting in the Model Business Corporation Act is extended to classes with limited or no voting rights when corporate changes that adversely affect the rights or privileges of that class are being considered.

CLOSE CORPORATIONS or **CLOSELY HELD CORPORATIONS** are corporations with relatively few shareholders and no regular markets for their shares. For a fuller discussion of the problem of definition see §§ 1.5, 12.1. There is no litmus test for when a corporation should be considered closely held and the definition may in part depend on the substantive context in which it arises. In addition to the small number of shareholders and lack of public market, close corporations usually have made no public offering of shares and the shares themselves are usually subject to restrictions on transfer. **CLOSE** and **CLOSELY HELD** are synonymous in this context.

CLOSELY HELD. See **CLOSE CORPORATION.**

COMMON SHAREHOLDERS are beneficial holders of common shares, the ultimate owners of the residual interest of a corporation. See **COMMON SHARES.**

COMMON SHARES represent the residual ownership interests in the corporation. Holders of common shares select directors to manage the enterprise, are entitled to dividends out of the earnings of the enterprise declared by the directors, and are entitled to a per share distribution of whatever assets remain upon dissolution after satisfying or making provisions for creditors and holders of senior securities.

CONSOLIDATION is an amalgamation of two corporations pursuant to statutory provision in which both of the corporations disappear and a new corporation is formed. See § 18.2. Compare **MERGER.**

CONTROL PERSON in securities law is a person who is deemed to be in a control relationship with the issuer. Sales of securities by control persons are subject to many of the requirements applicable to the sale of securities directly by the issuer.

CONTROL PREMIUM refers to the pricing phenomenon by which shares that carry the power to participate in or dominate the control of a corporation are more valuable per share than shares which do not carry a power of control. See § 14.16. The control premium is often computed not on a per share basis but on the aggregate increase in value of the "control block" over the going market or other price of shares which are not part of the "control block."

CONVERSION SECURITIES are the securities into which convertible securities may be converted. See **CONVERTIBLE SECURITIES.**

CONVERTIBLE SECURITIES are usually preferred shares or debentures. The conversion privilege consists of the right of exchanging the convertible securities, at the option of their holder, for a designated number of shares of another class, usually common shares, called the **CONVERSION SECURITIES.** The ratio between the convertible and conversion securities is fixed at the time the convertible securities are issued, and is usually protected against **DILUTION.**

COPROMOTERS. See **PROMOTERS.**

CORPORATION BY ESTOPPEL is a doctrine which prevents a third person from holding an "officer," "director," or "shareholder" of a nonexistent corporation personally liable on an obligation entered into in the name of the nonexistent corporation on the theory that the third person relied on the existence of the corporation and is now "estopped" from denying that the corporation existed. See § 5.9.

CUMULATIVE DIVIDENDS on preferred shares carry over from one year to the next if a preference dividend is omitted. An omitted cumulative dividend must be made up in a later year before any dividend may be paid on the common shares in that later year. However, cumulative dividends are not debts of the corporation but merely a right to priority in future discretionary distributions.

CUMULATIVE TO THE EXTENT EARNED DIVIDENDS on preferred shares are cumulative dividends that are limited in any one year to the available earnings of the corporation in that year.

CUMULATIVE VOTING is a method of voting that allows substantial minority shareholders to obtain representation on the board of directors. When voting cumulatively, a shareholder may cast all his available votes in an election in favor of a single candidate. See § 9.4.

D & O INSURANCE refers to directors and officers liability insurance. Such insurance, which is widely available commercially, insures such persons against claims based on negligence, failure to disclose, and to a limited extent, other defalcations. Such insurance provides coverage against expenses and to a limited extent fines, judgments and amounts paid in settlement. See § 14.18.

DEADLOCK in a closely held corporation arises when a control structure permits either of two or more factions of shareholders to block corporate action if they disagree with some aspect of corporate policy. A deadlock often arises with respect to the election of directors, *e. g.*, by an equal division of shares between two factions, but may also arise at the level of the board of directors itself.

DEBENTURES are long term unsecured debt instruments. Typically a debenture is payable to bearer and interest coupons representing annual or semiannual payments of interest are attached. See **BONDS.**

DEEP ROCK DOCTRINE is a principle applicable in bankruptcy cases by which unfair or inequitable claims presented by controlling shareholders of bankrupt corporations may be subordinated to claims of general or trade creditors. The doctrine received its name from the corporate name of the subsidiary involved in the leading case articulating the doctrine. See §§ 6.8, 7.14.

DE FACTO CORPORATION at common law is a partially formed corporation that provides a shield against personal liability of shareholders for corporate obligations; such a corporation may be attacked only by the state. See § 5.8.

DE FACTO MERGER is a transaction which has the economic effect of a statutory merger but is cast in the form of an acquisition of assets or an acquisition of voting stock. A few cases have reclassified a de facto merger as a statutory merger. See **REORGANIZATION.** See § 18.2.

DE JURE CORPORATION at common law is a corporation that is sufficiently formed to be recognized as a corporation for all purposes. A de jure corporation may exist even though some minor statutory requirements have not been fully complied with. See § 5.8.

DELECTUS PERSONAE is a Latin phrase used in partnership law to describe the power each partner possesses to accept or reject proposed new members of the firm.

DEREGISTRATION of an issuer occurs when the number of securities holders of an issuer registered under section 12 of the Securities Exchange Act of 1934 has declined to the point where registration is no longer required. See **REGISTERED CORPORATION.**

DERIVATIVE SUIT is a suit brought by a shareholder in the name of a corporation to correct a wrong done to the corporation. See § 17.1.

DILUTION of outstanding shares results from the issuance of additional shares. The dilution may be of voting power if shares are not issued proportionately to the holdings of existing shareholders, or it may be financial, if shares are issued disproportionately and the price at which the new shares are issued is less than the market value or book value of the outstanding shares prior to the issuance of the new shares. See § 7.16. See also **ANTIDILUTION PROVISIONS.**

DIRECTORY REQUIREMENTS are minor statutory requirements. At common law, a de jure corporation may be created despite the failure to comply with directory requirements relating to its formation. Important statutory requirements are called **MANDATORY REQUIREMENTS.** See § 5.8.

DISCOUNT SHARES are par value shares issued for cash less than par value. Discount shares are considered a species of watered shares and may impose a liability on the recipient equal to the difference between the par value and the cash for which such shares were issued. See § 7.7.

DISSENSION in a closely held corporation refers to personal quarrels or disputes between shareholders that may make business relations unpleasant and interfere with the successful operation of the business. Dissension, however, may occur without causing a deadlock or adversely affecting the corporation's business.

DISTRIBUTION is a payment to shareholders by a corporation. If out of present or past earnings it is a **DIVIDEND.** The word **DISTRIBUTION** is often accompanied by a word describing the source or purpose of the payment, *e. g.,* Distribution of Capital Surplus, or Liquidating Distribution.

DIVIDEND is a payment to shareholders from or out of current or past earnings. The word dividend is sometimes used more broadly to refer to any payment to shareholders though a more appropriate term for payments out of capital is **DISTRIBUTION.**

DOUBLE TAXATION refers to the structure of taxation under the Internal Revenue Code of 1954 which subjects income earned by a corporation to an income tax at the corporate level and a second tax at the shareholder level if the same income is distributed to shareholders in the form of dividends.

DOWN STREAM MERGER is the merger of a parent corporation into its subsidiary.

EQUITY or **EQUITY INTEREST** are financial terms that refer in general to the extent of an ownership interest in a venture. In this context, equity refers not to a legal concept but to the financial definition that an owner's equity in a business is equal to the business's assets minus its liabilities.

EQUITY SECURITY is a security that represents an interest in the equity of a business. See **EQUITY.** Equity securities are usually considered to be common and preferred shares.

EX DIVIDEND refers to the date on which a purchaser of publicly traded shares is not entitled to receive a dividend that has been declared and the seller of such shares is entitled to retain the dividend. The ex dividend date is a matter of agreement or of convention to be established by the securities exchange. See § 16.2. On the first day shares are traded without the right to receive a dividend, the price will decline by approximately the amount of the dividend; such shares are often referred to as "trading ex dividend."

EX RIGHTS refers to the date on which a purchaser of publicly traded shares is not entitled to receive rights that have been declared on the shares. Compare **EX DIVIDEND.**

FORCED CONVERSION. A conversion of a convertible security is said to be forced if it is called for redemption at a time when the value of the conversion security into which it may be converted is greater than the amount that will be received if the holder permits the security to be redeemed. Normally, a holder of a convertible redeemable security has a period of time after the call for redemption to determine whether or not to exercise the conversion privilege.

FREEZE OUT refers to a process, usually in a closely held corporation, by which minority shareholders are prevented from receiving any direct or indirect financial return from the corporation in an effort to persuade them to liquidate their investment in the corporation on terms favorable to the controlling shareholders.

GENERAL PARTNERS are unlimitedly liable for the debts of the partnership. **GENERAL PARTNER** is usually used in contrast with a **LIMITED PARTNER** in a limited partnership, but **GENERAL PARTNER** is also sometimes used to refer to any partner in a general partnership.

GOING PRIVATE refers to a transaction in which public shareholders of a publicly held corporation are compelled to accept cash for their shares while the business is continued to be owned by officers, directors, or large shareholders. A going private transaction may involve a merger of the publicly held corporation into a subsidiary in a **CASH MERGER.** See § 18.3.

GOING PUBLIC refers to the first public distribution of securities by an issuer pursuant to registration under the securities acts. If a corporation has been in business for several years, the initial registration by which the corporation goes public is apt to be difficult and expensive.

HYBRID SECURITIES are securities that have some of the attributes of both debt securities and equity securities.

INCOME BOND. See **BONDS.**

INCORPORATORS are the person or persons who execute the articles of incorporation. See § 3.4. In modern statutes only a single incorporator is required, the role of the incorporator is largely limited to the act of execution of the articles of incorporation, and restrictions on whom may serve as incorporators have largely been eliminated.

INDEMNIFICATION refers to the practice by which corporations pay expenses of officers or directors who are named as defendants in litigation relating to corporate affairs. In some instances corporations may indemnify officers and directors for fines, judgments, or amounts paid in settlement as well as expenses. See § 14.17. Broad indemnification rights may raise issues of public policy; on the other hand, the fear has been expressed that it might be difficult or impossible to persuade persons to serve as directors in the absence of indemnification.

IN PARI DELICTO is a common law principle that usually is referred to as the "unclean hands" doctrine. The principle limits a person intending to engage in wrongful conduct from suing another wrongdoer when things do not work out as expected.

INSIDE DIRECTORS are directors of a publicly held corporation who hold executive positions with management. See § 13.4.

INSIDER is a term of uncertain scope that refers to persons having some relationship to an issuer, and whose securities trading on the basis of nonpublic information may be a violation of law. See **INSIDER TRADING.** See also § 14.14.

INSIDER TRADING refers to transactions in shares of publicly held corporations by persons with inside or advance information on which the trading is based. Usually the trader himself has an employment or other relation of trust and confidence with the corporation. Such a person is often called an **INSIDER**; that term is broader than **INSIDE DIRECTOR**. See § 14.14.

INSOLVENCY may refer to either equity insolvency or insolvency in the bankruptcy sense. Equity insolvency means that the business is unable to pay its debts as they mature while bankruptcy insolvency means that the aggregate liabilities of the business exceeds its assets. Since it is not uncommon for a business to be unable to meet its debts as they mature yet have assets that exceed in value its liabilities, or vice versa, it is often important to specify in which sense the term **INSOLVENCY** is being used.

INSTITUTIONAL INVESTORS are large investors, such as mutual funds, pension funds, insurance companies, and others who largely invest other people's money. See § 13.2. Since World War II, institutional investors have accounted for an increasing portion of all public securities trading.

INTRA VIRES means acts within the powers or stated purposes of a corporation. Intra vires is the opposite of **ULTRA VIRES.**

INVESTMENT BANKERS are commercial organizations involved in the business of handling the distribution of new issues of securities. See **UNDERWRITERS.** An investment banker may also provide other investment and advisory services to corporations.

ISSUED SHARES are shares a corporation has actually issued and has not cancelled. Issued shares should be contrasted with **AUTHORIZED SHARES.** Issued shares that have been reacquired by the corporation are called **TREASURY SHARES.**

LEVERAGE refers to the advantages that may accrue to a business through the use of debt obtained from third persons in lieu of contributed capital. Such debt improves the earnings allocable to contributed capital if the business earns more on each dollar invested than the interest cost of borrowing funds. See § 7.12.

LIMITED PARTNER. See **LIMITED PARTNERSHIP** and **GENERAL PARTNER.**

LIMITED PARTNERSHIP is a partnership consisting of one or more limited partners (whose liability for partnership debts is limited to the amount originally invested) and one or more general partners (whose liability for partnership debts is unlimited). To create a limited partnership a certificate must be filed with a State official, and even if a certificate is filed a limited partner may lose the shield of limited liability if he actively participates in the management of the business.

MANDATORY REQUIREMENTS are substantive statutory requirements which must be substantially complied with if a de jure corporation is to be formed. See § 5.8.

MERGER is an amalgamation of two corporations pursuant to statutory provision in which one of the corporations survives and the other disappears. Compare **CONSOLIDATION.**

NEGATIVE CASH FLOW refers to a situation where the cash needs of a business exceed its cash intake. Short periods of negative cash flow create no problem for most businesses; longer periods of negative cash flow may require additional capital investment if the business is to avoid insolvency in the equity sense. See **INSOLVENCY.**

NIMBLE DIVIDENDS are dividends paid out of current earnings at a time when there is a deficit in earned surplus (or other financial account from which dividends may be paid). Some state statutes do not permit nimble dividends; these statutes require current earnings to be applied against prior deficits rather than being used to pay a current dividend.

NOMINEES are a form of securities registration widely used by institutional investors to avoid onerous requirements of establishing the right of registration by a fiduciary. See § 13.3.

NONCUMULATIVE VOTING or **STRAIGHT VOTING** limits a shareholder to voting no more than the number of shares he owns for a single candidate. Compare **CUMULATIVE VOTING**. In noncumulative voting, a majority shareholder will elect the entire board of directors. See § 9.4.

NONVOTING COMMON SHARES are shares that expressly have no power to vote. Such shares may be created in most states; in some states, however, nonvoting shares may be entitled to vote as a class on certain proposed changes adversely affecting that class as such.

NO PAR SHARES are shares which are stated to have no par value. See § 7.5. Such shares are issued for the consideration designated by the board of directors; such consideration is allocated to stated capital unless the directors or shareholders determine to allocate a portion to capital surplus. As a result, in many respects no par shares do not differ significantly from par value shares.

NOVATION is a contract principle by which a third person takes over the rights and duties of a party to a contract, such party thereby being released from obligations under the contract. In the law of corporations, the concept may be applied to the release of a promoter who is personally liable on a preincorporation contract when the corporation is formed and adopts the contract. See § 5.5. A novation requires the consent of the other party to the contract, but that consent may be implied from the circumstances.

ORGANIZATIONAL EXPENSES are the costs of organizing a corporation, including filing fees, attorneys' fees, and related expenses. Organizational expenses may also include the cost of raising the initial capital through the distribution of securities. Under the Model Business Corporation Act, § 22, organizational expenses may be paid out of capital without impairing it. Under the Internal Revenue Code of 1954, organizational expenses may be capitalized and written off against income over a five-year period.

OUTSIDE DIRECTORS are directors of publicly held corporations who do not hold executive positions with management. Outside directors, however, may include investment bankers, attorneys, or others who provide advice or services to incumbent management and thus have financial ties with management. See § 13.4.

PAR VALUE or **STATED VALUE** of shares is an arbitrary or nominal value assigned to each such share. At one time par value represented the selling or issuance price of shares but in modern corporate practice, par value has little significance and serves only a limited role. Shares issued for less than par value are usually referred to as **WATERED SHARES.** See §§ 7.4, 7.6, 7.7.

PARTICIPATING BONDS. See **BONDS.**

PARTICIPATING PREFERRED SHARES. See **PREFERRED SHARES.**

PENDENT JURISDICTION is a principle applied in federal courts that allow state created causes of action arising out of the same transaction to be joined with a federal cause of action even if diversity of citizenship is not present.

PHANTOM STOCK PLAN is an employee benefit plan in which benefits are determined by reference to the performance of the corporation's common shares. For example, a person receiving benefits based on 1,000 "phantom shares" will have credited to his account each year an amount equal to the dividends declared on 1,000 shares; the number of "phantom shares" will be increased by share dividends or splits actually declared on real shares; on his death or retirement the person will receive a credit equal to the difference between the market price of the "phantom shares" in his account on the date of death or retirement (or a related date) and the market price of the "phantom shares" in his account on the date he was awarded the rights.

POOLING AGREEMENT is a contractual arrangement among shareholders relating to the voting of their shares. So long as such agreement is limited to voting as shareholders, it is enforceable. See § 9.6.

PREEMPTIVE RIGHTS permit a shareholder to purchase or subscribe for a proportionate part of a new issue of shares in order to protect his interest in the corporation from dilution. In modern statutes, preemptive rights may be limited or denied. See § 7.16.

PREFERRED SHARES are shares that have preferential rights to dividends or to amounts distributable on liquidation, or to both, ahead of common shareholders. Preferred shares are usually entitled only to receive specified limited amounts as dividends or on liquidation. If preferred shares are entitled to share in excess distributions with common shareholders on some defined basis, they are **PARTICIPATING PREFERRED SHARES.** Participating preferred shares may also be called class A common, or some similar designation to reflect its open-ended rights.

PREFERRED SHAREHOLDERS are beneficial holders of **PREFERRED SHARES.**

PREFERRED SHAREHOLDERS CONTRACT refers to the provisions of the articles of incorporation, the bylaws, or the resolution of the board of directors, creating and defining the rights of holders of the preferred shares in question. Preferred shareholders have only very limited statutory or common law rights outside of the preferred shareholders' contract. However, even provisions creating and defining the rights of holders of preferred shares may usually be amended without the consent of each individual holder of preferred shares. The major protection provided by statute against onerous amendments is the right of preferred shareholders to vote as a class on such changes. See § 18.1.

PREINCORPORATION SUBSCRIPTION. See SUBSCRIPTION.

PROMOTERS are persons who develop or take the initiative in founding or organizing a business venture. Where more than one promoter is involved in a venture, they are usually described as **COPROMOTERS.** See Chapter Five.

PROXY SOLICITATION MACHINERY is a phrase commonly used to describe the phenomenon that incumbent management of a publicly held corporation may usually produce large majorities of shareholder votes on any issue it desires. This power is based in part on the ability of incumbent management to use corporate funds to communicate at will with the shareholders and partially on the ability to represent their views as the views of "management." See §§ 13.1, 13.2.

PUBLIC EXCHANGE OFFER is a technique by which an aggressor corporation seeks to obtain control over a target corporation by offering to exchange a package of its securities for the target corporation's voting shares. Usually, a specified number of target corporation shares must be presented for exchange before it will take place.

PUBLIC OFFERING involves the sale of securities by an issuer or a person controlling the issuer to members of the public. Generally, any offering that is not exempt under the private offering exemption of the Securities Act of 1933 and/or similar exemptions under state blue sky laws is considered a public offering. Normally registration of a public offering under those statutes is required though in some instances another exemption from registration may be available.

PUBLICLY HELD CORPORATION is a corporation with shares held by numerous persons. For a fuller discussion of the problem of definition see § 1.5. Typically, a publicly held corporation is registered under section 12 of the Securities Exchange Act of 1934, though such registration is not technically necessary. See § 13.5. Shares of publicly held corporations are usually traded either on a securities exchange or through brokers "over-the-counter."

RECORD OWNER of shares is the person in whose name shares are registered on the records of the corporation. A record owner is treated as the owner of the shares by the corporation whether or not he is the beneficial owner of the shares.

REDEMPTION means the reacquisition of a security by the issuer pursuant to a provision in the security that specifies the terms on which the reacquisition may take place. A security is **CALLED FOR REDEMPTION** when the issuer notifies the holder that the redemption privilege has been exercised. Typically, a holder of a security that has been called for redemption will have a limited period thereafter to decide whether or not to exercise a conversion right, if one exists.

REDUCTION SURPLUS. In a few states, reduction surplus is defined to be the surplus created by a reduction of stated capital. In many states, such surplus is treated simply as capital surplus. See § 16.6.

REGISTERED CORPORATION is a publicly held corporation which has registered under section 12 of the Securities Exchange Act of 1934. See § 13.5 for a discussion of the requirements of section 12 and the obligations imposed on a corporation registering under that section. Section 12 may apply to issuers other than corporations. The registration of an *issuer* under this section of the 1934 Act should be contrasted with the registration of an *issue* under the Securities Act of 1933. See § 1.3.

REORGANIZATION is a general term describing corporate amalgamations or readjustments. The classification of the Internal Revenue Code is widely used in general corporate literature. A *Class A reorganization* is a statutory merger or consolidation (*i. e.*, pursuant to the business corporation act of a specific state). A *Class B reorganization* is a transaction by which one corporation exchanges its voting shares for the voting shares of another corporation. A *Class C reorganization* is a transaction in which one corporation exchanges its voting shares for the property and assets of another corporation. A *Class D reorganization* is a "spin off" of assets by one corporation to a new corporation; a *Class E reorganization* is a recapitalization; a *Class F reorganization* is a "mere change of identity, form, or place of organization, however effected."

RIGHTS are short term options to purchase shares from an issuer at a fixed price. Rights are often issued as a substitute for a dividend or as a "sweetener" in connection with the issuance of senior or debt securities. Rights are often publicly traded. Compare **WARRANTS.**

SCRIP is issued in lieu of fractional shares in connection with a stock dividend. Scrip merely represents the right to receive a portion of a share; scrip is readily transferable so that it is possible to acquire scrip from several sources and assemble the right to obtain the issuance of a full additional share.

SECURITY FOR EXPENSES statutes require certain plaintiffs in a derivative suit to post a bond with sureties from which corporate or other defendants may be reimbursed for their expenses if they prevail. Designed as a protection against

STRIKE SUITS, security for expenses statutes have been widely criticized as being illogical and unnecessary. See § 17.4.

SERIES OF PREFERRED SHARES are sub classes of preferred shares with differing dividend rates, redemption prices, rights on dissolution, conversion rights, and the like. The term of a series of preferred shares may be established by the directors so that a corporation periodically engaged in preferred shares financing may readily shape its preferred share offering to market conditions through the use of series of preferred shares. See § 7.11.

SHAREHOLDERS or **STOCKHOLDERS** are the persons who own shares of stock of the corporation. Such shares may be either common shares or preferred shares. The Model Business Corporation Act and modern usage generally tends to prefer "shareholder" to "stockholder" but the latter word is deeply engrained in common usage.

SHORT FORM MERGER is a merger of a largely or wholly owned subsidiary into a parent through a stream-lined procedure permitted under the statutes of many states. See § 18.3.

SINKING FUND refers to an obligation sometimes imposed pursuant to the issuance of debt securities by which the issuer is required each year to set aside a certain amount to enable the issuer to retire the securities when they mature. A sinking fund may be allowed to accumulate or may be used each year to redeem a portion of the outstanding debt securities.

SQUEEZEOUTS are techniques by which a minority interest in a corporation is eliminated or reduced. Squeezeouts may occur in a variety of contexts, *e. g.*, in a "going private" transaction in which minority shareholders are compelled to accept cash for their shares (see § 18.3), or the issuance of new shares to existing shareholders in which minority shareholders are given the unpleasant choice of having their proportionate interest in the corporation reduced significantly or of investing a large amount of additional or new capital over which they have no control and receive little or no return. Many squeezeouts involve the use of **CASH MERGERS.** Squeezeout is often used synonymously with **FREEZEOUT.**

STATED CAPITAL in Model Business Corporation Act nomenclature represents the basic capital of the corporation. Technically, it consists of the sum of the par values of all issued shares plus the consideration for no par shares to the extent not transferred to capital surplus plus other amounts than may be transferred from other accounts. Distributions generally may not be made from stated capital. See §§ 7.4, 16.4.

STATED VALUE. See **PAR VALUE.**

STRAIGHT VOTING. See **NONCUMULATIVE VOTING.**

STREET NAME refers to the common practice of registering publicly traded securities in the name of one or more brokerage firms with offices on Wall Street. Such certificates are endorsed in blank and are essentially bearer certificates transferred between brokerage firms. See § 13.3.

STRIKE SUITS is a slang term for derivative litigation instituted for its nuisance value or to obtain a favorable settlement.

SUBCHAPTER S refers to a tax option under the Internal Revenue Code of 1954 which permits certain closely held corporations to be taxed in a manner similar to that applicable to partnerships. Under Subchapter S corporate income is taxable directly to shareholders whether or not actually distributed to them. Subchapter S was designed to eliminate the **DOUBLE TAXATION** problem; however, the provisions of

Subchapter S are complex and create a number of unique problems not present in the tax treatment of partnerships. See § 2.3.

SUBSCRIBERS are persons who agree to invest in the corporation by purchasing shares of stock. See § 5.2. Subscribers usually commit themselves to invest by entering into contracts defining the extent and terms of their commitment; at common law subscribers usually executed "subscriptions" or "subscription agreements." Modern contracts for the purchase of corporate shares from the issuer usually use the phrase "agree to purchase *and subscribe for* . . .."

SUBSCRIPTION is an offer to buy a specified number of theretofore unissued shares of a corporation. See § 5.2. If the corporation is not yet in existence, a subscription is known as a **PREINCORPORATION SUBSCRIPTION**, which is enforceable by the corporation after it has been formed and is irrevocable despite the absence of consideration or the usual elements of a contract.

STOCKHOLDERS. See **SHAREHOLDERS.**

TAINTED SHARES are shares owned by a person who is disqualified for some reason from serving as a plaintiff in a derivative action. The shares are "tainted" since for policy reasons a good faith transferee of such shares will also be disqualified from serving as a plaintiff.

TARGET CORPORATION is a corporation the control of which is sought by an **AGGRESSOR CORPORATION.**

THIN CORPORATION is a corporation with an excessive amount of debt in its capitalization. A **THIN CORPORATION** is primarily a tax concept. See §§ 7.12, 7.13.

THIN MARKET refers to a market for publicly traded securities in which the number of transactions and/or the number of securities offered for sale or purchase at any one time are relatively few. In a thin market a single substantial purchase or sale order may cause a significant price movement. A thin market is nevertheless a market, so that the phrase is not ordinarily used in connection with closely held shares for which there is no regular market at all.

TREASURY SHARES are shares that were once issued and outstanding but which have been reacquired by the corporation and "held in its treasury." Treasury shares are economically indistinguishable from authorized but unissued shares but historically have been treated as having an intermediate status. Many of the complexities created by treasury shares revolve around accounting concepts. See § 16.5.

TRIANGULAR MERGER is a method of amalgamation of two corporations by which the disappearing corporation is merged into a subsidiary of the surviving corporation and the shareholders of the disappearing corporation receive shares of the surviving corporation. See § 18.3.

ULTRA VIRES is the common law doctrine relating to the effect of corporate acts that exceed the powers or the stated purposes of a corporation. See Chapter Four. The modern view generally validates all corporate acts even though they may be ultra vires.

UNDERWRITERS are persons who buy shares with a view toward their further distribution. Used almost exclusively in connection with the public distribution of securities, an underwriter may be either a commercial enterprise engaged in the distribution of securities (an **INVESTMENT BANKER**), or a person who simply buys securities without an investment intent and with a "view" toward further distribution.

UP STREAM MERGER is a merger of a subsidiary corporation into its parent.

VOTING TRUST is a formal arrangement by which record title to shares is transferred to trustees who are entitled to exercise the power to vote the shares. Usually, all other incidents of ownership, such as the right to receive dividends, are retained by the beneficial owners of the shares. See **VOTING TRUST CERTIFICATES**. See §§ 9.7–9.9.

VOTING TRUST CERTIFICATES are certificates issued by voting trustees to the beneficial holders of shares held by the voting trust. Such certificates may be as readily transferable as the underlying shares, carrying with them all the incidents of ownership of the underlying shares except the power to vote.

WARRANTS are a type of option to purchase shares issued by a corporation. Warrants are typically long period options, are freely transferable, and if the underlying shares are listed on a securities exchange, are also publicly traded. The price of warrants of publicly held corporations will obviously be a function of the market price of the shares and the option price specified in the warrants. See also **RIGHTS**.

WATERED SHARES are par value shares issued for property which has been overvalued and is not worth the aggregate par value of the issued shares. Watered shares is often used as a generic term to describe all shares issued for less than par value—including discount and bonus shares. The issuance of watered shares may impose a liability on the recipient equal to the amount of the shortfall from par value. See § 7.7.

*

INDEX

References are to Pages

INDEX

INDEX

INDEX
References are to Pages

[*361*]

DERIVATIVE SUIT

Defined in Glossary

Defenses, 310–311

Described, 303

Direct recovery, 313–314

Distinguished from direct, 304–305

Plaintiffs expenses, 315

Prerequisites, 306–310

Res judicata effect, 314

Settlement, 312–313

DILUTION

Defined in Glossary

Discussed, 102–103, 105

DIRECTORS

Action without meeting, 179–181

Bylaw amendments, 134–135

Classification, 151

Committees, 182–184

Compensation, 177–178

Demand on, 306–307

Fiduciary duties, 237

Hold over, 178–179

Initial, 36–37

Inspection of books, 279

Interference with, 129–130

Liabilities of,

Loans, 46–47

Minimum capital, 34–35

Loans to, 256

Meetings, 175–177

Proxy voting, 179

Qualifications, 175

Removal,

In general, 128–129

Effect of cumulative voting, 152

Roles, 129–131, 213–214, 218–220

Vacancies, 178

Written dissent, 181–182

DIRECTORY REQUIREMENTS

Defined in Glossary

[*365*]

INDEX

INDEX

NAME
Discussed, 31–32

NEGATIVE CASH FLOW
Defined in Glossary

NO PAR SHARES
Defined in Glossary
Discussed, 93–94

NOMINEES
Defined in Glossary

NONCUMULATIVE DIVIDENDS
See Cumulative Dividends
Discussed, 104

NONCUMULATIVE VOTING
Defined in Glossary

NONVOTING SHARES
Defined in Glossary
Discussed, 107–108

NOTICE
Discussed, 141, 176
Waiver by attendance, 181–182

NOVATION
Defined in Glossary

OFFICERS
Authority, 185
Employment contracts, 196–197
Fiduciary duties, 192, 237
Liabilities of, 192–194
Loan to, 46–47
Roles, 131–132, 186–187
Tenure of, 196

ORGANIZATIONAL EXPENSES
Defined in Glossary
Discussed, 59–61

ORGANIZATIONAL MEETING
Described, 39–40

INDEX

INDEX

[*374*]

INDEX

INDEX

†